the fervent prayer

the fervent prayer

*The Worldwide Impact of the
Great Awakening of 1858*

by

J. EDWIN ORR

MOODY PRESS
CHICAGO

THE FERVENT PRAYER

Copyright 1974

J. EDWIN ORR
D. Phil., Oxford

ISBN: 0-8024-2615-8

Printed in the United States of America

CONTENTS

INTRODUCTION

EVANGELICAL AWAKENINGS

An Evangelical Awakening is a movement of the Holy Spirit bringing about a revival of New Testament Christianity in the Church of Christ and in its related community. Such an awakening may change in a significant way an individual only; or it may affect a larger group of believers; or it may move a congregation, or the churches of a city or district, or the whole body of believers throughout a country or a continent; or indeed the larger body of believers throughout the world. The outpouring of the Spirit effects the reviving of the Church, the awakening of the masses, and the movement of uninstructed peoples towards the Christian faith; the revived Church, by many or by few, is moved to engage in evangelism, in teaching, and in social action.

Such an awakening may run its course briefly, or it may last a lifetime. It may come about in various ways, though there seems to be a pattern common to all such movements throughout history.

The major marks of an Evangelical Awakening are always some repetition of the phenomena of the Acts of the Apostles, followed by the revitalizing of nominal Christians and by bringing outsiders into vital touch with the Divine Dynamic causing all such Awakenings—the Spirit of God. The surest evidence of the Divine origin of any such quickening is its presentation of the evangelical message declared in the New Testament and its re-enactment of the phenomena therein in the empowering of saints and conversion of sinners.

It is more than interesting to compare the characteristics of the Awakenings of various decades with the prototype of evangelical revivals in the Acts of the Apostles, a perennial textbook for such movements.

Our Lord told His disciples: 'It is not for you to know the times or seasons which the Father has fixed by His own authority. But you shall receive power when the Holy Spirit has come upon you; and you shall be My witnesses . . . to the end of the earth.' Thus was an outpouring of the Spirit predicted, and soon fulfilled.

Then began extraordinary praying among the disciples in the upper room. Who knows what self-judgment and confession and reconciliation went on? There were occasions for such. But, when they were all together in one place, there suddenly came from heaven a sound like the rush of a mighty wind and it filled all the house. The filling of the Holy Spirit was followed by xenolalic evangelism, not repeated in the times of the Apostles nor authenticated satisfactorily since.

The Apostle Peter averred that the outpouring fulfilled the prophecy of Joel, which predicted the prophesying of young men and maidens, the seeing of visions and dreams by young and old. He preached the death and resurrection of Jesus Christ. What was the response? The hearers were pierced, stabbed, stung, stunned, smitten— these are the synonyms of a rare verb which Homer used to signify being drummed to earth. It was no ordinary feeling; nor was the response a mild request for advice. It was more likely an uproar of entreaty, the agonizing cry of a multitude.

Those who responded to the Apostle's call for repentance confessed their faith publicly in the apostolic way. About three thousand were added to the church. Then followed apostolic teaching, fellowship, communion and prayers.

What kind of fellowship? Doubtless the words of Scripture were often used liturgically, but it is certain that the koinonia was open. What kind of prayers? There are instances of individual petitions of power and beauty, but there are also suggestions of simultaneous, audible prayer in which the main thrust of petition is recorded, as in the prophet's day.

The Apostles continued to urge their hearers to change and turn to God, which they did by the thousands. And no hostile power seemed for the moment able to hinder them. Persecution followed, but the work of God advanced.

The events recorded in the Acts have been repeated in full or lesser degree in the Awakenings of past centuries. From the study of Evangelical Revivals or Awakenings in cities and districts, countries and continents, generations and centuries, it is possible to trace a pattern of action and discover a progression of achievement that establish in the minds of those who accept the New Testament as recorded history an undoubted conclusion that the same Spirit of God Who moved the apostles has wrought His mighty works in the centuries preceding our own with the same results but with wider effects than those of which the apostles dreamed in their days of power.

Although the records are scarce, there were Evangelical Awakenings in the centuries before the rise of John Wycliffe, the Oxford reformer. But such movements in medieval times seemed very limited in their scope or abortive in their effect. What was achieved in the days of John Wycliffe—the dissemination of the Scriptures in the language of the people—has never been lost, nor has the doctrine of Scriptural authority. Thus the Lollard Revival led to the Reformation, which would have been unlikely without it; and the principle of appeal to the Word of God in the matter of reform has not been lost either. The Reformation thus led to the Puritan movement in which the essentials of evangelical theology were refined; and the Puritan movement prepared the way for the eighteenth, nineteenth and twentieth century Awakenings occurring in more rapid succession.

A student of church history in general and of the Great Awakenings in particular must surely be impressed by the remarkable continuity of doctrine as well as the continuity of action. Anyone could begin reading the story of the Gospels, continue on into the narrative of the Acts of the Apostles, then without any sense of interruption begin reading the story of the poor preachers of John Wycliffe, the itinerants of the Scottish Covenant, the circuit riders of John Wesley, the readers of Hans Nielsen Hauge in Norway, or the Disciples of the Lord in Madagascar.

Not only so, but the student of such movements would find in the preaching of the Awakenings and Revivals the same message preached and the same doctrines taught in the days of the Apostles. But non-evangelical Christianity, with its accretions of dogma and use of worldly power, would seem a system utterly alien to that of the Church of the Apostles, resembling much more the forces both ecclesiastical and secular that had opposed New Testament Christianity.

The reader of the Acts of the Apostles must surely notice that the Church began to spread by extraordinary praying and preaching. So too the 'upper room' type of praying and the pentecostal sort of preaching together with the irrepressible kind of personal witness find their place in Great Awakenings rather than in the less evangelical ecclesiastical patterns.

The first three centuries of progress were followed by a millenium of changed direction when the Church was united with the State and political force compelled the consciences of men. These centuries are rightly called the Dark Ages, though they were not entirely without light.

Before the fifteenth century, a change began, commencing a progression of awakenings that moved the Church by degrees back to the apostolic pattern and extended it all over the world. Not only were theological dogmas affected and missionary passion created, but society itself was changed.

From the times of the Lollards onward, the impact of the Evangelical Revivals or Awakenings was felt in the realm of personal liberty— knowing the truth made men free, and made them covet freedom for all. Thus the Social Rising of 1381 championed a charter of freedom based on evangelical conviction. Its daughter movement in Bohemia defended its freedom against the forces of tyranny for a century.

The consequent Reformation that soon began in Germany caused such a ferment in men's minds that a rising became inevitable— but it was crushed, only because some of those responsible for the hunger for freedom betrayed it. The hunger for righteousness of the early Puritans brought about another attempt to establish freedom under the law, but, like various ventures before it, the Commonwealth failed because it relied more upon secular force than persuasion.

In the eighteenth, nineteenth and twentieth centuries, the revived Evangelicals re-learned an earlier method. New Testament counsel began to prevail, helping persuade freethinkers and Christians, traditionalists and Evangelicals, that freedom was God's intent for every man, everywhere. Thus the nineteenth century became in itself the century of Christian action, taking Good News to every quarter of the earth, to every phase of life. Those whose hearts the Spirit had touched became the great initiators of reform and welfare and tuned even the conscience of unregenerate men to a sense of Divine harmony in society.

Yet Christians believed that the horizontal relationship of man to men was dependent upon the vertical relationship of man to God, that social reform was not meant to take the place of evangelism, 'so to present Christ in the power of the Spirit that men may come to put their trust in Him as Saviour and to serve Him as Lord in the fellowship of His Church and in the vocations of the common life.'

What may be called the General Awakenings began in the second quarter of the eighteenth century, among settlers in New Jersey and refugees from Moravia about the same time. The First Awakening ran its course in fifty years, and was followed by the Second Awakening in 1792, the Third in 1830, the Fourth in 1858-59, the Fifth in 1905.

The movements of revival in the English-speaking world were hampered by the outbreak of war between Great Britain and the American Colonies. Trevelyan noted the year 1776 as a low-water mark in the ebbtide of infidelity in Britain, while in the revolting American States the onslaught of war produced a sorry effect on all the Churches—even though there were sporadic local revivals on both sides of the Atlantic. Greater troubles soon followed.

The infidelity of the French Revolution represented the greatest challenge to Christianity since the time preceding the Emperor Constantine. Christians had endured the threat of the northern barbarians, the assault of the armies of the crescent, the terror of the hordes from the steppes, and an eastern schism and a western reformation. But, until 1789, there had never been such a threat against the very foundations of the Faith, against believing in the God revealed in the Scriptures. Voltaire made no idle boast when he said that Christianity would be forgotten within thirty years.

In France, even the Huguenots apostasized. Deism rode high in every country in Europe, and so-called Christian leaders either capitulated to infidelity or compromised with rationalism. The infant but sturdy nation on the American continent was swept by unbelief, so that the faithful trembled. Between the mailed fist of French military power and the insidious undermining of faith, there seemed no escape.

The spiritual preparation for a worldwide awakening began in Great Britain seven years before the outpouring of the Spirit there. Believers of one denomination after the other, including the evangelical minorities in the Church of England and the Church of Scotland, devoted the first Monday evening of each month to pray for a revival of religion and an extension of Christ's kingdom overseas. This widespread union of prayer spread to the United States within ten years and to many other countries, and the concert of prayer remained the significant factor in the recurring revivals of religion and the extraordinary out-thrust of missions for a full fifty years, so commonplace it was taken for granted by the Churches.

The outbreak of the Revolution in France at first encouraged lovers of liberty in the English-speaking world to hope that liberty had truly dawned in France. When the Terror began, and when military despotism rose, they were fearfully alarmed. The British people decided to fight. In the second year of the Revolution, John Wesley died.

The revival of religion, the second great awakening, began in Britain in late 1791, cresting in power among the Methodists who seemed unafraid of the phenomena of mass awakening. It was also effective among the Baptists and the Congregationalists, though manifested in quieter forms. It accelerated the evangelical revival going on among clergy and laity of the Church of England, strengthening the hands of Simeon and his Eclectic Club and those of Wilberforce in his Clapham Sect—an Evangelical party in the Anglican Establishment which soon became dominant in influence.

At the same time, the principality of Wales was overrun by another movement of revival, packing the churches of the various denominations and gathering unusual crowds of many thousands in the open-air. The revival accelerated the growth of the Baptists and Congregationalists, increased the number of Wesleyan Methodists, and caused the birth of a new denomination, the Calvinistic Methodist Church of Wales, now the Welsh Presbyterians, who separated from the Church of Wales because of its failure to provide either ministers or sacraments for its societies.

Phenomenal awakenings also swept many parts of the kingdom of Scotland, raising up such evangelists as the Haldanes, and such pastoral evangelists as Chalmers in Glasgow and MacDonald in the North. The Scottish revivals began in the teeth of majority opposition in the Church of Scotland but within a generation had evangelized the auld Kirk. The coverage of the Scottish Revival was patchwork, its occurrence sporadic, because of the desperate state of the country. The light prevailed over the darkness.

Not for the first time, nor the last, the unhappy kingdom of Ireland, a majority of whose inhabitants were disfranchized, was rent asunder by turmoil that boiled over into the Rebellion of 1798. In the midst of strife, local awakenings occurred among the Methodists, affecting the evangelical clergy of the Church of Ireland. The Presbyterians of the North were fully occupied contending for orthodoxy against a Unitarian insurgency. Revival brought forth societies for the evangelization of Ulster and the renewal of church life.

This period of revival in the United Kingdom brought forth the British and Foreign Bible Society, the Religious Tract Society, the Baptist Missionary Society, the London Missionary Society, the Church Missionary Society, and a host of auxiliary agencies for evangelism. It produced also some significant social reform, even in wartime.

Before and after 1800, an awakening began in Scandinavia, resembling more the earlier British movements of the days of Wesley and Whitefield, though borrowing from the later British awakening in adopting its home and foreign mission projects, its Bible societies, and the like. In Norway, the revival was advanced by a layman, Hans Nielsen Hauge, who made a lasting impact upon Norway as a nation. Another layman, Paavo Ruotsalainen, expedited the movement in Finland. There were several national revivalists operating then in Sweden, but the influence of George Scott, a British Methodist, later exceeded them all. In Denmark, the revival seemed less potent and was sooner overtaken by a Lutheran confessional reaction, which inhibited the renewal of revival in the 1830s—unlike Norway, Sweden, and Finland, which experienced extensive movements up until the mid-century, Gisle Johnson and Carl Olof Rosenius being the outstanding leaders in Norway and Sweden respectively.

In Switzerland, France, and the Netherlands, the general awakening was delayed until the defeat of Napoleon. A visit to Geneva by Robert Haldane triggered a chain reaction of revival throughout the Reformed Churches of the countries named, raising up outstanding evangelists and missionary agencies. In Holland, the movement was somewhat delayed, and was sooner cramped by confessional reaction among the Dutch Reformed, some of whom objected to state control as well as evangelical ecumenism.

In the German States, the general awakening followed the defeat of Napoleon, and raised up scores of effective German evangelists, such as the Krummachers, Hofacker, Helferich, von Kottwitz, and the von Belows; German theologians, such as Neander and Tholuck; social reformers, such as Fliedner; and noteworthy home and foreign missionary agencies. As in other European countries, the complication of state-church relationships provoked confessional reaction among Lutherans who repudiated the evangelical ecumenism of the revivalists in general. Next to British evangelical pioneers, the German revivalists achieved the most lasting social reforms. Close collaboration between British and German revivalists existed in home and foreign mission projects.

Confessionalism in Europe, whether Anglo-Catholic in England, Lutheran in Germany and Denmark, or Reformed in Holland and Switzerland, inhibited the renewal of revival in the 'thirties, unlike the United States, where the free church system accelerated it.

In the United States and in British North America, there were preparatory movements of revival in the 1780s that raised up leaders for the wider movement in the following decade. Conditions in the United States following the French Revolution were deplorable, emptying churches, increasing ungodliness and crime in society, infidelity among students. Sporadic revivals began in 1792. Then Isaac Backus and his friends in New England adopted the British plan for a general Concert of Prayer for the revival of religion and extension of Christ's kingdom abroad. Prayer meetings multiplied as church members devoted the first Monday of each month to fervent intercession.

In 1798, the awakening became general. Congregations were crowded and conviction was deep, leading to numerous thoroughgoing conversions. Every state in New England was affected, and every evangelical denomination. There were no records of emotional extravagance, and none among the churches of the Middle Atlantic States, where extraordinary revivals broke out in the cities of New York and Philadelphia as well as in smaller towns. In the western parts of New York and Pennsylvania, there were more startling displays of excitement. The population of these eastern States was three million, and the extent of the revival therein was three times more considerable than in the frontier territories, with three hundred thousand people.

In 1800, extraordinary revival began in Kentucky, long after its manifestation east of the Alleghenies. Among the rough and lawless and illiterate frontiersmen, there were extremes of conviction and response, such as trembling and shaking—described as 'the jerks,'—weeping for sorrow and shouting for joy, fainting. Extravagances occurred among a comparative few, but were exaggerated by critics out of all proportion, so that twentieth century historians have stressed the odd performances and ignored the major thrust of the awakening in the United States, even pontificating that the awakening actually began, extravagantly, on the frontier— an obvious misreading of history. It cannot be denied that the revival transformed Kentucky and Tennessee from an utterly lawless community into a God-fearing one.

On the frontier, there were minor schisms following the awakening, due largely to defects inherent in denominational organization than to the revival, which raised up voluntary evangelists among the laity. Reaction against evangelical ecumenism and lay evangelism forced some people out.

The awakening spread southwards into Virginia, North and South Carolina, and Georgia, again—as in Kentucky and Tennessee—attracting crowds so huge that no churches could possibly accommodate them, hence five, ten or fifteen thousand would gather in the forest clearings. The Negroes were moved equally with the whites.

In the Maritime Provinces of British North America, the revival of the 1780s was renewed among the Baptist and New Light Congregationalist churches. In Upper Canada— now Ontario—the Methodists promoted revival meetings and grew very rapidly, as did some Presbyterians and (later) the Baptists. American itinerants were most active in the movement, anti-American Churchmen and secular leaders most opposed to it. The war of 1812 interrupted the work, which resumed with the coming of peace, though still discouraged by conservative British leaders.

As the influence of infidelity had been so strongly felt in the American colleges, so the blessing of revival overflowed in collegiate awakenings. Timothy Dwight, erudite president of Yale, proved to be the greatest champion of intelligent evangelical Christianity on campus, but the movement among students soon became a spontaneous, inter-collegiate union. The revived and converted students provided the majority of recruits for the home ministry, educational expansion, and foreign missionary effort.

Revived Americans duplicated the formation of various evangelical societies in Britain, founding the American Bible Society, the American Tract Society, the American Board of Commissioners for Foreign Missions, the Foreign Mission of the American Baptists, and society after society. The order and extent of missionary organization reflected in some measure the degree of involvement of denominations in the Awakening.

The Dutch colony of 30,000 at Cape Town experienced an awakening under the ministry of Dr. Helperus Ritzema van Lier, and thrust out local missionaries to evangelize the Khoisan (Hottentot and Bushmen) in the Cape hinterland. A revival broke out in British army regiments in 1809, the Methodist soldier-evangelists gaining a hearing after an earthquake of great severity had shaken the Cape. There was little in the way of a free constituency to be revived in Australia, but the first chaplains to the settlements were Anglican Evangelicals, and revived congregations in Great Britain sent out evangelistically-minded laymen as settlers.

There is no doubt that the general awakening of the 1790s and 1800s, with its antecedents, was the prime factor in the extraordinary burst of missionary enthusiasm and social service, first in Britain, then in Europe and North America. Thomas Charles, whose zeal for God provoked the formation of the British and Foreign Bible Society, was a revivalist of first rank in Wales. George Burder, who urged the founding of the Religious Tract Society, was a leader in the prayer union for revival. William Carey, a founder and pioneer of the Baptist Missionary Society, was one of a group who first set up in England the simultaneous prayer union that spread throughout evangelical Christendom and achieved its avowed purpose in the revival of religion and the extension of the kingdom of Christ overseas. The London Missionary Society and the Church Missionary Society grew out of the prayers of other Free Church and Church of England Evangelicals in the awakening. Methodist missions came from the same source, as did other Scottish societies and the Church of Scotland missions. The revival provided dynamic.

The participation of Germans and Dutch in the Church Missionary Society and the London Missionary Society had its origin in the revival prayer groups in those countries, as did the proliferation of national missionary societies. A student prayer meeting in Williams College, the Haystack Compact, led to the foundation of the American Board and the American Baptist Missionary Union. The origins of the other denominational societies lay in the general revival.

It is all the more amazing to realise that these unique developments took place in Britain while that country was engaged in a titanic struggle with Napoleon, supported by ten times as many people. And the eager readiness of revived believers in Europe and North America transcended the political divisions and upheavals between them and Britain. The coming of peace in 1815 brought about a renewal of the revival in Britain, the rise of the Primitive Methodists to undertake an outreach to the masses somewhat neglected by Wesleyans. In the Church of England, Charles Simeon was at the height of his influence, and the Church Building Society with government help was building hundreds of parish churches. The Baptists and Congregationalists were active in revival in England, and in Wales there were local revivals in many places. In Scotland, local awakenings and pastoral evangelism and social service built up the Church of Scotland Evangelicals. Revivals occurred in Ireland.

As in Great Britain, revival was renewed in the United States and Canada after 1815, and for fifteen years there were revivals reported here and there. This renewal saw the emergence of outstanding evangelists, such as Asahel Nettleton in New England, Daniel Baker in the South, and Charles Finney in the 'burnt-over' area of western New York.

On the mission fields, the pioneers encountered three types of response to their evangelistic outreach and prayer: folk movements of unindoctrinated people, awakenings of instructed communities, and revivals of believers, in such places as South India, South Africa, Indonesia and Polynesia which were open to the Good News.

It seemed almost too good to be true that another general awakening of phenomenal power swept the United States in 1830-1831. Whether in the eastern, western or southern States, it was without reported extravagance. The movement began in Boston and New York and other cities in summer-time, 1830. It began in Rochester, New York, during the autumn in Finney's ministry, and reached its peak in mid-winter 1830-31, winning a thousand inquirers at the same time that a hundred thousand others were being enrolled in other parts from Maine to the borders of Texas. Finney, as a national evangelist, was made by the revival of 1830-31, not vice versa. In these years, several smaller bodies of evangelistic folk unchurched by their denominations united in the virile Disciples of Christ movement.

Bishop Asbury told his Methodist preachers: 'We must attend to camp-meetings; they make our harvest time.' The harvest was followed by as much work as that which preceded sowing. The Methodist Episcopal Church thrived in the 1830s, and doubled its numbers around 1840. Likewise, the Baptists, carrying on their ministry by means of their 'farmer-preachers,' covered the country with a network of Baptist associations, founding a Home Mission in 1832.

The revival of the 1830s was effective in Great Britain also, provoking local movements of great intensity among the various Methodist bodies in England, strengthening the Anglican Evangelicals and Free Churches. It was inhibited somewhat by a confessional reaction, the Tractarian movement, which stressed a sacramental-sacerdotal churchmanship and opposed the evangelism of the awakenings. James Caughey, an American evangelist, won many thousands in a series of campaigns in England—including William Booth, who commenced open air preaching.

First South Wales and then North Wales were moved in awakenings in the 1830s. Another general revival stirred Wales in the 'forties, influenced by Finney's philosophy of revival. In Scotland, revivals increased in number in the 1830s, culminating in an extraordinary outburst at Kilsyth under the ministry of William C. Burns, who witnessed a like revival in Dundee, then in various parts of Scotland, as spontaneous revivals broke out in the Highlands from 1839 onwards. This Scottish Awakening prepared the way for the Disruption and the formation of the Free Church of Scotland, a protest against lay patronage and government interference. So great was the revival in Ireland that the bishops of the Church of Ireland were talking about 'a second reformation,' somewhat prematurely, for the converts of the time were lost to Ireland by emigration following the potato famine. In the North, Evangelicalism triumphed over Arianism among Presbyterians, who multiplied their congregations.

The evangelical ecumenism of the times produced an interesting development. Dublin Evangelicals formed a group for 'the breaking of bread,' attracting many who were bewildered by denominationalism. From this gathering came the Christian Brethren, miscalled Plymouth Brethren. John Darby became the leader of the Exclusive Brethren, George Müller of the Open Brethren, who promoted evangelism and missionary enterprise.

The ministry of George Scott in the 1830s precipitated a lasting revival in Sweden, Carl Olof Rosenius taking up his work after his expulsion, awakenings general in the 1840s, when revival was renewed in Norway, all Scandinavia being moved in the 1850s, despite a confessional reaction under Grundtvig. There was confessional reaction in Germany also, although revivals continued. The continuing Reveil in France and Switzerland reached the Netherlands in 1830, provoking awakenings as well as a confessional reaction.

The 1830s were marked by some extraordinary revival-awakenings in Polynesia. In 1834, a phenomenal movement began in the kingdom of Tonga, described by the Wesleyan missionaries as a 'baptism from above.' In 1837, a similar movement began in the kingdom of Hawaii, Titus Coan taking in 1705 tested converts in one day at Hilo, 7557 in one church during the movement. Revivals were felt in other parts of Polynesia, and a movement in Tonga in the 1840s paralleled a great ingathering in the Fiji Islands, among a Melanesian population fearfully addicted to cannibalism.

The Netherlands Missionary Society entered Sulawesi in Indonesia in 1822. While revival moved the Netherlands, a folk movement of great proportions swept Minahassa, the northeastern peninsula, making that field Christian within a couple of generations.

In the 1830s, there were renewed revivals in Grahamstown in South Africa, and an overflow to the Bantu folk round about. Robert Moffat witnessed an ingathering in Botswanaland. At the same time, pioneers were pouring into southern Africa from missionary societies renewed or founded in the movements going on in the sending countries. Pioneers were at the same time entering the Gold Coast and Nigeria, while freed slaves settled Sierra Leone and Liberia.

Missions of help to the Oriental Churches in the Near and Middle East resulted in revivals and awakenings, sometimes in disruption and reformation. The pioneers coming from revived churches in Britain, Europe, and North America gained barely a foothold in China, where resistance to the foreign faith was strong. Japan and Korea remained closed to all missionary enterprise.

There were folk movements in various parts of India. Missionaries flocked to India after 1833 and accelerated the work of evangelism and social reform in the sub-continent. There were local revivals, among them a striking movement sparked by the ministry of Samuel Hebich. A folk movement of the Karens of Burma to Christ followed the conversion of Ko Tha Byu through Baptist evangelism. There was 'a time of revival' in Ceylon.

The work of James Thomson, who pioneered education and Bible distribution in the Latin American republics, was systematically destroyed in the political and religious reaction throughout the continent. In the West Indies, newly-liberated slaves flocked to the churches of the missionaries who had defended them against oppression.

After Finney became a national figure, he was invited to campaign in Boston, New York, Philadelphia and the larger cities. His 'new measures' aroused opposition, and his theology moved away from a Presbyterian-Congregational brand of Calvinism to a middle course between Calvin and Arminius. Reacting against a kind of fatalism in his own denomination, he deplored the notion that sinners should continue under conviction of sin until God should deign to grant them repentance; rather he felt that they should, by an act of the will, surrender to God.

As a gospel tactician, Finney was second to none. As a strategist, his practice was better than his theory. Finney went to the extreme of stating that revivals of religion were nothing more or less than a result of the right use of the appropriate means. His own expectancy of revival seemed justified by the results almost everywhere reported in his services. His theories, based on the assumption that times of refreshing were automatically assured, have not always applied during serious declines in community religion.

Unfortunately, besides encouraging many a local pastor or evangelist to expect revival, Finney's theory encouraged a brash school of evangelists who thought that they could promote genuine revival by means chosen by themselves in times chosen by themselves. The use of means was often blessed with Spirit-filled men, but with less-spiritual agents it gave rise to a brand of promotional evangelism, full of sensationalism and commercialism.

Neither the 1792 Awakening, at Finney's birth, nor the 1830 movement, nor the 1858-59 Awakening, nor the 1905 Revival after his death, was planned, programmed or promoted. It must be concluded that Finney's theory applied to evangelism, not outpourings of the Spirit.

One among many influenced by the writings of Finney, George Williams, converted in his 'teens, commenced in London in the 1840s the Young Men's Christian Association, at first as thoroughly evangelistic as it was social. The formation of the Y.W.C.A. followed in the 'fifties. These movements experienced a remarkable expansion during the mid-century awakening in the United States and Great Britain —two of many voluntary organizations assisting Churches.

Out of the evangelical ecumenism of the 1830s and 1840s came the Evangelical Alliance, founded in 1846 by leaders of the revival movement on both sides the Atlantic.

The Third Great Awakening came to an end about 1842 in the United States. The unfulfilled predictions of William Miller regarding the Second Coming, the affluence of society in an expanding economy, and the divisive effect of chattel slavery tended to hinder further expansion of the Churches. In 1848, political turmoil affecting most countries brought it to an end in Great Britain and other parts of Europe. But after a decline which lasted about fifteen years, there came another great awakening, surpassing previous movements in its extent, wholesomeness, effects, and lasting impact, while sharing their theology and objectives.

1

THE SOURCES OF THE REVIVAL

Between 1845 and 1855, religious life in the United States of America was in decline. There were many reasons for decline, political and social as well as religious.[1] The question of slavery was of paramount importance, and men's passions and energies were being diverted into channels of debate and contention.[2]

Many people at the time lost faith in spiritual things because of the extremes of apocalyptists who followed William Miller and others in predicting Christ's return and reign in 1843 and in 1844.[3] Public confidence became shaken as the excitement died down, some disappointed victims becoming bitter infidels while others embraced a cynical materialism. So widespread was the delusion that the churches became the subjects of ridicule and faith in religion was impaired, so that between 1845 and 1855, there were several years in which church accessions scarcely kept pace with severe losses due to a relenting discipline and a relentless death rate. There was cause for concern.

There were secular factors operating as well. Financial and commerical prosperity had had an adverse effect upon the American people of the mid-century.[4] The zeal of the people was devoted to the accumulation of wealth, and other things (including religion) took a lesser place. Cheap and fertile land attracted multitudes of settlers, as the frontier was pushed farther and farther west. Cities and states were founded in rapid succession and the population in them increased at an astounding rate. Harvests were plenteous; boom times caught the public fancy and turned men's hearts from God and His commandments.

Secular and religious conditions combined to bring about a crash.[5] The third great panic in American history swept the giddy structure of speculative investment away. Thousands of merchants were forced to the wall as banks failed, and railroads went into bankruptcy. Factories were shut down and vast numbers thrown out of employment, New York City alone having 30,000 idle men.[6]

By October of 1857, the hearts of the people had been thoroughly weaned from speculation and uncertain gain, while hunger and despair stared them in the face. But this financial collapse was not the only major factor involved. There had occurred a commercial revulsion, quite as widespread or unexpected, in the year 1837. It was tenfold more disastrous, yet then produced no unusual turning to religion, no revolution of the popular mind, no upheaving of social foundations.[7] People as a whole were far more intent upon examining the political and economic causes of their pecuniary pressure than searching for a spiritual explanation. Now, in the United States, distress preceded an awakening. There was another factor at work, Divine sovereignty.

For beginnings of the 1858 religious revival which was soon to sweep the United States, it is necessary to look beyond the boundaries of the Union. The first unusual stream of blessing arose not in New York, as commonly supposed, but in the city of Hamilton, in Ontario, in Canada.[8]

Walter and Phoebe Palmer, a physician and his talented wife, were the evangelists involved. On the 5th November 1857, prominent headlines in a national journal announced from New York that in a 'Revival Extraordinary' three or four hundred converts had made a public profession of faith. Twenty-one persons had professed conversion on the first day of the movement and, as the work steadily increased, the number of public professions grew from a score to forty-five daily, a hundred people having been converted on the Sunday prior to the penning of the report for publication. Hence the enthusiastic correspondent stated:[9]

> The work is taking within its range . . . persons of all classes. Men of low degree, and men of high estate for wealth and position; old men and maidens and even little children are seen humbly kneeling together pleading for grace. The mayor of the city, with other persons of like position, are not ashamed to be seen bowed at the altar of prayer beside the humble servant.

Walter and Phoebe Palmer reported converts by the hundreds in camp meetings in Ontario and Quebec in the fall of 1857, the attendances ranging from 5000 to 6000 during the 'Indian summer' in the northland.[10]

Hamilton's 'gust of Divine power' sweeping the entire community had its origin in the stirring of the laity and was entirely spontaneous. This rise to leadership on the part of laymen became typical of the great movement that followed.

In fact, the Hamilton Revival bore all the marks of the subsequent American Awakening, save one, the union prayer meeting feature developed in New York, and popularized throughout the States.

The account of this extraordinary revival of religion was read by hundreds of wistful pastors in the Methodist Episcopal Church, America's largest and most evangelistic body of believers at that time.[11] The appearance of the account of the Hamilton Revival in Christian newspapers was followed by a steadily increasing number of paragraphs describing local awakenings in various states.

Among the signs of preparation of heart for an awakening was the calling of a convention at Pittsburgh, 1st December 1857.[12] This was under Presbyterian auspices, and largely attended by the ministers from the Synods of Pittsburgh, Allegheny, Wheeling, and Ohio.[13] The convention continued in session for three days, considering the necessity of a general revival of religion in the churches represented and in others as well. Agenda of the meetings included discussion of the means, the encouragements, and the hindrances, the demand of the times, the indications of divine providence and all related questions on revival.

It was a solemn, anxious, melting and encouraging meeting. Two hundred ministers and many laymen attended, and much of the time was spent in prayer. Then many local ministers of Presbyterian and other churches delivered messages on the first Sunday of the New Year (1858) on the subject of revival, and the first Thursday was observed as a day of humiliation, fasting and prayer. It was the same in its effects as in a convention at Cincinnati.[14]

In December, Baptist pastors throughout New York set aside one day each week for an all-day meeting of intercession for an outpouring of the Spirit. Baptists were being prepared also.[15] Among Methodists, these prayer meetings multiplied, and all other evangelical denominations interceded with God for a Divine visitation.

Meanwhile, in metropolitan New York, events were about to take place that would capture the attention of the nation. On 1st July 1857, a quiet and zealous businessman named Jeremiah Lanphier had been appointed as a city missionary in downtown New York.[16] Born in Coxsackie, in upper New York in 1809, he had been converted in 1842 in Broadway Tabernacle built by Charles G. Finney a decade earlier, toward the end of the earlier movement of spiritual revival.

A journalist described Lanphier as 'tall, with a pleasant
face, an affectionate manner, and indomitable energy and
perseverance; a good singer, gifted in prayer and exhortation,
a welcome guest in any house, shrewd and endowed with much
tact and common sense.'

The North Dutch Reformed Church in Lower Manhattan
had been suffering from a depletion of membership due to
removal of population from downtown to better residential
quarters, and the new city missionary was engaged to make
diligent visitation in the immediate precincts to encourage
church attendance among the floating population of the lower
city streets.[17]

The movement of population away from the heart of the
city has posed problems for city churches ever since the
industrial revolution began.   Members moving out to the
suburbs generally attach themselves to a suburban church
of like faith or congenial atmosphere.   It is not so easy to
attract the unchurched people downtown to attend a place of
worship hitherto frequented by the better classes.   These
unchurched people are often handicapped by sorry poverty.

Burdened by the need, Jeremiah Lanphier decided to invite others to join him in a noonday prayer meeting, to be
held on Wednesdays.   He therefore distributed a handbill,
placing it in the offices and warehouses:[18]

How Often Shall I Pray?
As often as the language of prayer is in my heart; as
often as I see my need of help; as often as I feel the
power of temptation; as often as I am made sensible
of any spiritual declension or feel the aggression of a
worldly spirit. In prayer we leave the business of time
for that of eternity, and intercourse with men for
intercourse with God.

Lanphier announced on the other side of the bill that the
meeting was intended to give merchants, mechanics, clerks,
strangers and businessmen generally an opportunity to stop
and call upon God amid the perplexities incident to their respective avocations.   It was planned to last for an hour, but
was also designed for those who found it inconvenient to
remain more than five or ten minutes, as well as people
able to remain the full hour.

Accordingly at noon, 23rd September 1857, the door was
opened. The time went by, and nobody appeared.   At 12:30,
a step on the stairs was heard, and another and another,
until six men gathered and prayed together.[19]

The attendances increased by the Wednesday following. In the first week of October 1857, it was decided to hold meetings daily instead of weekly. In the same week, the extraordinary revival of religion swept over Hamilton in far away Canada. The New York prayer meetings as well as the Hamilton awakening preceded the third event. In the second week of October, the great financial panic of that year reached a crisis and prostrated business everywhere. It is impossible not to connect the three events, for in them was demonstrated the need of religious revival, the means by which to accomplish it, and the provision of Divine grace to meet the serious situation in church and society.

It is the fashion among the uninformed and the sceptical to dismiss the 1858 Revival as hysteria following the bank panic of October 1857.[20] This view, which is ideological rather than historical, ignores the fact that the prayer meetings began during the month before the financial crisis prostrated business; its evangelistic phase began in Canada which was not affected by the crash; rural areas remote from the city experienced revivals three months after the panic; and the cities were not swept by the enthusiasm until six months after the crash, when the newspapers at last publicized it. It is foolish to ignore the bank failures as a factor, but even more foolish to consider them the major factor, in the light of the fact that most bank failures (including 1929) have not at all produced religious revivals.

The promise of renewal, given Solomon in the days of the Kings, has made it clear that the humbling of the people of God, their diligence in intercession, their seeking of the Divine Will, and their turning from recognized sin—these are the factors in Revival, bringing about in God's good time an answer to their prayers, forgiveness of their sin, and a healing of their community. And these were the real factors recognized at the time by authorities qualified to judge, rather than the notions of facetious journalists of the day or opinions of the prejudiced a century or so later.

From tiny springs of prayer in New York and preaching in Hamilton came a flood soon to envelope the world. The United States received the blessing first, then the United Kingdom, Australia, South Africa and South India.

Within six months, ten thousand business men were gathering daily for prayer in New York. Within two years, a million converts were added to the American churches. No part of the nation remained untouched by fervent prayer.

Not only was the population of the United States involved, but within a year or so the people of the United Kingdom— Ulster, Scotland, Wales and England—were moved by an awakening as extensive and lasting as the Evangelical Revival of Wesley's day.

It was to be expected that such an awakening would also touch the ministry of American missionaries working overseas. Not only was that effected, but a reviving of the work of God occurred wherever there was an evangelical cause of any size, particularly in India and Southern Africa.

The 1858 Revival must therefore be considered in its worldwide context, and not as an American phenomenon only. It becomes ludicrous to name the movement 'the bank panic revival' in the absence of bank panics elsewhere. Its contemporaries rightly called it 'the prayer meeting revival,' for it was universally marked by fervent prayer.

2

THE RISING TIDE

At the New Year 1858, New York City had a population of eight hundred thousand that included neither inhabitants of Brooklyn nor of the other boroughs of the present city. New York was by no means an irreligious city, for therein were church sittings for fully one quarter of the inhabitants and church attendance was fairly good.[1]

Notices of 'revivals of religion' began to appear in the religious press at the beginning of the year. Meanwhile the faithful Fulton street company was ever growing in strength and prayers were being answered in 'drops' and 'showers' of blessing.[2] The Gothic Church in Brooklyn reported seventy-five conversions in a local awakening in January. During the same month a thorough revival moved the Hudson River town of Yonkers, when nearly ninety conversions occurred.[3] Over in New Jersey towns, unusual awakenings were beginning, and throughout the whole country was increasing an expectancy of a downpour of Divine blessing. As yet, the revival was in its preparatory stage, with the quickening quite obvious to the ministers of the various churches but unnoticed by the public at large.

In February, the secular press, noticing that something unprecedented was happening, began to give space to revival news. On 10th February, a New York daily newspaper gave widespread publicity to the movement in an editorial telling of the crowds at the Fulton Street meeting and elsewhere in lower Manhattan.[4]

> We understand that arrangements are being made for the establishment of one or two additional meetings in the upper portion of the city; soon the striking of the five bells at 12 o'clock will generally be known as the signal for the 'Hour of Prayer.'

Indicating a move from prayer to evangelism, the same journal announced two weeks later that 'Religious Inquiry Meetings' were being carried on daily in the Norfolk Street Church, of which Dr. Armitage was the pastor. The hour was from 4 until 6 p.m., attendance already noteworthy.[5]

Prayer meetings multiplied. Meanwhile, in the original meeting place in Fulton Street, the sponsors were trying to accommodate crowds by holding three simultaneous prayer meetings one above the other in rooms in the same building; the seats were all filled and the passages were so crowded that it was scarcely possible for people to pass in or out. Hundreds were unable to gain admission, and a demand arose for more meetings at noon.[6]

Undoubtedly the greatest awakening in New York's varied history was sweeping the city and it was of such an order to make a whole nation curious. There was no fanaticism, no hysteria, simply an incredible movement of the people to pray. The services were not devoted to preaching. Instead anyone was free to pray.

In Washington, it was noted that in New York 'religious interest has been growing in the midst of the rowdyism everywhere so long prevalent,' adding that the 'religious revivals were never more numerous or effective.'[7]

Then churches began to feel the impact of the noonday meetings,[8] which were largely laymen's voluntary efforts. One typical example of happy reaction in the churches was that Thirteenth Presbyterian Church received one Sunday, by a public profession of faith, 113 people: twenty-six were heads of families, ten teachers in their Sunday School, and more than half the total over twenty years of age.[9]

On March 17, Burton's Theatre in Chambers Street in Brooklyn was thrown open for noonday prayer meetings organized and financed by local merchants. In fact, Mr. Burton as the owner of the building was perfectly willing for them to operate religious services there, and himself expressed a desire to be prayed for. Half an hour before the time appointed for the service, the theatre was packed in every corner from the pit to the roof.[10] By noon, the entrances were so thronged that it required great exertions to get within a hearing distance, and no amount of elbowing could force an entrance so far as to gain sight of the stage! People clung to each projection along the walls, and they piled themselves upon the seats, and crowded the stage beneath, above and behind the curtain. The street in front was crowded with vehicles, and the excitement was 'tremendous.' Almost all the assembly were businessmen, only two hundred being ladies. With fifty clergymen, the Rev. Theodore Cuyler led the service. Also occupied at noon by businessmen desiring to pray were the public halls in other parts of greater New York.[11]

The local newspapers increased their coverage of news. A two-column write-up upon a front-page gave a significant review of the movement in New York City (Manhattan without Brooklyn). At least 6110 people were in attendance at daily prayer meetings. A partial survey on March 26 showed:[12]

Fulton Street	Dutch Reformed	300
John Street	Methodist Episcopal	600
Burton's Theatre	Union service	1200
Ninth Street	Dutch Reformed	150
Pilgrims Church	Congregational	125
Broome Street	Dutch Reformed	300
Waverley Place	Y.M.C.A.	200
Mercer Street	Union service	150
Madison Square	Presbyterian	200
34th Street	Methodist Episcopal	250

The estimates were made by reporters using horse cabs to rush from place to place. Another dozen places listed gave a very incomplete review of the total situation.

Meanwhile, the noonday prayer meetings had flowed over into weeknight services in many of the churches, where conversions were common. The most sensational conversion in March was that of Orville Gardner, a pugilist better known as Awful Gardner. Gardner's public testimony had greatest impact on a certain class of citizen. Before very long ten thousand New Yorkers had been converted to God and were in the care of the churches,[13] and in May a good authority gave the total for the city as fifty thousand converts.[14] The national press from coast to coast carried news of the great awakening in the metropolis, citizens everywhere being challenged by the movement.

The most publicized work of grace undoubtedly was the condition prevailing in the metropolis of New York, but the phenomenon of packed churches and startling conversions was reported everywhere inquiries could be made. Three streams of blessing seemed to flow out from the Middle Atlantic States, one northwards to New England, another one southwards as far as Texas, and a third westwards along the Ohio valley.

In a leading secular newspaper[15] an observer stated it well, when he wrote that 'the Revivals, or Great Awakenings, continue to be the leading topic of the day . . . from Texas in the South to the extreme of our Western boundaries and our Eastern limits; their influence is felt by every denomination.' Papers from Maine to Louisiana reflected his view.

Denominational organs confirmed the news of extraordinary happenings. As early as the beginning of February, 'extensive revivals' prevailing in the Methodist Episcopal Church all over the country were reported to the denomination's leading journal, which observed that its exchanges with Methodist contemporaries in the Central, Pittsburgh, Northwestern, Western, and its own territory told of a total of eight thousand people converted in Methodist meetings in the course of one week.[16]

A Baptist journal reported 17,000 converts: [17]

Maine	411	Ohio	1148
New Hampshire	82	Indiana	737
Vermont	304	Illinois	1146
Massachusetts	2575	Michigan	604
Rhode Island	387	Wisconsin	465
Connecticut	795	Iowa	278
New York	2386	Minnesota	388
Pennsylvania	746	Missouri	424
New Jersey	698	Tennessee	711
Delaware	40	Virginia	205
Canada	287	Other States	207

The Baptist figures were very incomplete—simply numbers reported to a metropolitan office by odd correspondents.

There was another attempt at estimating the actual number of converts, again 'exceedingly incomplete' and valuable only for the relative proportions in various states. In May 1858, an editor in New York collected interdenominational figures from as many sources as possible. They showed that a total of 96,216 people had become converted to God in the few months past, and this was considered very heartening. The smaller number from States of the Deep South or California may be attributed to delay in transmission long distance by land or by sea:[18]

Maine	2670	Illinois	10460
New Hampshire	1376	Wisconsin	1467
Vermont	770	Minnesota	508
Massachusetts	6254	Iowa	2179
Rhode Island	1331	Missouri	2027
Connecticut	2799	Kentucky	2666
New York	16674	Tennessee	1666
New Jersey	6035	Delaware	179
Pennsylvania	6732	Maryland	1806
Ohio	8009	Virginia	1005
Michigan	8081	Deep South	1494
Indiana	4775	California	50

The number of conversions reported reached a total of fifty thousand a week. For a period of two years, there were ten thousand additions to church membership weekly.

The well-known New York editors, Horace Greeley and James Gordon Bennett, had enthusiastically begun to feature revival news from February 1858 onward, adding editorials to news items.[19] Newspapers throughout the country followed suit. Because this Awakening was so thoroughly interdenominational, newspaper men felt free to give fullest reports, in contrast with earlier times.[20] The stage was being set for a nationwide movement without precedent in world history and never repeated since.

The influence of the Revival was felt everywhere in the nation. It first captured the great cities, but it also spread through every town and village and country hamlet. It swamped schools and colleges. It affected all classes regardless of condition. A Divine influence seemed to pervade the land, and men's hearts were strangely warmed by a Power that was outpoured in unusual ways. There was no fanaticism. There was a remarkable unanimity of approval by religious and secular observers alike, with scarcely a critical voice heard anywhere. It seemed to many that the fruits of Pentecost had been repeated a thousandfold.

Nowhere was the Awakening more effective and without fanaticism than in the colleges and universities, from New England to the western frontier, from Virginia to the heart of Texas. Few were the institutions untouched by it.

As early as November 1857, an awakening was reported in Oberlin College, a citadel of evangelism.[21] The historic colleges of New England were moved in 1858, Dartmouth in 'quiet good order and serious deportment,' Middlebury with half the students inquirers, Williams witnessing the sound conversion of some of the wildest on campus, Amherst the whole college penetrated, only three or four seniors still unconverted—these typical of New England colleges.[22]

At Harvard, predominantly Unitarian, it was regarded as 'poor form' to preach the Gospel; but the leading professor of religion, Frederic Dan Huntington, initiated a well-attended mid-week devotional meeting in Appleton Chapel, and thereafter entering the Episcopal ministry. The movement at Yale in 1858 was unprecedented, 45 seniors, 62 juniors, 60 sophomores, and 37 freshmen professing conversion, more than a hundred of these applying for membership of Yale's Congregational College Church.[23]

Similar awakenings occurred in the colleges of Middle Atlantic states, in New York and New Jersey. Of 272 men at Princeton, 102 professed faith and 50 entered Christian ministry.[24] There were awakenings in the colleges of the South, 'great power and blessed results' at Davidson as in other North Carolina campuses, 'scarcely a solitary young man without conviction of sin' at Oglethorpe University, and awakenings at the other colleges in Georgia. There was a noteworthy revival at Baylor University in Texas.[25]

There were awakenings at Denison and Miami in Ohio, and movements far to the west in Beloit College (Wisconsin) and William Jewell (Missouri).[26] The general awakening in newly settled California led to the foundation of colleges, one becoming the University of California at Berkeley.[27]

Frederick Rudolph, a historian of American colleges and universities,[28] named Williams, Wofford, Amherst, North Carolina, Wake Forest, Trinity, Wabash, Georgia and Emory as universities and colleges touched by the Revival of 1858, which moved 'dozens of other colleges as well.' However, he was mistaken in designating 1858 as 'the last great revival year,' in view of later movements such as 1905:[29]

> Evangelical religion—with its emphasis on a great outpouring of spirit, individual professions of experience, with its goal of total victory always waiting to be achieved—would never have as good a year again as 1858.

The state universities, which increased in numbers after the Civil War, experienced the same religious movements as private institutions during 1858, and, in fact, produced a new development in student religious life. The first Y.M.C.As. for students were organized at the University of Michigan and the University of Virginia during the Revival[30] of 1858. Prayer meetings multiplied among the 633 students at the state University of Virginia in 1858, becoming permanent. All the evangelical churches of Ann Arbor in Michigan had shared in the movement, and President Henry Tappan became a leader in the awakening at the state University. The Y.M.C.A. of those days was ardently evangelistic. As university campuses became more and more secularized, the collegiate Y.M.C.A. became the main vehicle of witness to the ever-increasing student population.

Instead of dissipating, the 1858 Awakening began to intensify throughout the United States. The crisis of the War between the States was approaching, but a harvest of souls was reaped before the storm burst on the nation.

3

THE EASTERN STATES

Throughout the 'fifties, church attendance in New England had remained high,[1] with fully one-quarter of the population attending church regularly and another quarter occasionally. But New England had always been a fruitful ground for theological controversy, producing the most rigid conservatives and the most volatile radicals in America. Finney visited the city of Boston in the winter of 1856, and found that his vital evangel was opposed strongly by various very orthodox theologians.[2] Boston thus was the happy hunting ground of controversialists, and a divisive spirit was prevalent.

Nevertheless, there were many faithful intercessors. A daily prayer meeting had been held in Boston for several years before the 1858 Awakening. An interest in religious revival continued to increase, so it was decided to commence a businessmen's prayer meeting in the Old South Church, which was convenient to the business district of the city. To the surprise of the sponsor, a businessman, the place was overcrowded the first day, and many could not get in at all.[3]

Early in March 1858, the secular press began to take notice of the revival, declaring that religious excitement was on the increase. Finney all the while was holding forth in Park Street Church, preaching on evangelistic topics. By that time, the revival had swept the city, and had become (to quote Finney) 'too general to keep any account at all of the number of converts, or to allow of any estimate being made that would approximate the truth.'

By March 1858, the awakening in Boston (like its counterpart in New York City) had become news to the whole nation. The Boston correspondent of a Washington newspaper affirmed that religion had become the chief concern in Boston and throughout New England.[4] The meetings for prayer, he reported, were crowded and solemn, with the whole assembly sometimes in tears, under the melting power of the Spirit. The movement in Boston was wholly interdenominational in character, not only Baptist minority and Congregational majority supporting it, but often the Unitarian churches.

The movement to prayer was by no means urban only. The awakening in New England generally was even stronger than in the metropolis. The most numerous denomination reported in the revival period[5] 11,744 added on profession; and another claimed 8,479 in a few months.[6] Two hundred and sixty smaller communities announced over ten thousand conversions in two months.[7]

In New Bedford, one in twenty of the people made a profession of faith in a few months, and similar awakenings were reported in Lynn and Haverhill. In a revival at Holliston, two hundred and fifty conversions occurred, a like number of additions being registered at Winchester. Unprecedented awakenings occurred at Lowell and Williamstown. Orange, 'a stronghold of error,' was transformed by the movement. In Massachusetts, a total of one hundred and fifty towns were moved by this revival of religion, with five thousand converted before the end of March.[8]

Great crowds in Portland, Maine attended the morning, noon, afternoon, and evening meetings and the church bells daily summoned thousands to prayer.[9] An extensive revival arose in Bangor and the nearby towns; while in Biddeford, the movement was distinguished for the remarkable rapidity of the work of grace, adults and heads of families being the outstanding fruit of the revival.[10] Large accessions were made by churches in Saco, a hundred and ten added at Deer Isle.

The city of Providence in Rhode Island had a time of religious interest never before known. Nearly every church was awakened, conversions becoming very numerous. Morning prayer meetings overflowed and other meetings were crowded —making a strong impression. It was noteworthy that there was no unhealthy excitement reported.[11] At Pawtucket, the revival increased until over a hundred people were professedly born again. At Warren, a single Baptist church experienced a wave of blessing that resulted in the conversion of more than one hundred people. Another thirty-six towns reported a thousand converts.[12]

In the State of Connecticut, the revival swept the communities in an unprecedented way.[13] One of the largest churches in New Haven was full to capacity for an 8 a.m. prayer meeting, repeating that proceeding daily at 5 p.m. Equally large prayer meetings were begun in Hartford and in New London. At Bethel, business was suspended for an hour every day between 4 and 5 p.m., and two hundred persons were reported converted in two months, three-quarters of whom joined the Congregational Church. In Connecticut also was reported a town where no unconverted adult could be found.[14] No fanaticism was reported anywhere.

In the contiguous states of Vermont and New Hampshire, revivals occurred in Dartmouth College and in Brattleboro, Claremont, Northfield, St. Alban's, Burlington, Castleton, Middlesbury, Derby and Manchester, in each of which a daily prayer meeting had met with success.[15] Two hundred conversions were reported from Dover and New Ipswich, while forty other New Hampshire towns reported four hundred and twenty-five conversions, and forty Vermont towns reported over six hundred. And in Rutland, Vermont, two hundred or more people were led to decision for Christ, seventy in a single meeting.

Walter and Phœbe Palmer, as a husband and wife team, had already experienced a remarkable awakening in upper Canada, significantly at Hamilton, but also in great series of meetings in the Ontarian towns. The summer and autumn were filled with great camp meetings, which affected first the Canadian Methodists, but other denominations as well. Across the border in Canada, awakenings began in St. John's in Newfoundland in January 1858, with 'remarkable scenes.' In the Maritime Provinces, the revival continued for years — 'scarcely a church westward but has been refreshed and quickened, and in very many, souls have been converted.' The movement later affected Montreal, in French Quebec, when Payson Hammond visited the city.[16]

The State of New York was soon swept by a wave of religious interest comparable to the one being experienced in its greatest focus of population. Along the beautiful Hudson River, busy little towns and cities witnessed unusual happenings. At Hudson, the Dutch Reformed, Baptist, Methodist, and Presbyterian churches launched a daily prayer meeting as a union effort, people coming 'as doves to their windows' to throng the place beyond every precedent.[17] At Yonkers, more than two hundred people were converted in a few weeks. The Washington Street Methodist Episcopal Church, where meetings were held every day in Poughkeepsie, found its altar rails crowded with inquirers, and in three weeks of special meetings in all the churches, three hundred people sought salvation.[18] Peekskill, a reputedly wicked town, saw the same means used and the same results achieved. The union prayer meetings at Kingston, Ulster County, overflowed one church after another.[19]

Farther up the Hudson river at Troy, clerks, merchants, and particularly professional men showed an interest in their own spiritual welfare, hence meetings were held daily and nightly in the churches which gained several hundred additions.[20] Catskill, noted for its religious indifference, saw a revival commence through the conversion of a young Bible class attender; each other member became converted and 115 new members were soon afterwards received in church membership.[21]

Albany, the state capital, with 60,000 population, was the scene of unusual happenings.[22] An early morning prayer meeting was initiated by state legislators who began with six participants in the rooms of the Court of Appeals opposite the Senate Chamber; soon afterwards the rooms were overflowing. The noon prayer meetings attracted great crowds in Albany as elsewhere. The Baptist pastor at Union Village baptized 111 converts and expected soon to baptize more, saying he had never witnessed a revival of such extent where there was manifest so little mere sympathetic excitement. More than fifty of those baptized were heads of families, between the ages of 25 and 50, one being a man in his eighty-third year.   A hundred and forty people 'decided' in Olean; two hundred in Cold Spring.[23]

All this was accomplished without devices of any kind, other than the call to prayer. No series of advertised and promoted evangelistic meetings were arranged, and no itinerant evangelist was called in. Typical of the spontaneous revivals in New York State's little cities was a report from Salem: [24]

> Without any alarming event, without any extraordinary preaching or any special effort or other means that might be supposed peculiarly adapted to interest the minds of people, there has been within a short time past in several towns and villages in Washington and Warren Counties, and in towns and villages along the western part of the State of Vermont, revival so extraordinary as to attract the attention of all classes . . .
> . . . In one town, over a hundred have been brought to conviction and conversion, and the glorious work is still going on; they expect the whole town will be converted —for this they pray. This work does not appear to be confined to the churches; hundreds are converted at prayer meetings, in private homes, in the workshops, and at their work in the fields.

Farther west, on the strategic Mohawk River, like revivals occurred in the towns and villages. In Schenectady,
church bells sounded every evening, calling the crowds to
meetings, filling each church.[26] Two popular prayer meetings daily bore much fruit, and converts came into church
fellowships with surprising rapidity; the ice on the Mohawk
was broken for believers' baptism. From the month of
December onwards in Utica, the pastors of the evangelical
churches united in union prayer meetings held in rotation in
various churches, the movement being so well supported that
the early morning prayer service in a large church was
crowded with worshippers, some frequently having to stand.
Syracuse held union services in Convention Hall.[27] Geneva
produced a revival of unusual stillness and solemnity, with
numerous conversions and the usual prayer meetings, one
church trebling membership. Buffalo witnessed a powerful
revival of religion. Examples could be multiplied, for two
hundred towns reported six thousand specific cases of real
conversion.[28]

One of the first sections of the country to experience an
awakening was the New Jersey area, which reported stirring
revivals of religion as early as late October 1857.[29] In both
Readington and Pennington, a hundred and twenty conversions
occurred before New Year, while blessing began in Newark
in January with sixty additions in Mount Lebanon Circuit.
Orange Methodists rejoiced in no less than one hundred and
twenty-five additions in early February. The Baptists also
reported unusual awakenings, as did other denominations.

By the month of March, the awakenings in New Jersey
matched anything observed on the American continent. The
city of Newark, population 70,000, witnessed startling evidences of a sweeping movement there. In a couple of months,
2785 in all professed conversion, averaging one hundred
conversions in each reporting congregation. It became a
common sight to see business houses closed, with a notice
'will reopen at the close of the prayer meeting,' and the union
meetings thus advertised were crowded to oveflowing. Extra
efforts were made to reach members of the Fire Department
with the gospel, and on one occasion, nearly two thousand
firemen attended one such meeting at the National Hotel in
Market Street. Dr Scott, a leading Newark pastor, testified
that the revival was winning the most mature minds in the
community, judging by the forty-five people who had just
united with his congregation.[30]

Similar scenes of revival were witnessed in Paterson (New Jersey) where a successful union meeting was begun as well as evening meetings, all churches reporting accessions to membership. In Jersey City, large numbers professed conversion, and there also a union meeting was held daily from 7 to 9 a.m. in the Lyceum on Grand Street. In New Brunswick (New Jersey) 177 joined the Methodist Church, 112 of whom were heads of families, including steamboat captains and pilots; and in Trenton the Methodists alone gained upwards of 1700 additions. Sixty towns in revival in the State of New Jersey reported approximately six thousand conversions.[31] There was not a single instance of fanaticism reported anywhere in the state.

Among the first attenders of the original Businessmen's Prayer Meeting in New York City was a young man, not yet twenty-one years of age, hailing from Philadelphia. Upon his return to his home, he and some of his fellow Y.M.C.A. men approached trustees of the Methodist Episcopal Church on Fourth Street below Arch Street and requested the use of their lecture room for a similar meeting. The request was granted, and the first noon prayer meeting in Philadelphia was held there on 23rd November 1857.[32]

For a long time, however, the response of Philadelphia's businessmen was disappointing, the average attendance being about a dozen men. But on February 3, the meeting was removed to a little ante-room in the spacious public hall owned by Dr. Jayne, popularly known as Jayne's Hall.[33] Throughout February, increase in attendance was gradual; twenty, thirty, forty, fifty, then sixty attending. In March, revival came.

At first, only the small room was occupied, with a few in attendance. Then it became overflowing, and the meeting removed to the main saloon, meetings starting there on 10th March. Twenty-five hundred seats were provided, and were filled to overflowing.[34] The sponsors next removed a partition from the main floor space and platform; next the floor, platform and lower gallery; then floor, platform, and both galleries filled;[35] fully six thousand people gathered daily. It was here that George Duffield wrote 'Stand Up for Jesus.'

For months on end, each separate church was opened at least every evening, some of them as often as three to five times a day, and all were filled. Simple prayer, confession, exhortation and singing was all that was heard, but it was 'so earnest, so solemn, the silence...so awful, the singing... so overpowering' that the meetings were unforgettable.[36]

In order to continue the work, which (as in New York) flooded churches with inquirers and converts, a big canvas tent was bought for $2000 and opened for religious services on 1st May 1858. During the following four months, an aggregate of 150,000 people attended the ministry under the canvas, many conversions resulting.[37] The churches in Philadelphia reported five thousand converts thus won.

The Awakening in Philadelphia was to have a long-range effect across the Atlantic, for fraternal delegates from the Irish Presbyterian Church observed the movement and told their fellow-Christians of the wonders that they saw. It was in Ireland that the Awakening made its first trans-Atlantic appearance, spreading all over the British Isles.

It was impossible to keep record of all the Pennsylvania towns and villages and country places that reported blessing, for even the most enthusiastic editors wearied of the task. West in Pittsburgh two daily prayer meetings were begun to accommodate intercessors desiring to pray at noon between the hours of 11.30 and 12.30, about a thousand attending in these two places, and as many more in meetings elsewhere in the city. The churches of Pittsburgh reaped a harvest.[38]

In Maryland, the revival began in December, when there were sixty conversions reported in Havre de Grace and over a hundred from Monroe Circuit, in Baltimore Conference —both instances Methodist.[39] The Baptists were reporting similar results. In Baltimore, during the spring of 1858, a daily prayer meeting was begun by the Y.M.C.A. with an encouraging attendance. Religious journals continued to report great numbers of conversions from all around the State, all the denominations sharing equally in the stirring.

Within the Nation's capital, five daily prayer meetings were started, commencing respectively at 6:30 a.m., 10 a.m., 5 p.m. and 7 p.m., the Y.M.C.A. and the churches sponsoring the effort.[40] The capital's newspapers described the meeting as 'still and solemn,' and on April 1 commented editorially that the religious excitement in the city was unabated, five thousand or so attending the prayer service in the Academy of Music Hall in Washington.[41] There was general consensus of opinion that a Divine visitation had occurred.

Washington was a sorely divided city at the time. The slavery issue was transforming itself into one of secession, soon to develop into civil war. Apparently, the revival of spiritual life became effective in personal morality first, the larger social issue requiring much longer time.

4

WEST OF THE ALLEGHENIES

By the New Year of 1858, it appeared that the wave of religious revival had crossed the mountains and was pouring down the Ohio following the line of settlements established by the pioneers. Within two months, four hundred and eighty towns reported some fifteen thousand professed conversions in prayer meetings in their churches.[1]

The leading Presbyterian magazine announced that the entire western country was sharing in a great revival movement.[2] It added the details of great awakenings occurring in all major cities—in Cleveland, Cincinnati, Louisville, Indianapolis, Detroit, Chicago, St. Louis and Dubuque, also saying that cities, villages and country places of Kentucky, Ohio, Michigan, Indiana, Illinois, Wisconsin, Missouri and Iowa were receiving revival increase. So also the regional Methodist journals, exulting in the spiritual winning of 'the West,' described awakenings in Ohio, Illinois and Indiana, claiming that forty-two Methodist ministers had reported 4384 conversions in three months, 750 being in one place.[3]

In Wheeling, West Virginia, it was reported that the past winter (1857-58) would long be remembered for its revivals. The Methodist leaders declared that there had been nothing to equal the movement in strength, not even the glorious days of 1839-40 which added to the Methodist Episcopal churches 154,000 converts. In some communities of West Virginia, almost the entire adult population had been brought under the influence of the Awakening, with various churches reporting one hundred to two hundred accessions.[4]

On the south bank of the Ohio River, Kentucky experienced unprecedented stirrings of religion. So many people were turning to God that Louisville churches were opened by day and by night.[5] Union prayer meetings were soon begun in the big Kentucky city, secular journalists observing that the meetings were growing in such interest, it was impossible to accommodate the crowds.[6] The Masonic Temple was overflowing with more than a thousand eager people in attendance as the prayer meeting began with:

Amazing Grace, how sweet the sound
That saved a wretch like me!
I once was lost, but now am found,
Was blind, but now I see.

The meeting of March 29 broke all records, the largest crowd yet seen there being unable to find proper space in the Masonic Temple. Meanwhile the daily prayer meetings were increasing, their influence pervading the city, with more than a thousand conversions resulting to the praise of Almighty God.[7]

In early April, four popular prayer meetings attracted an 'immense concourse'; there was no abatement of interest or diminution of attendance and such had been the improvement in the morals of the city and state that it was said by the press that the millennium had arrived at last.[8]

The Spirit of God seems to have produced an unusual degree of tenderness and solemnity in all classes... Never in the city have we seen so fair a prospect for a general and thorough work of grace as is now indicated.

Revival had already commenced in Lexington, Covington, Frankfort and other Kentucky towns. On the river steamer, Louisville journalists were informed, the religious Revival was a universal topic on the voyage up river, a spontaneous and crowded prayer meeting having been held in the main saloon until a late hour.[9]

Across the river in the State of Ohio[10] two hundred towns reported twelve thousand conversions in a couple of months. In Cincinnati, attendance at daily prayer meetings became so large that the venue chosen was unable to accommodate the crowds, necessitating a move to the First Presbyterian Church. The religious excitement in April raged unabated, and the churches were becoming more popular every day with citizens unaccustomed to the means of grace.[11] To the north, revival swept town after town.

In Cleveland, population forty thousand, the attendance at the early morning prayer meetings throughout all the city churches was two thousand, and the whole community was stirred up. The Plymouth Congregational Church held five meetings daily from six in the morning until nine at night. One thousand people were received into fellowship in just a couple of months.[12] The Methodist Episcopal Church of Circleville, Ohio, received two hundred and ten accessions, while other churches in the same town were receiving their thirties and forties.[13]

In Indiana, a hundred and fifty towns reported from four to five thousand converts in two months of revival.[14] Noonday prayer meetings were begun in Indianapolis, the State capital, and a religious interest pervaded the whole city, filling the churches with intercessors and inquirers.

In Michigan, morning prayer meetings held in the down-town Baptist and Congregational places of worship in Detroit were crowded by business men of all denominations. The Congress Street Methodist Episcopal Church reported over one hundred and forty conversions, and numerous inquirers and converts were reported in the other churches. In six Michigan towns, revivals with between fifteen hundred and two thousand conversions to God were recorded.[15]

There was a striking instance of the power of prayer demonstrated in Kalamazoo in Michigan.[16] There Episcopal, Baptist, Methodist, Presbyterian and Congregational people happily united in announcing a public prayer meeting. The ecumenical effort was begun in fear and trembling, it being wondered if the public would consider attending.

At the very first meeting a request was read: 'A praying wife requests the prayers of this meeting for her uncon-verted husband.' All at once a burly man rose and said: 'I am that man; I have a praying wife, and this request must be for me. I want you to pray for me!'[17]

As soon as he was seated, another man arose, ignoring his predecessor, to say with tears: 'I am that man; I have a praying wife. She prays for me. And now she asks you to pray for me. I am sure I am that man. I want you to pray for me!' Five other convicted husbands requested prayer, and a spirit of conviction moved that assembly. Before long, there were between four and five hundred conversions in Kalamazoo, and the churches thrived in the revival.

Farther west, an unusual interest manifested itself in St. Louis, Missouri, both in the churches and in the business circles of the city. The union prayer meetings were well attended by all classes of people among whom great serious-ness existed; and all the churches were crowded.[18] In St. Joseph, a great awakening began, churches of the city uniting to carry on the work. Whole families were converted. Simi-lar blessing was reported from St. Charles. A nephew of the renowned English Baptist minister, the Rev. Andrew Fuller, a converted actor J. B. Fuller, produced great excitement in Missouri by his preaching.[19] Fifty Missouri towns reported two thousand converts.

Uncounted intercessors and upward of a thousand converts were registered in Wisconsin in the early part of 1858, and about the same number was reported in Minnesota territory, three hundred converts being made by Minneapolis churches while a private correspondent[20] in nearby St. Paul wrote that 'the good work of the Lord goes on. The interest is still on the increase. St. Paul never saw a time like the present. The Holy Spirit seems to pervade the entire community, in every department of business.' In Iowa, the Congregational journal observed that never before had such a general interest in religion existed in Dubuque. Sixty other towns sharing in the awakening reported fifteen hundred converts. In weeks of beginning, a hundred and fifty towns in Illinois announced between three and four thousand conversions.[21] Baptists in Illinois were receiving a thousand additions a month. In Dixon, Rockford, Peoria and Springfield, unprecedented revivals of religion occurred.

Chicago in 1860 could boast of more than a hundred thousand inhabitants, for it was then enjoying a local boom due to the opening-up of the Middle West. There were few signs of revival in 1857, but the turn of the year 1858 brought news of 'a very interesting revival of religion.'[22]

By the month of March, the state of religion had become phenomenal.[23] Two hundred people had already been converted in four Methodist churches, and more than a hundred in as many Presbyterian churches, where 8 a.m. prayer meetings were in full swing daily. The Trinity Episcopal Church had a noonday prayer meeting, and the Dutch Reformed Church reported marked interest. First Baptist Church noted an increase and in Tabernacle (Second) there had been fifty conversions in meetings begun before New Year. In many cases, the proportion of heads of families converted was noticeably high, up to 50%. On March 13, it was stated:[24]

> In all these religious efforts there had been no appearance of excitement and no unusual means used: the movement has been quiet, deep and effective. The pastors of the churches have had very little assistance.

On March 19, a proposal was made to organize a general prayer meeting of the union type, similar to New York and Philadelphia meetings. Morning prayer meetings increased all the while; on March 25, the newspapers (in observing the 'unusual and almost unprecedented' events) were reporting that two thousand people now gathered daily at noontime for prayer in the Metropolitan Hall. A letter (March 21) stated:

> The Metropolitan Hall is crowded to suffocation. The interest in the First Baptist Church is beyond anything ever known in this city, and exceeds anything I have ever seen in my life. Some who have come to the city on business have become so distressed about their condition as sinners before God that they have entirely forgotten their business in the earnestness of their desire for salvation.
>
> I am amazed to see such evidences of God's grace and power manifested among men. I might add that the First Baptist Church has daily meetings from eight to nine in the morning, twelve to one at noon, and at six-and-a-half o'clock in the evening. The church today has had an all-day meeting.

At the end of that week, the press reporting commented on the perfect union of all evangelical Christians.[25] A religious review of the week told of morning and noontime meetings in churches of all denominations, with conversions daily. First Presbyterian Church reported seventy-five and St. John's Episcopal nearly forty added while Union Park Baptist gave a week's increase as forty and Tabernacle Baptist twenty-four on the Lord's Day. The Negro community was strongly affected by the revival, and conversions were reported by Baptist and Methodist churches of Negro stock in Chicago— as in other great cities.

The coming of temptingly good weather in April brought about a slackening of attendance at main meetings in Metropolitan Hall.[26] A thousand people were still regular supporters of prayer meetings, but the curious and spurious had now dropped off. By April 20, the noonday meeting at Metropolitan Hall was transferred to the First Baptist Church.[27] The revival had begun to run in different channels, there being an increase in the evening meetings of an evangelistic nature, with a thousand conversions in all churches to date.

In May, the revival interest in the city gradually retired from the union meetings into individual churches. The number of prayer meetings increased, but not the attendance, 1800 in daytime and 5000 at night. Large numbers joining the churches so constantly excited curiosity no more among the newspapermen.[28]

On May 24, the Moderator of the Presbyterian General Assembly (meeting that year in Chicago) declared that they were witnessing 'scenes of revival such as the Church of Christ had never enjoyed as richly before.' His remarks applied to Chicago and the rest of the country, of course.

During that winter, D. L. Moody received his first great challenge to Christian work, writing to his mother in New England to tell of his constant attendance and joy at services, though he dated his New Year letter with the previous year-date, as often happens in the first week of January.

Moody was impelled to convert inspiration into service. It was during a hot summer in 1858 that Moody got together a class of boys off the street, its first sessions being held on a beach at Lake Michigan.[29] The rapid growth of the city providing all the raw material for evangelism needed in Chicago, Moody became interested in winning young people to Christ through the Sunday School and the Young Men's Christian Association. He became an expert in 'drumming up' scholars for Sunday School.

Before very long, Moody, in 1858, started one of his own in a vacant saloon, and soon it became the largest Sunday School in Chicago. All the while, he continued active in his business as a salesman, but in 1860 he gave up his lucrative business to live 'by faith' in extending the revival in the city, resigning $5000 a year for uncertainty.[30]

The year 1858 was outstanding in the history of many Chicago churches.[31] Union Park Baptist Church recorded great revivals in the winters of 1858 and 1859, in which considerable numbers were added to the membership. Trinity Episcopal, which had 152 members in 1855, 186 in 1856, and 121 in 1857, built a new church to seat 1400 in 1860.

Third Baptist Church remembered an extended meeting of three weeks beginning 28th January 1858, when the pastor (as evangelist) enlisted twenty converts in the church. Second Presbyterian, after a lean year with the smallest number of converts (only nineteen in 1857), recorded 1858 as of very special interest, having provided large numbers of converts exceeding a hundred both among the adults and the children of the congregation.

In the same way, First Presbyterian enrolled seventy-five upon profession of faith in 1858 in 'consequence of a powerful revival' which gave an impulse to the spiritual activities there. Alas, South Presbyterian Church reported only a limited number of additions, due to an unfortunate church quarrel about the property and about the 'slavery issue.' Other churches that engraved the Revival in their congregational histories were the Church of the Atonement which noted large additions to the membership in 1858, and Plymouth Congregational Church where Moody enrolled.

The Mennonites, including the newly organized Mennonite Brethren, began to emigrate from Russia to Canada and the United States in the 1870s. They came in tens of thousands. Not only did they bring the influence of the 1860 Awakening in Russia with them, but they found their Mennonite friends in North America moved by the same mid-century Revival.

The Old Mennonites, organized in North America under a form of church government combining episcopal, synodical and congregational elements, were profoundly moved by the 1858 Awakening in Pennsylvania and the Middle West. The most important figure in the life of the Old Mennonites in the nineteenth century was John Fretz Funk, who moved to Chicago in 1857.[32] Converted in 1858 under Presbyterian influence, he was baptized in 1859. An ardent Sunday School worker for D. L. Moody, he helped the Mennonites organize Sunday Schools, mission boards, and publishing houses. He served as evangelist from 1872, as bishop from 1892 onward.

The General Conference Mennonite Church was born in the Middle West in the wake of the 1858 Revival.[33] Meetings in 1859 and 1860 launched the new denomination, to which most of the incoming Russian Mennonites adhered. Foreign missionary interest developed in the revival period.

Revival among the Indians was observed in happenings in Minnesota in the early 1860s. Provoked by frauds practised on them and led by medicine men, the savage Sioux ravaged an area of about twenty thousand square miles with torch and tomahawk, cruelly butchering six hundred people, burning the mission and the homes of Christian Indians. The revolt was suppressed by military force and the braves hunted down.

At Mankato, after thirty-eight of the worst offenders had been executed, more than four hundred Indian warriors were imprisoned. Williamson and Riggs of the American Board seized the opportunity to preach to the prisoners, teaching them also to read and write.[34] A deep work of grace began that winter among the braves, until in the spring some three hundred asked for baptism.

At Fort Snelling, eighty miles away, families of the prisoners camped in tents and tepees. A school was begun for them. When Riggs came, bringing letters from prisoners to their families, he told of the revival at the Mankato stockade. The camp was deeply moved, and conviction of spirit stirred the squaws to burn their idols. After four years, prisoners and their families were reunited in Nebraska. By that time, four hundred converts constituted a church of their own.

News of the awakening 'back east' reached California in 'hundreds of thousands of affectionate letters,' provoking an immediate flocking of the Christians to prayer meetings in the churches and other gathering places.[35] By May of 1858, a steadily growing religious interest in San Francisco had resulted in a 'very considerable number of conversions,' membership in the more than a dozen churches in the San Francisco area exceeding nine thousand.[36] An increasingly great interest was reported from the interior of California, with prayer meetings multiplying in Sacramento, Stockton, Marysville and San Jose.[37] One small church east of San Jose reported that great numbers had joined the church and a large majority of the adult population of the area round about had been brought under the influence of the Gospel.[38]

In June, it was said that the daily prayer meetings in the San Francisco area were continuing with unabated interest, with many converts, and as the weeks of summer went by, the religious interest extended in a multiplication of daily prayer meetings and the conversion of many inquirers.[39] In Southern California, somewhat isolated from the Bay area, news of the Awakening reached the tiny churches overland and by sea directly, with similar results. To the north, the Oregon settlements received the news directly overland, a proliferation of prayer meetings heralding the inrush into the church memberships. No instances were reported of an outbreak of revival on the Pacific coast earlier than the spring of 1858, when the news delayed by the time taken in transit over sea lanes or pony express tracks first reached the settlers from families and friends back east.

5

THE PROBLEM OF THE SOUTH

At the time of the 1858 Revival, the two great problems of the South were secession and slavery. The passions of the people were being inflamed by the attacks being mounted against their way of life by ardent abolitionists far up north. Defiance was rising in the States which later confederated to fight a total war.

Slavery was the 'peculiar institution' of the South. In spite of all of its inhumanity, it must not be forgotten that the evangelization of the Negro race in modern times began in the eighteenth century among the slaves of the Southern plantations in the United States.[1] In the years between the Declaration of Independence and the wartime Proclamation of Emancipation, many slave-owners provided both a fair education and religious services for their households. At first, Negro slaves worshipped with their masters in assigned sectors of the same churches, but, as the Christian faith gained ground, the Negroes preferred to organize their own church in which members with understandably lower grades of education could minister[2] in pastoral and lay capacities. Before long, the greatest work of evangelizing the Negroes was being done by Negroes themselves, with Caucasian workers initiating enterprises or educating leadership.

The pioneer advocates and engineers of the abolition of slavery within the British Empire were almost all products of the Evangelical Revival. It has been well established that many ardent Evangelicals in the United States likewise espoused the cause of the slaves. Charles Finney (the leading evangelist in the years before the 1858 Revival) announced a very simple solution to the problem of slavery: convert the slave-owners. And in his meetings, he called for slave owners in repentance to manumit their slaves on the spot.[3]

In the year of the Awakening, it was observed by a writer at Oberlin College, a base of anti-slavery agitation from its foundation: 'If this great Revival revives pure religion, it will purify the public conscience and ... beget a deeper abhorrence of slavery.'[4]

This hope was fulfilled in many parts of the country, and (to quote Prof. Timothy L. Smith) the 'revivalists were convinced that the conquest of social and political evil was at hand.'[5] The 'terrible logic of events' cited by an evangelical journal which had enthusiastically chronicled the Revival, crystallized the anti-slavery feelings of Northern Christians into anti-slavery action when God 'loosed the fateful lightning of His terrible swift sword' as His Truth went marching on to the liberation of the slaves.[6]

The Southern slave-owners resented Finney's brand of evangelicalism, and the people of the States contemplating secession built up a wall of ready rejection of its arguments. But they could not resist a movement of the Spirit which called Christians north and south to prayer.

Northern abolitionists in turn were unwilling to believe that the Lord could bless the South. Writing of the Revival of 1858, Charles Finney stated:[7]

> Slavery seemed to shut it out from the South. The people there were in such a state of irritation, of vexation, and of committal to their peculiar institution which had come to be assailed on every side, that the Spirit of God seemed to be grieved away from them. There seemed to be no place found for Him in the hearts of Southern people at that time.

These were strange words for one trained to sift evidence. Beardsley, a more recent historian, echoed Finney thus:[8]

> One section of the country alone was not powerfully affected by this revival. Slavery seemed to rest like a great pall upon the Southern States, and apparently prevented this divine visitation from extending thither to any remarkable degree. The contentions about the 'peculiar institution' were so numerous, and the public mind seemed so occupied with questions relating there to, that the operations of the Holy Spirit were shut out and no great results were realized.

Beardsley's opinion, held by many Northern historians, is patently an adaptation of Finney's. The writer considers both inexcusably untrue in the light of abundant evidence.

Bishop Candler, on the other hand, insisted that the results of the revival were 'in proportion to the population, greater in the South than in any other section,' and his good account of amazing revivals of religion in Confederate Armies in the War between the States seemed to contradict the contention that pro-slavery sentiment inhibited revival in the South.[9]

A Southern Presbyterian reviewer in July 1859 countered the Northern claim strongly, saying 'it is not Northern, nor Southern, Eastern nor Western,' while declaring that the revival in the South had reached as far as the Florida reefs. Revivals were as widespread in the South as in the Northern states, as any reading of periodicals will confirm.[10]

Some allowance should be made for the fact that the South then possessed no great industrial cities like the Northern metropolitan areas, and that its population was scattered over an agricultural countryside; hence it was less spectacular down South, where newspapers could not immediately influence crowded cities as north of the Mason-Dixon Line.

A Northern authority testified, nevertheless, that revival of more or less power was sweeping Wilmington, Baltimore, Washington, Richmond, Charleston, Nashville, Memphis, New Orleans, Mobile, Savannah, Augusta, Columbia, Raleigh and other Southern cities.[11] There is no contrary testimony.

In Richmond in Virginia, a daily prayer meeting was launched with success. In Lynchburg, in the same state, a revival of no mean dimensions converted many young men to the Christian faith.[12] In Mobile, Alabama, sermons were preached in the Catholic, Episcopal, Baptist, and Methodist churches daily, with 'unusually numerous converts.'[13]   In April, when the secular press reported that the revival was declining in New York City, it assured its readers that the awakening was increasing in Southern States where revivals were breaking out in Nashville, Mobile, New Orleans and Charleston, and was by no means confined to the cities.[14]

With these facts in mind, it must be confirmed that the 1858 Revival swept the South in spite of the slavery issue. Bishop Candler quoted official statistics to show that in the years 1858, 1859 and 1860, more than one hundred thousand converts were received by the Methodist Episcopal Church, South, insisting that the equally large Baptist denomination shared similar blessing.[15] That being so, the Revival in the South won as many converts proportionately as the North.

When secession was followed by war, did the strife obliterate revival? The period of the War between the States saw an increase of Christian concern on a larger scale than ever existed before in the United States.[16] Increased giving to Home Missions, to the Bible and Tract Societies, and to every charity was noted. In five years, foreign missionary giving doubled, though the war was absorbing so much of the wealth and energy of the nation.

The 1858 Awakening carried over to the War between the States, affecting both Federal and Confederate Armies. The War Department in Washington appointed chaplains indorsed by their appropriate denominational authorities; as William Warren Sweet observed: 'If the chaplain was an evangelical, a long stay in camp was likely to be improved by holding a revival meeting among the soldiers.'[17] A majority of these chaplains were active evangelicals, of course.[18]

The records of the war are full of instances of such awakenings and evangelism in the battlefield. In one New York regiment, evangelistic meetings ran for thirty nights in succession in a tent furnished by the commanding general, and more than a hundred soldiers professed faith.

Supplementing the work of the chaplains was the United States Christian Commission, a part-ministerial, part-lay organization which served the troops by word of mouth and printed page, offering care and comfort.

George H. Stuart, an active Y.M.C.A. leader, served as president of the Christian Commission; W. E. Boardman, whose writings upon the Higher Christian Life made a profound impression on Christian life in Britain as well as the United States, became executive secretary; and more than thirteen hundred ministers and clergy served faithfully as volunteer chaplains in camp.[19] An insight into their work is supplied by a report:[20]

> . . . We were taking a large number of wounded men down the Tennessee River after the battle of Pittsburg Landing. A number of young men of the Christian Commission were with me. I told them that we must not let a man die on the boat that night without telling him of Christ and heaven . . . The cry of a wounded man is 'Water! Water!' As we passed along from one to another giving them water, we told them of the water of life.

The one reporting was D. L. Moody. With the backing of the evangelistic Y.M.C.A. at home, he made frequent trips to the front to preach in the camps and minister on the battle field. Nor did he forget the enemy prisoners of war wearing the Confederate grey.

Religion in the armies of the Confederacy was even more conspicuous than among Union troops.[21] Converts numbered 150,000, according to some.[22] In the main Army of Northern Virginia, a major evangelical awakening occurred, sustained by Baptist, Episcopalian, Methodist and Presbyterian clergy and ministers. A chaplain recorded in his diary:[23]

> . . . May 17, 1863, 10 a.m., I preached in the Presby-
> terian Church: the house crowded with officers and
> soldiers; serious attention. At 3 p.m., I preached in
> Bates's brigade: a very good time, revival in the bri-
> gade; thirty to forty mourners: glorious work in this
> command. May 20, I preached in General Polk's bri-
> gade: forty to fifty mourners; fifteen to twenty con-
> versions. May 22, I spoke in General Riddle's brigade:
> a great work here; already more than one hundred
> conversions in this command.

After the bloodiest slaughter of men in all American history, the war ended. How did the Emancipation itself affect the evangelization of the American Negro?

Percentages of Negroes and whites in church membership was the same in 1800, but in 1860 (when there were four-and-a-half million Negroes in the country) only half a million were members of churches, the percentage of Negro church members in the population being half that of Caucasian Americans.[24]

The startling changes in the status of Negroes after their Emancipation was one for which neither they nor their white masters were prepared. Emancipation found the Negroes uneducated and untrained to fend for themselves, the Southern whites impoverished, inhibited, and uncertain of the future.

Latourette considered what followed one of the greatest of all achievements of the Christian faith. Numerical gains of Protestant Christianity among American Negroes, 1815-1914, equal the total made in all Africa and Asia in the same period. Never had such a large body of depressed people made such gains in civilization in so few decades of opportunity, and it was the Christian message given to Negroes by Negroes that counted most.[25] In fifty years, Negro church membership grew to four-and-a-half million, to 22% of the Negro population, a fourfold increase.[26]

The vast effort of conversion and organization of Negro churches following Emancipation and the conclusion of the Civil War has been assessed and appreciated by scientific writers, such as W. E. B. DuBois. Missionaries began to evangelize and educate the Negro freedmen, as soon as the smoke had lifted from the battlefields. Until the end of the century, Negro religious leadership developed chiefly by means of evangelism and education promoted by dedicated white people, northern and southern. As Negroes took over control, their churches grew in an unprecedented way.[27]

The parabola of the West Indies stretches from southern Florida, through the Greater Antilles (including Jamaica) and Lesser Antilles (including Trinidad) to the north coast of the continent of South America. The Bahamas, Jamaica, and various of the Leeward and Windward Islands were Anglo-African in population, similar to the plantation folk of the southern United States.

The impact of the 1858-59 Revival was felt immediately in the British West Indies among emancipated slaves and their children who had suffered spiritual decline following a first blessing after their Emancipation.

Primarily through the influence of the American Revival of 1858, awakenings began in the Bahamas, in Jamaica, in the Leeward and Windward Islands before the 1859 Revival had made its appearance in the British Isles. There were 'gracious outpourings of the Spirit' in Barbados before the end of 1858, for example.[28]

In 1859, a remarkable evangelical awakening begun in a Moravian church spread throughout the chapels of the island of Jamaica.[29] Beginning in the south, it moved the Christian congregations throughout the island—in the central parishes, on the north and south coasts, from Spanish Town to Savanna-la-Mar, Montego Bay to Ann's Bay.

> Chapels became once more crowded. There was a widespread conviction of sin. Crime diminished. Ethical standards were raised. There was renewed generosity. Old superstitions which had reasserted themselves once more declined in power. As the movement spread, unhealthy excitement and religious hysteria showed themselves in places, but the testimony of almost all observers of whatever denomination was that the Revival did permanent good.

The 'unhealthy excitement and religious hysteria' cited by Dr. Ernest Payne were understandable in a population of recently liberated slaves. But so great was the improvement of Jamaicans that the London Missionary Society in 1867 decided to withdraw from the field as evangelized.

The L. M. S. withdrew from other West Indian islands. The Awakening of 1859 rekindled the zeal of Trinidad Negro Christians descended from rebel slaves who were removed from the Carolinas by the British in the War of 1812. In the following decade, the churches began their missionary work among East Indians working the Trinidad estates, and East Indian churches were formed also.[30]

6

APPROVAL–AND DISAPPROVAL

One of the most remarkable features of the 1858 Revival in America was the almost unanimous chorus of approval that it received from its contemporaries. It was indeed difficult to find someone who had unkind words to say.

Critics were unable to lay the charge of fanaticism or hysteria, or any of the usual accusations against revivals. So they contented themselves with declaring that a revival which filled other churches, but not their own could not be of Divine origin.[1] Their criticism provoked very little attention or controversy in either secular or religious press.

As the Awakening of 1858 occurred in the modern newspaper age, its course was bound to be affected by the attitude that the press generally took to the movement. That the religious press should support the Revival is not at all surprising, but the overwhelming enthusiasm of the secular press is wholly astounding; the historian cannot but conclude that the secular press was the Revival's greatest earthly ally. A Presbyterian periodical expressed its wonder thus:[2]

> . . . Since the first settlement of our country, no religious movement has attracted more attention than the present. As might be expected, the religious press has chronicled numerous incidents connected with this work. But, what has seldom occurred before, the secular newspapers have also appropriated a portion of their columns almost daily, for two or three months, in giving detailed notices of prayer meetings in our large cities and various other particulars concerning the movement.

The beginning of the alliance between the Revival and the press is seen in the modest diary of Jeremiah Lanphier who, on 5th January 1858, 'called with some of the editors of the daily papers in regard to having some of the incidents which occur in the prayer meetings inserted in them.'[3]

By March 1858, the secular press was giving whole columns to intelligence of the Awakening. The headlines, 'The Hour of Prayer,' 'the Revivals,' 'the Great Awakening,' 'the Religious Awakening,' 'the Religious Movement,' and the like literally loaded the printed page. Why did the editors of the various papers give such space to a purely religious movement? There are two good reasons. It is obvious that the Revival was engrossing the whole nation and that the people demanded revival news. When a Western editor saw a column so generously devoted to religion in a New York contemporary, he noted the trend and found that the example was good. Another good reason was found in the startling effect of the Revival on editors and journalists themselves.

The news of the Revival displaced other news, and held premier place for several months. In ordinary times, the most successful religious movement rated a bare mention in the national papers, so overwhelmed is religious news by the welter of political, international, social, market and sports intelligence, not to mention crime and divorce. While life in 1858 was not as complex as life four generations later, it should be noted that the Awakening had as its rivals such topics as the Indian Mutiny, which stirred Americans to sympathy with their massacred cousins in India, the Slavery Question, which was causing bloody rioting and fighting in many places and was soon to rend the nation in twain, and the Financial Depression, which scared people everywhere.

The decline in the amount of space given the Awakening must not be thought of as paralleling a decline in the strength of the Revival. It was a natural result, for when the Revival got under way, it became so commonplace that it was no longer regarded as startling news. Instead of astounding instances, editors began featuring a summary of results.

The secular press became the instrument of revival in no small way. A pastor wrote to the editor of one of the newspapers saying: 'The glorious summary, with the editorial remarks on the Great Revivals in your paper of the 4th instant, stirred my soul so powerfully that I felt that something must be done in our village; so I have called on the other ministers, and we have started a meeting, and the dews are falling on us.'[4] A contemporary writer narrated the account of the part played by the press:[5]

> The Press, which speaks in the ears of millions, is taken possession of by the Spirit, willing or unwilling, to proclaim His wonders and go everywhere preaching the Word in its most impressive, its living forms and examples ... a new thing and, under God a mighty thing in the religious world. . . . . The barest statement in figures . . . is more eloquent of divine love than the voice of an apostle.

As the secular press had received revival news with the utmost enthusiasm, the religious press rejoiced in language of thanksgiving and exultant praise. Opposition came from two widely separated camps, from two schools of thought as far apart as the poles.

In the first instance, the American organ of the School of German Rationalists was torn between desires to explain the revival and to depreciate it. It declared:[6]

> Germans who come to America, be they freethinkers or believers in God, Protestants or Catholics, will find little relief in their minds of religion in the manner exhibited by the American people. There is a closer relationship between the German Rationalists and the extreme German Pietists, than there is between either of these and any of the religious sects in America.

The strongest attack upon the Revival came from another rationalist source, this time one within the pale of organized religion, the Rev. Theodore Parker of Boston.[7] Theodore Parker, described as an American theologian of rationalist views and one of the brightest intellects of his day, had already shocked Unitarian confreres with his advanced views. At one time, the Unitarian ministry wanted to expel him, but did not; he refused to resign, for he felt strongly that, as a Unitarian minister, he was free to express himself. So Mr. Parker continued to shock even Boston with extreme statements, such as his opinion that in all probability there would be new Christs manifested in the generations to come. The Unitarians of that day taught the uniqueness of Jesus.

It appears from one of Mr. Parker's sermons that he attended one of the union prayer meetings in Boston, and indeed offered a prayer there; whereupon, some zealous conservative rose to draw attention to the fact that the man who had just prayed was really outside the fold, and proceeded to pray earnestly for Theodore Parker's conversion. This unfortunate incident riled the rationalist theologian beyond measure.[8] Soon his bitter words were in the leading papers of the country, causing one to remark that 'Mr. Parker has evidently been sorely bruised by the hard hits of the revivalists, not to say by their prayers.' Many ardent souls tried hard to convert Theodore Parker personally, but they wasted their sweetness upon the desert air, leaving their victim decidedly agitated.

A Boston newspaper, 5th April 1858, carried a lengthy report of Parker's sermon on 'False and True Revival.'[9]

In this city, in March 1858, in a meeting-house, on a
Saturday afternoon, we find honest and respectable men
and women met together for prayer and conference;
most exciting speeches are made; exciting stories are
told; fanatical prayers are put up; a part of the assembly
seems beside themselves and out of their minds; they
say, 'The Lord is in Chicago and a great revival is going
on there; the Lord is in Boston and He has poured out
His Spirit here.'

Such remarks, according to Mr. Parker, would show that
the people making them were somewhat unbalanced mentally.
He went on to pour out his vials of wrath upon Park Street
Church, which was the antithesis of all that he stood for
theologically. In a more general way, he thought that the
Revival was demonstrating that the people could not get
enough of preaching, the poorer the article (in his opinion)
the more they wanted of it. Some Unitarian churches had
been revived, but in Mr. Parker's judgment 'as well might
we expect to produce fire by friction of ice blocks, as to
expect a revival among the Unitarians.'

The Evangelicals of Boston redoubled their prayers for
Mr. Parker's conversion, but with less assurance of fulfill-
ment. They sought to defend evangelical principles, to attack
rationalism and its advocate. A week later, the press commented that 'Theodore Parker is determined that blows which
have fallen on his heterodoxy shall not go unreturned.' He
preached another sermon, on 'True Revivals.'[10]

Prof. T. L. Smith has pointed out that the 1858 Revival
evoked surprising support from Unitarians and Universalists.
Unitarian churches in New York and Boston[11] were densely
crowded for weekday prayer meetings. Prof. Frederic Dan
Huntington conducted one such at Harvard weekly. The main
denominational newspaper featured the news regularly, and
voiced approval of the absence of sectarianism and excitement.[12] A Unitarian monthly published three articles defen-
ding the awakening.[13] But there were other Unitarian clergy
who were less enthusiastic, none as extreme as Theodore
Parker in utterance.

Apparently Boston was the only place where the Revival
stirred up violent controversy. The work of grace in Boston
was less in extent than in the other larger cities. Perhaps
if the zealous believers had shown a kinder spirit towards
Theodore Parker, his obvious early interest in the Revival
might have blossomed into a spiritual experience.

In the second instance, there was criticism from Roman Catholic and Anglo-Catholic circles, for the same kind of reason—the 'Catholic' view of the Church. The sight of multitudes flocking to Protestant churches and the report of church memberships being swollen (with only a little increase to Catholicism reported) left 'the Pope biting his nails' as a leading Methodist journal described it.[14] This same journal rejoiced that the majority of Churchmen of Anglican affiliation were in sympathy with the Revival, the most notable exception being their contemporary New York periodical which, being High Church, bewailed the fact that the converts of the Revival were entering the sects, not the true Church. It was said that '. . . the revival is an epidemic; an extravagant manifestation of a spirit of religious fervor, or perhaps furor, which is rapidly becoming fanaticism.'[15]

Spokesmen for all the other Protestant denominations were outraged by this attack by an Anglo-Catholic. It was quickly pointed out that a majority of Churchmen of Anglican affiliation were in sympathy with the movement. A responsible Lutheran weekly,[16] among dozens of religious periodicals, commented on a moderation of opinion of the Anglo-Catholic journal which 'a few weeks ago sneered at this "epidemic"' but 'now counsels Episcopal ministers to engage in the work' of the Revival.

Protestant Episcopal authorities reviewed the situation and considered the Revival 'an era in the religious history' of the country. They recognized the movement so widely spread as to be almost universal, a disruption with very little noise and disorder. As proper Anglicans, they noted that the Revival had occurred just before Lent, hence it was possible to turn it into proper channels, Lenten services being adequate to meet the needs of awakened penitents who overcrowded all the churches, augmenting the number of confirmations to unprecedented figures.[17]

Bishop Charles P. McIlvaine, addressing the Convention of the Diocese of Ohio on the Revival of Religion, observed: 'It is a work so extensive, so remarkable in its rise and progress and influence . . . I have no doubt 'whence it cometh'——it is the Lord's doing.'[18]

Bishop McIlvaine noted that the 1858 Awakening was (1) simple in means, prayer, reading, brief exposition, and singing; (2) quiet, marked by calmness and freedom from unwholesome excitement; (3) harmonious, showing brotherly affection; (4) restrained, having a conservative influence;

(5) far-reaching, of a very wide extent; and (6) reputable, commanding the respect of the world in unprecedented ways, all of which was easily substantiated.[19]

The state of New York was an Episcopal stronghold. The diocese of New York reported a twenty per cent increase in communicant membership between 1856-57 and 1858-59. The annual conference of the diocese of Western New York heard its Bishop, not a Low Churchman, announce that he had confirmed 1503[20] instead of the usual 600 candidates. Low Churchmen welcomed the Awakening heartily, Stephen Tyng and his sons being outstanding leaders in the movement in New York and Philadelphia.[21] High Churchmen were advised to conduct continuous evening services in parish churches during the Lenten and Easter seasons, popular singing and preaching being advertised.

What of the other major liturgical denomination, the Lutherans? Among Lutherans there were two emphases, evangelistic or sacramental, evangelical or traditional— and the former were considered the more numerous in the opinion of the Lutheran scholar, Philip Schaff.[22]

In January 1856, it was conceded in a Lutheran journal that revivals were lamentably rare in American Lutheran churches.[23] Two years later, the same journal announced to its readers:[24]

> It is with feelings of gratitude to the Great Head of the Church that I am able to communicate to numerous readers . . . the cheering intelligence of the outpouring of the Holy Ghost upon another of our congregations.

And there followed report after report weekly of a unique operation of the Spirit in Lutheran churches. A Philadelphia conference of Lutheran Churches noted the state of religion: an unqualified vote of confidence:[25]

> . . . Increased attendance . . . all pews taken . . . week day services well attended... conversions. . . reviving of many members...numbers awakened, convicted and hopefully converted—more than half the converts heads of family.

A Harrisburg Lutheran pastor reported to a Pennsylvania journal the conversion of a score of people in his congregation at Kutztown, between Reading and Allentown:[26]

> Revivals and protracted meetings were something new in Kutztown and were looked upon as a thing not belonging to the Lutheran Church. Yet we had not much opposition.

Reports of awakenings in Lutheran congregations came from the far frontiers.[27] A church in Iowa received three-score upon public profession of faith. In Cedar Rapids, a congregation of six became forty. Revivals were reported from Illinois and Indiana. There was a wide open door among the Scandinavians in Minnesota, Wisconsin and the north-west. Closer to the seaboard, a five week's meeting held in Franklin, Pennsylvania, resulted in 22 new members, six of whom were baptized and 16 confirmed.

Lutheran pastors continued to report 'the house filled with a sacred atmosphere . . . hearts begun to melt . . . a deep solemnity' in Maryland; while on the frontiers, in Dixon (Illinois) it was claimed that 'all Illinois appears to be in an awakened and inquiring state.'[28] The Lutherans in Ohio reported local and general happenings:[29]

> An extraordinary event is now taking place in our land. Eyes unused to weeping are weeping over sin . . . men are awed with a sense of the Divine presence . . . (there is) prayerful reading of the word of God.

By March 1858,[30] a Lutheran weekly giving two columns of news of the awakenings observed:

> The religious interest in our churches as well as in other denominations is so general and widespread that we are compelled to give mere extracts from the numerous accounts that have reached us. . . It is impossible to chronicle in full all the accounts we receive of the great work that is filling the land with rejoicing.

Old School Presbyterians methodically surveyed the impact of the 1858 Revival among them. Of 117 presbyteries, less than a dozen regretted a lack of glad tidings: a larger proportion reported a marked increase of activity resulting in the conversion of sinners and the edification of saints; the largest class rejoiced in 'deep and powerful revivals.' Seventy presbyteries were named as most blessed, from the Hudson to the Missouri. The most remarkable features of the awakenings were the social prayer meetings and the zeal and activity of ruling elders.[31]

In 1859, eleven new presbyteries were established, and new congregations blossomed in almost all the presbyteries. It was affirmed that all who had been revived in 1858 retained the spirit of those refreshing seasons; that prayer was prevalent; that instruction of youth was flourishing; that the preaching of the doctrines of the Word of God was plain and practical.[32]

years	1857[33]	1858[34]	1859[35]
communicants	244,825	259,335	279,630
adults baptized	3,376	5,170	6,672
certificated	9,719	10,558	10,879
examined	13,296	20,792	23,945
contributions	$2,742,704	$2,544,692	$2,835,147

Giving in 1858 was generous in view of 1857 bank failures. New School Presbyterians made similar gains, although the secession of fifteen thousand Southerners over the issue of slavery prevented statistics from showing the picture. New School Presbyterian leaders, such as George Duffield, were in the front rank of the revival evangelists.[36]

Congregational statistics for the year 1858 indicated an approximate 10% increase in church membership, 21,582 having been added to bring the total to 230,094.[37] Authorities in 1860 declared that the Revival of 1858 resulted in a very considerable ingathering, great harmony and quietness, the spontaneous conversion of sinners, the advance of home missions, and an increase of individual activity on the part of members of the churches. It can be documented that New England Congregational leaders enthusiastically supported the 1858 Revival, and continued to advocate its ideals.

American Quakers gave their approval to the Revival of 1858,[38] emphasizing that the movement had begun with the laity, and had gained the attention of men of all classes in society. There was much of Quakerism in the meetings but clear differences of procedure were evident.

The Baptist welcome of the work of grace in 1858 was, as far as humanly possible to ascertain, a unanimous one. Baptist journals were full of revival news. Baptist editors were not blind to dangers in revival movements, but the movement of 1858 appeared to them to be without serious blemishes. There were no Baptists then to question the emphasis upon personal salvation; and the prejudices of traditionalists rarely bothered them.

Between 1848 and 1858, the net increase made by the regular Baptist denomination was somewhat in excess of an annual 25,000. The average for 1856 and 1857 was about 26,000.[39] The net gain in 1858 was approximately 70,000. Illinois was a typical frontier state, with a membership of about 25,000 in 1855. In 1856 and 1857, Illinois Baptists added 3,000 a year: in 1858, more than 6,000. Baptisms in the three years preceding the Revival averaged less than 2,500; in 1858, there were more than 5,000.[40]

After the crest of the Revival had passed, the Baptists extended its impact by evangelistic campaigns and by social action. In 1860, Jacob Knapp conducted meetings in Boston for months on end.[41] A new star among Baptist evangelists arose: A. B. Earle, who ministered acceptably among various denominations united in city-wide efforts. Earle preached consecutively eighty times in an 1859 campaign in Boston, returned to Tremont Temple there for a three month's effort in 1862, coming back for an inter-church series in 1866.[42]

Methodists also were of one mind regarding the Revival of 1858. As early as January of that year, their leading journal singled out ten notable features of the Awakening: (1) few sermons had to be preached; (2) lay brethren were eager to witness; (3) seekers flocked to the altar; (4) nearly every seeker had been blessed; (5) experiences enjoyed remained clear; (6) converts were filled with holy boldness; (7) religion became a day-time social topic; (8) family altars were strengthened; (9) testimony given nightly was abundant; and (10) conversation was marked by a pervading seriousness.[43]

Three months later, it was agreed that thousands had been converted, churches had been invigorated, firemen, police, financiers and others had been born again, and there was then occurring the greatest demonstration of Christian catholicity of modern times.[44]

For every seven members on record in 1857, the various Methodist bodies added another member in 1858, a total of 200,000. In the year 1858, the Methodist Episcopal Church received by profession of faith 135,517 new members, the Methodist Episcopal Church South 43,338.[45]

The Baptists received by believer's baptism 111,647, an incomplete figure not allowing for smaller Baptist bodies, raising the total to 150,000.[46] Presbyterian additions, Dutch Reformed included, amounted to 44,715.[47] Congregationalists added 21,582.[48] Episcopalians took in 14,822.[49] Denominations with an aggregate membership of 3,500,000 added 357,931 members in 1858. It is supposed that this ten per cent figure applied to those whose statistics are unknown. Therefore, in 1858 alone, the increase in membership amounted to half a million. It is not unreasonable, comparing known figures of additions for the whole revival period of three years from the beginning of the movement, to estimate the numerical gain at more than a million, which was the estimate of the Methodist Bishop Warren A. Candler.[50]

Did the movement of 1858 continue into the tragic 1860s? After ten years, which included the bloodiest war of the nineteenth century, the tide of revival had risen high again, for in 1877 a qualified observer commented that[51]

> the Revival of 1868 did not come 'after long continued peace'. . . rather out of the darkness and fearful years of sorrow, war and blood did that beautiful flower bloom.

It would scarcely be practical to examine in detail all the records of all the American denominations. Halfway between the informalist Methodists and Baptists and the liturgical Lutherans and Episcopalians were the Presbyterians. Was the Great Awakening of 1858 an ephemeral phase? Minutes of Presbyterian General Assembly indicated otherwise. In 1863, it was reported that in 1862 'symptoms of incipient revival are widespread over the land,' with fervent and united prayer continuing. The following year, there were special awakenings reported in twenty-two presbyteries, especially in the war areas. In 1864, thirteen presbyteries announced 'gracious revivals.' At the end of the Civil War, 72 out of 91 presbyteries rejoiced in revivals which (in some ways) exceeded those of 1857-58. In 1866, a committee was appointed to bring about reunion of divided Presbyterians. In 1866-67, General Assembly reported that, not since 1857-58, were such widespread and fruitful revivals occurring, 'unparalleled' in some presbyteries, the next year bringing a report of 'convicting a multitude of souls,' the following year of a large number of extensive works of grace.[52]

One of the more prestigious of American quarterlies, in a survey of the three preceding eras of religious revival in the United States—those of 1734 onward, 1797 onward, and 1830 onward—designated 'the great religious movement of the past year, 1858,' as 'memorable in all future time as the fourth revival era of our country.'[53]

Dr. S. B. Halliday endorsed the judgment of Theodore Cuyler that the 1858 Awakening was probably the most extraordinary and widespread ever known in America, adding that the Churches, with a million new members, were soon 'belting the globe with their enterprises.'[54]

Contrary to the unwarranted opinions of a century later, everything in newspapers and journals of the time confirms and nothing in those of the following fifty years contradicts that opinion. Alas, the Revival of 1858 was 'too perfect' an example of the outpouring of the Holy Spirit to warrant the objective attention of certain sceptics.

Charles G. Finney declared that 'a revival is the result of the right use of the appropriate means.' Analysts who have espoused the notion that Finney's philosophy and influence forever changed the course of revivals will find no support in the records of the 1858 Revival, which, like the 1830 movement that preceded it and the 1905 awakening that followed it, was utterly unplanned, unpromoted and unprogrammed. Finney and several generations of evangelists and historians that followed him confused 'revival' with 'evangelism.'

Anti-evangelical sociologists have too often made the most of the emotional extravagances of the Awakening of 1800 on the frontiers of the United States, conveniently ignoring the fact that at the same time there were stirring awakenings in the cities and college towns of the eastern seaboard without any such emotional extravagance in fact. There was nothing of this extravagance in the Revival of 1858. In the compilation of factual details for this dissertation, only one case of falling, jerking or the like was discovered in the records—unrelated to the prayer meeting movement. Students of the psychological sciences would find the records of the Awakening of 1858 rather dull. Critics of evangelical revival have found them rather disappointing, but lovers of the New Testament have found in them deep satisfaction.

7
THE AWAKENING IN ULSTER

The news of the Mid-Century Awakening in the United States reached Europe in early 1858—by cable. The connection between the people of the United States and those of the United Kingdom was always immediate, but most intimate was the connection between Ulster and the tens of thousands of Ulster-Americans in America. So it is not surprising that the General Assembly of the Presbyterian Church in Ireland sent an official deputation of two of its most trusted members to visit the United States.[1] Professor William Gibson, soon to be elected to the highest Assembly office, with the Rev. William McClure visited the various American scenes of awakening, and published his impressions of the work of God in Philadelphia, which he described as a 'pentecost,' a quickening of believers and evangelizing of sinners.

Throughout Ulster, the reports of the American Revival tended greatly to quicken the minds of both ministers and people.[2] Many sermons upon Revival were preached and the prayer meetings multiplied. The first appeared to be one begun in Kells near Ballymena by a young man named James McQuilkin who had been busy reading the testimony of George Müller, the man of faith, as well as hearing of the Revival in America. James McQuilkin said to himself: 'Why may we not have such a blessed work here?'[3]

James McQuilkin and his prayer helpers held a meeting on the 14th March 1859 in the First Presbyterian Church in Ahoghill. Such a large crowd attended that 'it was deemed prudent to dismiss the meeting lest there be a fatal accident from the falling in of the galleries which threatened to give way under the alarming pressure.'[4] Whereupon, a layman addressed the three thousand people outside in the chilling rain and, moved by his fervency and his apostolic language, hundreds fell on their knees in the muddy street.

This apparently was the first outbreak of mass conviction of sin to occur anywhere in the British Isles during the mid-nineteenth century awakening about to spread throughout the United Kingdom.

Three miles from Ahoghill is the prosperous marketing town of Ballymena, the hub of middle Antrim, and nearby is the parish of Connor in which was begun the original prayer meeting. At that time, Ballymena had a population of six thousand, largely Presbyterian. The Ballymena newspaper first noticed the Revival on March 26, then for six months was chronicling the events of the Awakening, and its many extensive social, moral and religious improvements.[5]

The Rev. Samuel J. Moore noted several cases of deep conviction among his charges. On returning from a meeting of the Presbyterian Synod in Dublin, he found the town in a great state of excitement, many families having neglected their overnight sleep for two preceding nights.[6]

A number of prepared young laymen devoted almost all of their time to the giving of spiritual and physical comfort to the scores of people in need of such. Prayer meetings were held all hours of the day and night, and all evangelical churches were open for evening services. The Presbyterian, Anglican and Methodist ministers and people united in mass meetings, including a gathering of five thousand in a quarry.[7]

In the month of May 1859, the Awakening first made an appearance in Belfast, a busy city of 120,000 people, a third of whom were Roman Catholic. By the end of May, a Belfast newspaper was giving daily a half-column or a column of space to Revival news.[8] This outbreak of fervent revival in Belfast came through a visit of some of the 'converts from Connor.' It was in Berry Street Presbyterian Church that the greatest demonstation came. So many people lingered after the service that the Rev. Hugh Hanna reopened the church and took charge.[9] On the Lord's Day following, most of the evangelical churches of the town were utterly overcrowded by seekers after God.

Dr. Knox, the Bishop of the United Dioceses of Down, Connor and Dromore, invited all his clergy to early breakfast in order to hear their opinion respecting the Revival, which apparently had his careful support.[10] All at length agreed that it was a work of God, but there was a difference of opinion among the clergymen regarding the 'prostrations' of sinners coming under conviction, some regarding them as hysteria, and others as a Divine method of conviction. The Belfast Presbytery met and expressed gratitude to God for the Revival, but also urged caution regarding the physical manifestations.[11] Ministers of the Wesleyan, Independent and Baptist churches supported the work from the start.

With something approaching unanimity, the ministers of Belfast commenced a united prayer meeting in the Music Hall, with the Mayor in the chair. The building was crowded to excess. A week later, the Bishop took the chair, assisted on the platform by 146 clergymen, including the Moderator of the General Assembly and all Presbyterian ministers, the President of the Wesleyan Methodist Conference, and the Anglicans, Baptists, Congregationalists, Methodists and Moravians, and even the well-known Dr. Montgomery of the Unitarian communion.[12] Hundreds participated in overflow meetings, and thousands were turned away, disappointed.

By June, most evangelical churches remained open and overcrowded for weekday services. Friends of the Revival estimated that ten thousand people were converted (only a small proportion violently by prostration) in the weeks that followed.[13] Soon the movement was affecting all six counties of the North, the historic city of Derry, the town of Armagh, and many parts of the South, including Dublin.

Another development of the Revival in Belfast came with organizing mass open-air meetings for prayer in the beautiful Botanical Gardens. At the end of June, the first meeting attracted an assemblage 'never before seen' in the north of Ireland.[14] The Presbyterian Moderator presided and among 15,000 attending, 'results exceeded anything hereto known.'

In July, the efforts of ministers, visitors and converts in Belfast continued unabated in energy and zeal and success. The Rev. H. Grattan Guinness preached to at least 15,000 people in the open-air.[15] In August, churches of every denomination were crowded to excess, with visiting ministers busy officiating in local pulpits to relieve exhausted but rejoicing Belfast preachers.

Another of the Botanic Gardens prayer meetings attracted 20,000 on 16th August, the proceedings being undertaken by the Y.M.C.A. In September, the churches remained crowded, without any signs of weariness on the part of ministers or people; and in October the attendances were still 'in no wise abated,' although the novelty had worn off. The October meetings of the Maze Racecourse drew 500 people instead of the customary 10,000. A large distillery capable of turning out a million gallons of whisky annually was put up at auction to be sold or dismantled. These Belfast reports were confirmed by the Evangelical Alliance meeting there that year,[16] drawing observers from all parts of Britain. There was an immediate impact on Christians across the sea.

Meanwhile the Ulster Revival began to spread into County Down. Writing from Holywood Palace, the Bishop notified his opposite number in the Presbyterian Church (Professor Gibson) that,[17] of 106 replies from clergy, seventy five gave gratifying testimony of spiritual blessing in their parishes.

Townsfolk of Coleraine, in that part of County Derry close to revived County Antrim villages, witnessed some of the most amazing scenes in the whole movement in Ireland. A school-boy under deep conviction of sin seemed so incapable of continuing his studies that a kindly teacher sent him home with another boy, already converted. The two boys on their way home observed an empty house and entered to pray. At last the unhappy boy found peace, and returned immediately to class to tell his teacher: 'I am so happy: I have the Lord Jesus in my heart!' This innocent testimony had its effect on the class, as boy after boy slipped outside. The master, standing on something to look out of the window, observed the boys kneeling in prayer around the schoolyard, each apart. The master being overcome, he asked the converted schoolboy to comfort them. Soon the whole school was in strange disorder, and the ministers sent for remained all day dealing with seekers after peace— schoolboys, schoolgirls, teachers, parents and friends, the premises being thus occupied till eleven o'clock at night. These happenings stirred the whole district.[18]

On 7th June 1859, an open-air meeting was held on Fair Hill to hear the converts. So many thousands attended that it was deemed advisable to divide the crowd into separate meetings, each addressed by an evangelical minister of one denomination or another. The people stood motionless until the very last moment, when an auditor cried in distress. Several others likewise were prostrated, bewildering the ministers who, having had no previous similar experience, scarce knew how to help the distressed in soul and body. The clergymen spent all night in spiritual ministry, and, when the sun rose, the day following was spent in like manner. A union prayer meeting was begun and attracted the crowds for many months.[19]

Dr. H. Grattan Guinness addressed more than 6000 people in a single meeting in Coleraine.[20] In August the work progressed steadily and in September the churches were as full as ever. By October there were very few cases of prostration but the prayer meetings continued as numerous and well attended as before.

A Coleraine observer stated in an editorial article that 'No one can deny that a change for the better, which all must believe to be permanent, has taken place in the case of hosts of individuals.'[21] In 1860, the Grand Jury of the Coleraine Quarter Sessions was informed that moral and religious reform had reduced crime to almost negligible proportions, there having been only one unimportant case to try.[22] There were instances in Ulster of judges being presented with white gloves, signifying not a case to try.

The Revival spread into the towns and villages of County Derry, and soon reached the historic city of Londonderry, appearing with great suddenness among all denominations. It began on 12th June through a visit of Ballymena converts who moved hearers to tears.[23] Further open-air meetings attracted 5000 people. In County Tyrone, revivals spread rapidly southward.[24] The people of County Armagh experienced movements in their towns and villages simultaneously with Tyrone, but later than Antrim and Down and the city of Belfast with their heavier Protestant populations.

In Ireland's ecclesiastical capital, the city of Armagh, there was the usual evidence of strange happenings. On Wednesday 21st September 1859, a prayer meeting for all Ireland was arranged.[25] People came from a hundred miles around, riding on roofs of railway carriages or stowing away in cattle trucks and goods vans. Scenes at Armagh were overpowering, for 20,000 people gathered in a large field, to be addressed in part by a distinguished Englishman, the Hon. and Rev. Baptist Noel. In October, local ministers reported that 'a great and good work of conviction and conversion' was progressing.

County Fermanagh shared in the Revival, though rather belatedly. Unlike the other northern counties, Fermanagh possessed 38 per cent Episcopalians, and only six per cent other Protestants, chiefly Methodists, while there were 56 per cent Roman Catholics in the county.

Outside the six northern counties, the Revival movement was felt—but in degree inversely proportionate to Roman Catholic majorities in each county as well as directly proportionate to the numbers of Presbyterians, Methodists, Baptists, Congregationalists, Moravians and Friends among the Protestants. This was especially true of the remaining three of the nine counties of Ulster—Donegal and Monaghan and Cavan,[26] where limited revivals occurred. Elsewhere a hostility or indifference was manifested.

There was more encouragement around Dublin which then possessed a large Protestant population amounting to 22 per cent in the city itself, no less than 40 per cent in the suburbs around, and 20 per cent in the County of Dublin. When tidings of the Revival in Ulster reached the Irish capital, many clergy and ministers repaired thither. Among them was the Rev. J. Denham Smith of Kingstown, who was profoundly moved by all that he saw and heard.

In September 1859, Kingstown Christians had a new spirit of prayer that became the forerunner of blessing, and in October and November there were inquiries after salvation in every meeting.[27] A union prayer meeting in Dublin was supported by the members of all three major evangelical denominations.[28] The large Metropolitan Hall, seating 3000, was made the venue of special meetings, Spurgeon preaching five times in January 1860, with many other speakers, including S. J. Moore of Ballymena who gave a discourse on the Revival in the North of Ireland.

Metropolitan Hall was opened on Tuesdays for free prayer, 3000 attending with more than 100 inquirers in each of the first three meetings. In July, an 'increasing interest' was reported from Metropolitan Hall, the inquirers undiminished in number, and Sunday open-air meetings drew 3000 to the evangelistic outreach.

On the whole, the Revival in the south and west of Ireland had none of the startling effects of the Ulster Awakening; nevertheless, a work of grace among isolated Protestant communities launched many eager and faithful evangelists, clerical and lay, who worked against overwhelming odds to evangelize warmly their Roman Catholic fellow-countrymen in the South.[29]

The Hibernian Bible Society issued in Ulster, between April and August 1859, more than twenty thousand Bibles, which was double the 1858 quota.[30] A desire to learn to read the Scriptures moved many adult converts to enroll in night schools, and a significant impulse towards popular education was felt in the North.

At the 14th annual conference of the Evangelical Alliance held in Belfast in 1859, Dr. John Motherwell gave a full medical report of the physical and psychic peculiarities of the Revival. Prof. James McCosh, a Scotsman famed as a philosopher at Queen's University and afterwards president of Princeton University, delivered a scholarly address on the physiological accidents of the Ulster Revival.[31]

The Hon. and Rev. Baptist Noel told the conference of the Evangelical Alliance that he thought 100,000 converts in the Ulster Revival was probably under the mark.[32] In all Ireland, there were more. Thus it was that this movement, which originated in a prayer meeting of four young men in the village schoolhouse of Kells in the parish of Connor in the county of Antrim made greater impact spiritually on Ireland than anything else known since the days of Saint Patrick. In that same county of Antrim, it was noted with wonder there was not one prisoner in custody, not one crime reported to the police.[33]

In 1860, the Bishop of Down and Connor circularized his clergy in the united diocese, asking for a report upon the effectiveness of the '59 Revival in their parishes.[34] Of about seventy parishes, 51 reported a marked improvement, 13 some improvement, 5 no change; and the average increase at matins and evensong was substantial. These were the results among Anglicans, other denominations reporting far greater impact in almost every way.

Before the end of 1860, the Ulster Revival was viewed in retrospect, and summarized as follows: (1) the preaching services were thronged; (2) numbers of communicants were unprecedented; (3) prayer meetings were abundant; (4) family prayers were increased; (5) scripture reading was unmatched; (6) Sunday Schools were prosperous; (7) converts remained generally steadfast; (8) liberality seemed greatly increased; (9) vice was abated; and (10) crime was much reduced.[35]

Although the Irish Revival of 1859 was paralleled by the Welsh Revival of that same year, and followed by the 1860 Awakenings in Scotland and England, the movement among the Ulster folk remained the unsurpassed example of the power of God in the lives of intercessors and converts. It was long remembered in the North of Ireland, renewed in 1905 and 1922 in less spectacular awakenings. It provided the dynamic for evangelism, which always remained lively in the face of a militant Roman Catholicism.

In 1959, six major denominations in Ireland cooperated officially in a commemoration of the centenary of the Year of Grace, as the Revival year of 1859 was designated. The council arranged meetings in St. Patrick's Cathedral in Dublin, and in tiny little country churches, in the market towns of the North, and in the shrinking congregations of the far South. More than a thousand churches cooperated in the commemoration.[36]

8

THE AWAKENING IN SCOTLAND

After a year's observation of the Awakening, the Church of Scotland, meeting in Edinburgh in May 1860, declared:[1]

> . . . General Assembly, taking into consideration the gratifying evidence manifested in many countries, and in various districts of our own land, of an increased anxiety about salvation and deepening interest in religious ordinances, followed in so many cases by fruits of holy living, desires to record its gratitude to Almighty God.

In the same month, Scotland's equally large Free Church Assembly heard a moving address by its new Moderator:[2]

> Two years ago, our Assembly was deeply stirred by the intelligence of what God was doing in the United States of America. One year ago, the impression was deepened... the pregnant cloud had swept onwards and was sending down upon Ireland a plenteous rain. This year, the same precious showers have been and are even now falling within the limits of our own beloved land. We, as a Church, accept the Revival as a great and blessed fact. Numerous and explicit testimonies from ministers and members alike bespeak the gracious influence upon the people. Whole congregations have been seen bending before it like a mighty rushing wind.

And, in the same month of May, the Synod of the United Presbyterian Church, the third largest church organization, had 'resolved to recognize the hand of God in the measure of new life outpoured upon our churches, and appointed the second Sabbath of July as a special Day of Prayer for the Revival.'[3]

Thus the three main branches of the dominant Presbyterianism of Scotland, whose adherents formed 70 per cent of the population, declared in no uncertain way that Scotland was experiencing a Revival of Religion as deep as Ulster's. Their repeated jubilation, without a note of discord, and the continued rejoicing of survivors for fifty years, has stood in stark contrast to an historical opinion written from the vantage point of a full century afterward that these Scottish

Presbyterian Churches 'soon dissociated themselves from the movement'—a capricious notion without foundation.[4]

Already Scotland's Christian life was being quickened by evangelists, often drawn from the higher ranks of society. The news of the revival of religion in the United States provoked much interest and not a few prayer meetings,[5] as in Edinburgh, Glasgow, and Aberdeen, where there was united intercession for an abundant outpouring of the Holy Spirit.

A measure of prayer in preparation of heart for revival is indicated in the offical report of the United Presbyterian Church that one in every four of its 162,305 communicants was attending its regular prayer meetings, an average of some 40,549 at prayer in 1205 regular meetings, with 129 new prayer meetings and 16,362 new attenders, in 1859.[6]

The first recorded outbreak of revival was reported from Aberdeen, which enjoyed the first-fruits of the movement to follow. In the autumn of 1858, a united prayer meeting was begun in the County Buildings in Aberdeen.[7]

In the middle of August 1859, the revival became news in Glasgow with all the suddenness of a summer thunderstorm. Almost a column in a newspaper was devoted to a public meeting held in the City Hall, which crowded gathering was presided over by Bailie Playfair.[8] Another newspaper described a similar meeting (to hear about the Revival) in the Stockwell Free Church in the city, a meeting crowded to excess in which the interest was so deepened that great excitement and tears were in evidence. Four days later, at 6.30 p.m. on August 19, a public meeting was held on Glasgow Green, with 20,000 people crushing to hear the speakers.

Religious writers were very little ahead of secular in recognizing the outbreak of Revival in Glasgow. One such, on 2nd August 1859, claimed that[9]

> . . . the Holy Spirit has been manifesting His gracious power in a remarkable manner in this neighbourhood during the last few days. Our readers are aware that ever since news of the Great Revival in America reached Scotland, prayer meetings for the special purpose of imploring a similar blessing have been held in Glasgow as well as in other places. The intelligence which has reached us recently leaves no room to doubt that these prayers have been heard.

The report referred to increased attendances at prayer meetings as well as increased numbers of conversions among those waiting behind for counsel by the ministers and workers.

Three weeks later, the same Glasgow weekly paper commented on increased attendance at union prayer meetings. As in America and in Ireland, noon prayer meetings gave rise to prayer meetings and preaching services in the various evangelical churches on week-nights, and in these meetings there were scores of conversions reported. After a year or so, Glasgow was still enjoying 'times of refreshing.' One church built a stone pulpit outside the building: [10]

> Every Sabbath evening service since the Bridegate Church was opened, the crowds around the stone pulpit have been increasing, until on Sabbath evening last, there could not have been fewer than 7000 hearers, probably more. We say 'hearers,' for, notwithstanding the vastness of the congregation, the voice of the preacher appeared to be perfectly audible at the furthest extremity. At the close of the open-air service, an invitation is given from the pulpit to all who wish to come to a decision in the matter of religion to attend the prayer meeeting... Within ten minutes the church is generally packed, and, being seated for 900, it will receive probably upwards of 1100 when thus crowded ...
> About ten o'clock, the meeting was brought to a close and those only were asked to remain who wished conversation with the minister and other friends. About 500 waited including, of course, the friends of those who were in distress. This meeting continued till 11.45 p.m.

Just as 'approximately 20,000' had gathered on Glasgow Green at the start of the movement, a similar-sized crowd gathered on 6th September 1860. An adjoining theatre was opened for the inquirers.[11] The outstanding speaker, whose powerful voice seemed to fill the Green, was a butcher named Robert Cunningham. So great was the interest and so heavy the work entailed that the visiting speakers, Gordon Forlong, Reginald Radcliffe, and Richard Weaver collapsed tired out.

The Awakening of 1859-60 permeated every corner of southwestern Scotland down to the vale of Dumfries and the borders of Cumberland.[12] The movement repeated the phenomena of the Ulster Awakening, but most reporters seemed to stress the dispensability of 'prostrations' and the other physical phenomena, recognizing their value in first startling observers, but relieved when they gave way to much quieter manifestations.

In the New Year of 1861, a second wave of revival blessing was felt in both the Vale of Dumfries and in Glasgow.[13] The occasion was the visit of an American student of theology,

Edward Payson Hammond, who was invited to conduct revival services in Annan on the Solway Firth. It was stated by the Dumfries newspaper that the revival spirit reached a degree of intensity unparalleled in the religious history of the burgh. Hammond, his assistant Drysdale, four ministers and many helpers often had to counsel inquirers (as many as 500 at a time) until the early hours of the morning. The work among children was noteworthy, and this factor shaped Hammond as a children's evangelist in future years. In Dumfries, a secular newspaper described the response as 'marvellous.' Payson Hammond carried the revival influence to Glasgow again, where such a work was wrought that a thanksgiving meeting drew 12,000 to the City Hall, a third of whom gained entrance. The effect of Hammond's preaching was felt for many months, and permanent results were claimed by his gratified sponsors. The lasting result of his work was the creation of an interest in child conversion.

The Highland Revival sweeping up the western islands and the northern highlands jumped across the Pentland Firth to the Orkney Islands,[14] from which a Kirkwall gentleman reported: 'There is a most marvellous, miraculous work of God's Spirit going on here. . . . I believe that the whole character of this end of the island is changed.' In 1860 there were eight special prayer meetings in the Shetlands and the general interest grew until 1862, when Dr. Craig and Mr. John Fraser commenced an evangelistic campaign to which up to 1200 people came, overcrowding the parish church night after night.[15] This work continued for many months till the spring of 1863, spreading from town to rural districts.

In northeast Scotland, from Moray Firth to the Firth of Tay, including the counties Nairn, Moray, Banff, Aberdeen, Kincardine and Angus, the Awakening was felt immediately and intensely in 1859. Following the prayer movement in 1858, and limited Revival in early 1859,[16] there were ambitious open-air services in the city of Aberdeen in the spring and summer of 1859. In London, religious editors were credibly informed that there was scarcely a town or village between Inverness and Aberdeen that had not been moved by the quickening power of the Spirit.

As to the nature of the awakenings, the Rev. W. T. Ker of Deskford stated: 'It is indeed a most wondrous work of the Lord, and it is passing along this whole coast like a mighty wave, having assumed a character identical with that of the work in Ireland.'[17]

Almost every parish in the county of Perth felt the quickening influences of the Spirit during the wonderful years of
1859-60.[18] Wherever there was a living Christian community,
revival was long prayed-for and its arrival hailed with joy.
More than fifty ministers and lay workers addressed 4000
people between 11 a.m. and 6 p.m. on one occasion (22nd
August 1860) in which the sponsors avowed that they 'buried
sectarianism in the South Inch of Perth that day and saw no
Christian weep over its grave.' Church of Scotland, Church of
England, United Presbyterian, Congregational and Baptist
ministers participated. In Perth City Hall, 2000 attended,
three churches being used simultaneously that evening for
many inquirers dealt with by the ministers. Seven weeks
or so later, local ministers reported no abatement of this
movement, 'all the country around on fire.'

There was a remarkable outbreak of revival phenomena
in Fifeshire, to the south of Dundee. An Army officer of high
rank summed up his impressions of Cellardyke thus:[19]

> Those of you who are at ease have little conception
> of how terrifying a sight it is when the Holy Spirit is
> pleased to open a man's eyes to see the real state of his
> heart. Men who were thought to be and who thought them-
> selves to be good, religious people . . . have been led
> to search into the foundation on which they were resting,
> resting on their own goodness, and not upon Christ.
> Many turned from open sin to lives of holiness, some
> weeping for joy for sins forgiven.

The forerunner of the Edinburgh Revival was a united
prayer meeting begun in April 1858, when the news of the
American Revival crossed the Atlantic, held every Monday
for twenty-one months, becoming a daily meeting in January
1860.[20] In this meeting, the Church of Scotland, Free Church
and United Presbyterian ministers worked together in unity
and fraternity.

In November, it was reported from Edinburgh that 'a very
general expectation of a manifest outpouring of the Holy
Spirit exists.'[21] The American revivalist, Prof. Charles G.
Finney, was in Edinburgh for a short visit at that time, and
his meetings,[22] very well attended, produced many converts.
Strange things were already happening in the Carrubber's
Close Mission (which had opened its doors eighteen months
before by ejecting an Atheist Club from the premises) where
scores of people of all ages were being converted. Only two
of these converts displayed any physical manifestations.

By March, the work of revival was making progress in Edinburgh and surrounding district, prayer meetings having been established in many towns and villages nearby, as well as in the city.[23] Gospel meetings began to attract huge crowds, with good results. Radcliffe and Weaver, English evangelists, could not get a location large enough for their meetings. On one occasion, 1800 people packed Richmond Place Chapel, while thousands crowded a street outside; the evangelists were compelled to walk upon the shoulders of stalwart men, in order to alternate in ministry inside and outside the chapel. Hundreds remained behind for conversation, even though the preaching had gone on intermittently from seven till eleven at night. Such a response was not unusual.

In the Border counties south of Edinburgh, the Awakening began with prayer meetings that were quickened by news brought by their ministers from northern Ireland and western Scotland.[24] It continued effective for many years in the historic towns north of the Roman Wall.

What began as a movement of prayer among Christians in Scotland continued as a remarkable movement for the evangelization of Scotland. The incoming Moderator of the influential Free Church of Scotland, in 1861, paid tribute to the high quality of the work: 'Fathers and Brethren, I congratulate you on your meeting again in the midst of such an outpouring of the Spirit of God and a remarkable work of grace pervading the whole church and the whole land.' [25]

Judging from available material, there was not the same degree of controversy in Scotland as in Ireland about the work. This might be due to the fact that the manifestations in Ireland were novel in the British Isles in that century. They had been known in Scotland in Whitefield's day.

Five years after the initial outbreak of revival, a typical Presbytery reported: [26]

> (1) The Awakening had continued throughout the years, and was not so much a completed period of Revival but rather the beginning of a better state of things in the spread of vital religion.
> (2) All classes were influenced, and only its earliest stages were accompanied by excitement.
> (3) Agency was both lay and clerical, method both united prayer and expository preaching.
> (4) Revival had resulted in the quickening of believers, increase of family religion, decrease of cases of discipline in all congregations since.

Special conversions of remarkable character had stood the test of time, but it was difficult to state accurately what proportions of the number of converts had been genuine, as no attempts to count such conversions had been made.

A prominent evangelist was quoted as saying that thousands stood of the fruit of 1859-60, and many were going on well; and another added that in the first stages of revival there was a seeking of the evangelist, while later it became a seeking of the lost by the evangelist.

It is exceedingly difficult to compile accurate statistics of lasting conversions in the Scottish Revival of 1859-60, not only because of the divisions and the varying standards in Presbyterianism but because masses of the ordinary people customarily in formal membership in the Kirk made up most of the converts, hence were uncounted as accessions.

This was least true in the case of the non-established bodies. The United Presbyterian Church of Scotland stated that 477 of their congregations added 15,314 new members, presumably in the latter months of 1859.[27] Checking with Irish figures, it is found that the average Scottish and Irish Presbyterian congregation each gained thirty-three per cent. Upon the basis of incomplete Scottish statistics and comparisons with the results in the sister-Presbyterian Church in Ireland, it is calculated that the number of conversions in Scotland was ten per cent of the population of three million, or three hundred thousand people.

R. C. Morgan's Revival journal was the real day-to-day historian of the movement, and its trusted correspondents in 1865 summed up the Scottish results thus:[28]

> The wave of Divine blessing came to us apparently from Ireland four or five years ago. It struck first the west coast of Scotland, then spread over a great part of the country. It was a very blessed season, perhaps the most extensive in its operation that we have ever known amongst us. But it has, in a great measure, passed away. Still, fruit remains—living, active, consistent Christians who keep together, cherishing the memory of the time, blessing and praying for its return . . .
> The number of students entering our divinity halls this season will be double or triple that of former years; this is the blessed fruit of the Revival. Such men are likely to be of the right stamp.

Thus a prepared Scottish ministry welcomed Moody, the greatest evangelist produced by the 1858-59 Awakenings.

9

THE AWAKENING IN WALES

The 1859 Revival in Wales can be traced to the influence of the American Revival of 1858, but, unlike its Scottish counterpart, it owed nothing to the Ulster movement.[1] Indeed, there is evidence to suggest that the outbreak of revival in Wales actually preceded that experienced in Ulster.[2]

Nevertheless, the primary place must be given to the Ulster movement on account of its influence on the remainder of the United Kingdom, for English and Scottish religious life was comparatively uninfluenced by happenings in Cymric-speaking Welsh churches. In fact, in the summer of 1859, thousands of English Christians journeyed through North Wales to embark at Holyhead on their way to study the 'work of grace' in Ireland, without realizing that as profound an Awakening was stirring the villages and towns passed by whose inhabitants spoke the incomprehensible Welsh.[3]

There were local awakenings in Wales before 1858, but news of the Revival in the United States quickened the interest of churches and associations of ministers and laymen. Conditions were difficult. There were many who had seen the impact of earlier Awakenings in Wales, but the life of the churches was lukewarm and life outside the churches displayed boldness in sin.

'Before the '59 Revival,' asserted Principal Edwards of Bala College, 'the churches were withering away in our country; a wave of spiritual apathy and practical infidelity had spread over Wales.'[4]

Beside the general influence of the American Awakening upon the prayers of Welsh Christians, there was a more particular link with that Revival. A Welsh lad, Humphrey Rowland Jones had been born in North Cardiganshire about 1832.[5] He became converted fifteen years later and in 1854 he applied to the Wesleyan District Meeting of South Wales for admission to the ministry. He was rejected, then emigrated to the United States to rejoin his parents. There the Methodist Episcopal Church ordained him.[6] He became a revival preacher, itinerating widely.

Caught up in the American Revival movement in 1857-58, he returned to his native Wales in the summer of 1858. His evangelistic efforts had a measure of success, but this success created unconcerned and good-natured scepticism in the mind of a nearby Calvinistic Methodist minister, Rev. David Morgan, who greatly distrusted anything of American extraction or of Wesleyan dispensation.[7]

David Morgan himself had been awakened in a local revival in his native Cardiganshire in the year 1841.[8] His ministry was recognized in 1857, when he was ordained by the Trevine Association. For ten years he had prayed for an outpouring of the Divine Spirit. Hence, in spite of his deep prejudice, he went to hear young Humphrey Jones at a Wesleyan Chapel near Ysbytty Ystwyth and was deeply convicted by an address on the words: 'Because thou art neither hot nor cold, I will spue thee out of my mouth.' David Morgan entered into an experience of spiritual deepening a few days later. He began to preach with power.

The new dynamic immediately caused a movement to God. In David Morgan's village of Ysbytty Ystwyth, the population did not exceed 1000, yet 200 adult converts had been won before the end of 1858.[9] A feature of the revival was 'moliannu' or praising, a peculiar form of worship described as a chorus of rapturous praise from preacher and people in turn. In early 1859, David Morgan began to visit the nearby village churches. In Pontrhydfendigaid, more than half the population of 800 united themselves to the Calvinistic Methodists. An unordained Pontrhydfendigaid lad carried word to Tregaron, where all the congregation burst into praising, and eighty-seven people were converted in the service. By mid-summer the whole country of Cardigan had been pervaded with the most fervid religious feeling, Calvinistic Methodist converts alone numbering 9,000 in June, 15,000 in August, out of a population of 70,000.[10]

Every county in Wales experienced blessing.[11] Following the week of prayer in January 1860, a second wave of revival swept Wales, with even greater strength in some places and with the same happy interdenominational unity.[12] North and South Wales alike enjoyed its benefits.

In Monmouthshire, culturally a Welsh county though a part of England, the revival movement may be traced to the Congregational Association meetings at Beaufort, 29th and 30th June 1859.[13] Then the churches of every denomination participated enthusiastically in intercession and evangelism.

Cardiff, the Welsh metropolis, shared in the evangelistic movements stirring England in the 1860s.[14] In the spring of 1862, the American evangelists, Dr. and Mrs. Walter Palmer, began to experience stirring times in Cardiff. For thirty days 'a remarkable work of the Spirit' was acknowledged and felt throughout the town, affecting public morals, bringing hundreds to prayer meetings—so much so that an Episcopal town councilman with long experience testified that police cases were dwindling in number, a detective adding 'Cardiff has become a different place.' Local ministers supported the work well, and 800 people became inquirers in their churches. The Palmers were followed by Richard Weaver, and 'half the people could not get in.' The largest building in South Wales, the Music Hall, filled up with 4000 people, and each evening hundreds were turned away.

In the spring of 1863, William and Catherine Booth, fresh from a revival of great power in Cornwall, began preaching in Cardiff, and won 500 people to the faith.[15] Mrs. Booth preached with simplicity and modesty. So great was the interest in the Booth campaign that it became necessary to use a large circus building accommodating 2000 to 3000 people. The effort was supported by Christians of every denomination. Quite a number of the converts of the Cardiff meetings were Cornish people, one couple having voyaged by sea to Wales on account of conviction produced by the revivalist in Cornwall. The Booths were followed by Richard Weaver on another visit, and crowds of 3000 attended, 500 professing faith in Christ.[16]

It should be emphasized that in all the Cardiff series, English was the medium of preaching. Reports of revival in Cardiff during the earlier Welsh Revival movement were so scarce that it underlined the notion that Cardiff was looked upon as a cosmopolitan city within Wales. That the English movements of the 1860s affected Cardiff so powerfully bears this contention out.

Principal Charles of Trevecca College noted three main characteristics of the Welsh Revival thus:[17] first, an extraordinary spirit of prayer among the masses; second, a remarkable spirit of union among all the denominations of Christians; and third, a powerful missionary effort for the conversion of others—three characteristics obvious in the American, Irish and Scottish movements which, like the '59 Revival in Wales, were independent of great personalities, even David Morgan in Wales being a simple country pastor.

In what way did the Welsh movement differ from its contemporaries? There were fewer cases of physical prostration in Wales, if any, but just as many evidences of intense
conviction or agony of mind. In Ulster, the physical prostrations were the stimulating incidents which first created
public interest; but, in Wales, the rapture of praise seemed
to be the catalyst.

The Baptist churches gained about 14,000 new members
from the converts.[18] The Rev. Thomas Thomas, Principal of
the Baptist College at Pontypool, reported 'tens of thousands'
added, with many new churches formed for Welsh-speaking
and English-speaking converts, and the number of students
preparing for the ministry actually doubled.

The Calvinistic Methodist Church of Wales—later the
Presbyterian Church of Wales—reaped a rich harvest from
the Awakening of 1859. The number of the converts who
subsequently joined their churches was recorded as 36,190,
a high percentage of the total membership.[19]

Congregationalists claimed a similar total of converts
gained by their churches, about 36,000.[20] In the county of
Carnarvon, Congregationalists built a score of chapels to
house the new recruits.

The Wesleyan Methodists gained 4,549 new members in
1859-60,[21] and support of the Revival by the Methodists also
seemed unanimous. Hugh Price Hughes was converted in
that awakening and lived to become a great leader in British
Methodism, next in rank to John Wesley, said some.

The Church of England in Wales supported the movement,
but its accessions could be estimated only—in the absence
of reliable figures—as 20,000 new communicants. Converts
were made among many nominal church members.

The Rev. John Venn, M.A., the Prebendary of Hereford,
spoke before an Evangelical Alliance gathering in the autumn
of 1860. He claimed that almost every county in the principality had been influenced by a more or less remarkable
work of grace.[22] He attempted to assess the lasting worth
of the movement by giving details of great numbers already
received into church membership by various authorities and
adding a proportionate number for additions in the Established
Church, his own denomination. Prebendary Venn estimated
that about 100,000 persons in all had been received into full
communion in the course of two years. Carefully, he was
willing to deduct 10 per cent or so to avoid going beyond the
truth, a deduction that could be ignored if one desired to

estimate the numbers of professed conversions rather than additions to church membership, for it can be demonstrated that great numbers of actual church members are professedly and dynamically converted in every revival movement.

In his history of Protestant Nonconformity in Wales, published 1861, Thomas Rees stated the number of conversions in the Revival to Nonconformity alone as 85,000 to 95,000, declaring 'the numerous converts with comparatively rare exceptions hold on remarkably well.'[23] And a full fifty years after the Revival, one reliable authority declared on the basis of additions to church membership that it could be 'safely accepted that the whole harvest of the Revival in Wales did not fall short of a hundred thousand souls,' the great majority of whom satisfied the test of time.[24] Thus approximately a tenth of the population of Wales was permanently influenced by the Awakening, there being about a million people in Wales in 1859.

Family worship was begun and extended in the Awakening of 1859. A movement of temperance in the use of alcoholic beverages made its influence felt in church life, not insisting upon total abstinence for membership but recommending it to young and old.

Crime was diminished very considerably by the Revival of 1859 in Wales. In the year that followed the Revival, the number of criminal cases before the Welsh Courts decreased from 1809 to 1228.[25] And Wales shared in the social reforms which followed in the United Kingdom after 1860.

A year after the outbreak of Revival in Wales, a survey of the work was published in a book by Thomas Phillips. From it, the following has been summarized: (1) additions to the churches numbering many thousands broke all records to date; (2) not one convert in fifty relapsed; (3) the morals of the people were vastly improved; (4) a missionary spirit took hold of the churches; (5) ministers were anointed with fresh zeal, and lay-workers filled with 'first-love'; (6) an increase of brotherly love between individuals, churches and denominations produced more cordial cooperation.[26]

The follow-up of the 1859 Awakening in Wales was very thorough. Care was taken to instruct the people in principles. They were cautioned that excitement was not conversion, an awakening of conscience not regeneration. It was urged that unless their experience issued in hatred of sin and love of holiness and respect of moral obligation, it was a delusion. They were told to treat the Bible as the standard.

10

AWAKENING IN NORTHERN ENGLAND

The pattern of the Awakening in England was noteworthy, for it included full scale revival of the spontaneous and immediate type experienced in Ulster, Wales and Scotland; evangelistic movements in the metropolitan areas; and movements of delayed action until the Revival produced the right atmosphere and leaders for evangelism.

North of the Tyne in Northumberland, late in the summer of 1859, there was an early stirring due to the visit of Dr. and Mrs. Walter C. Palmer.[1] The Palmers had been participants in the original outbreak of revival in Hamilton, two years earlier, and their ministry provided a climax to the year of prayer meetings going on in Newcastle-on-Tyne.

The press in London reported that Newcastle had become 'the scene of a religious "Awakening" which bids fair to rival anything of the kind which has occurred either in America or the North of Ireland.'[2]

By October 1859, there seemed to be a more or less general awakening going on in the Tyneside city,[3] Anglican and Nonconformist clergy and ministers conducting special services, in one of which a saloon keeper who had invested in the brewery business created a sensation by renouncing the liquor traffic. The Rev. Robert Young reported:[4]

> The Revival with which this town is favoured is advancing with increased power and glory. In Brunswick Place Chapel, we hold a united prayer meeting from twelve o'clock to one; another meeting for exhortation and prayer from three to five; and a similar service from seven to ten. Many seem 'filled with the Holy Ghost' and pray 'as the Spirit gives them utterance.' All attempts to proselytize are utterly repudiated: hence some designate the work as 'the Evangelical Alliance Revival.' The meetings, although often crowding our spacious chapel, are orderly, and generally are marked by deep solemnity. It is true that occasionally there is the cry of the spirit-stricken sinner and the bursting joy of the newly emancipated captive, but that is music in our ears.

A month later, this Methodist minister stated that the Newcastle Awakening had accounted for 1300 conversions in his church, all the converts being willing to publish their names.[5] At the end of the year there were 1400 confirmed converts.[6] Five years later in Newcastle, evangelism in church and public hall was still effective, going 'gloriously' on among the working men.[7]

In the county of Durham, there was immediate response to the prayer challenge of 1859-60. In Sunderland, a meeting of ministers[8] unanimously resolved to commence prayer meetings, and in September 1859 these were held 'morning, noon and night,' attended by professing Christians and anxious inquirers. The first phase of revival had begun. Later that year the ministers claimed that an extensive revival had moved Sunderland. No less than 3444 persons joined local Wesleyan Societies in a movement led by the Palmers.[9]

Another productive hub of revival evangelism in County Durham was the Tyneside city of Gateshead. The Palmers visited the city in May 1860,[10] winning 500 or more converts. A New Connexion (Methodist) Church there experienced a time of revival in 1859 under its pastor, William Booth. Four years later, a circuit chapel reported that of the forty-nine professed conversions occurring within its walls that year thirty people were known to have joined the society, of whom eleven were still in fellowship, another fourteen in fellowship elsewhere, and yet another three had just been restored from backsliding, showing a loss of only two out of thirty.[11] In the second phase of the revival, 200 conversions were reported in 1861, a total in three years of 300 new members thus added to the New Connexion circuit. And so many sinners were brought to repentance that this Bethesda Chapel, Gateshead, earned the name, 'the Converting Shop.' Who can judge its influence in the birth of an organization?

It was during these revival times that Mrs. Catherine Booth (8th January 1860) announced her intention of preaching —to the astonishment of her husband[12] and his congregation. Likewise, during this local revival, William and Catherine Booth began to preach the doctrine of full salvation, now an integral part of Salvationist teaching. The Booths conducted a preaching mission in Hartlepool, attracting up to 1000 people, turning many away disappointed, and winning 250 converts.[13] In spite of this success, Methodist New Connexion Conference tried to set a limit upon Booth's evangelism, leading to his resignation in 1862.[14]

Dr. and Mrs. Palmer campaigned in Carlisle in February. A year later, there was a further movement also attributed to the melting and subduing influence of the Holy Spirit, in which numbers of converted youths were found bringing in 'young heathen' from the streets to be converted by scores. It was reported six months later that the work of grace was increasing, supported by a united prayer meeting combining five churches using a theatre for preaching services.[15]

In the 1860s, evangelism continued in strength in Liverpool, including meetings of between 700 and 1000 young men, many becoming converted. The American evangelist, E. Payson Hammond, was visiting Liverpool in the summer of 1861 and addressed larger gatherings, following which hundreds of inquirers remained for counsel.[16] In the autumn, Reginald Radcliffe began Sunday evening meetings in the Concert Hall which was overflowing. About that time, the Americans, Dr. and Mrs. Palmer, came to Liverpool for a rest from heavy duties and were immediately caught up in 'an extraordinary work of the Holy Spirit,' with converts in the hundreds.

On Christmas Eve 1859, Prof. Charles Finney arrived in Bolton with Mrs. Finney, and became the spearhead of a revival movement there among the Congregationalists and Methodists.[17] The chapel was filled from its first meeting, and when Finney called for inquirers on the fourth night, he found the vestry filled. Meetings were then transferred to a larger Temperance Hall, and under Finney's direction the whole town was canvassed with happy results. Three months later, more than 1200 were attending the weeknight services, and hundreds were being turned away on Sundays.

In Manchester, the religious revival appeared in full strength two years after the initial prayer meetings.[18] The work continued till the end of 1861, and it proved neither superficial nor evanescent. Finney's Manchester campaign was disappointing to him, but produced many converts:[19]

> His preaching is marked by strong peculiarities. It is highly argumentative—keenly logical—yet, being composed of good strong Saxon, is intelligible to the common people. Boldness, verging to severity, is one of its characteristics. Unpalatable truths are urged with a fearless courage ... masks, pretexts, subterfuges of all sorts, are exposed; and the selfish, the worldly, the cowardly and inconsistent, are driven from their retreats. Then comes the Gospel with its full and free antidote to despair, its gracious invitation to the penitent, its pardon and peace to the believing.

One convert of the 1861 meetings was Harry Moorhouse, whose companions were irreligious as himself. Moorhouse heard much shouting and noise from within the Alhambra, buttoned up his coat ready for whatever fray was provided, and rushed in, only to be confronted by a sight of ex-pugilist Richard Weaver preaching the gospel in his own inimitable style.[20] Before long Moorhouse and his companions found the same salvation preached by Weaver, and Harry Moorhouse was set upon his worldwide career as an evangelist.

In 1867, Harry Moorhouse crossed the Atlantic and began to preach to American congregations. In Chicago, Moody absent, Moorhouse was invited to preach, his appearance of insignificance causing much misgiving. But night after night, the Lancashire lad preached on John iii, 16, impressing all who heard him. Moody on his return was equally impressed, Moorhouse preaching all week on the same text. Said Revell, Moody's brother-in-law: 'D. L. Moody had great power before, but nothing like what he had after dear Harry Moorhouse came into our lives and changed the character of the preaching.'[21]

There were two phases of the Evangelical Awakening of 1859 in the middle belt of English counties, the first being the movement to prayer begun in summer 1859 and developed beyond all description after the second week of January in 1860, whereas the second was the evangelistic phase, sometimes following directly after the prayer movement but more often breaking out in the autumn of 1861 or later.

In the West Midlands,[22] the ministers of the great city of Birmingham convened general prayer meetings late in 1859. In early 1863, Dr. and Mrs. Palmer with Methodist support began holding special services at noontime and evening, a total of 133 inquirers recorded in the first six days.[23] The movement spread to all denominations and affected a number of nearby towns and villages. The pattern of the Awakening, with prayer meetings and evangelistic services, was being repeated in the industrial heart of England.

The Palmers were followed in September 1863 by another pair who had been inspired by their joint ministry at Gateshead in 1859, none other than William and Catherine Booth, who enjoyed a successful time in the Moseley Street Chapel, with 150 professed conversions recorded. The Booths were followed by their friend and patron, James Caughey, who had deeply impressive meetings in Bath Street Chapel and the Alhambra Circus seating 3,000.[24] Thus it might be said that the Awakening developed evangelism in Birmingham.

In 1863 a religious Revival began in the Black Country, that intensely industrialized area to the north of Birmingham. Dr. and Mrs. Palmer, the lay evangelists, ministered for a month in Walsall, using the midday prayer meetings and evening preaching service technique.[25] As a result, 300 folk made profession of conversion, including people as old as eighty years. Some converts requested prayer on behalf of personal friends and had tte joy of seeing them make decision in subsequent meetings.

The Palmer visit to Walsall (February 1863) was followed by one of the Booths, who ministered there until the summer. One of William Booth's open-air meetings attracted about 5,000 people,[26] three-quarters of whom were men, and on these working men were turned loose a team of converted laymen, as Booth found another weapon to use in future: 'just of the stamp to grapple with this class, chiefly of their own order, talking to them in their own language, regarding themselves as illustrations of the power of the Gospel.'

One had been a drunken, gambling, prize fighting hooligan who had needed six policemen to take him to jail. Another had been a horse-racer, professional gambler and drunkard. And yet another was nicknamed 'the Birmingham Rough', a wicked and abandoned character before his conversion. That evening a local chapel was crowded to hear Catherine Booth speak, and some forty decisions were recorded there. It is interesting to note that one of the converts of the Walsall Mission was a lad, Bramwell Booth, who without parental urging came under conviction and joined the penitents.[27]

In the autumn of 1863, William Booth was still working in the Black Country, and a letter to a friend described his experiences in Cradley Heath—three miles from Dudley— population exceeding 20,000.[28] The chapel was full on the first Sunday morning but too overcrowded for comfortable speaking or hearing at night. William Booth began by calling on the leaders of the church to make a renewed consecration of themselves to God, so 'a gracious melting and breaking up of heart followed, blessing a great number throughout the chapel.' Conversions began to be declared in the days that followed the time of reviving.

At Walsall,[29] William Booth's converts were announced to take part in the proceedings as the 'Hallelujah Band.' It was through their ministry that William Booth adopted as a lasting principle that the masses would be most effectively reached by converts of their own kind.[30]

11

AWAKENING IN SOUTHERN ENGLAND

The news of the Ulster Revival increased intercession in England. Early in 1860, Elizabeth Codner, a London lady, published anonymously a poem which became a much-used devotional hymn for several generations:[1]

> Lord, I hear of showers of blessing
> Thou art scattering full and free,
> Showers the thirsty land refreshing—
> Let some drops now fall on me.

Dr. Eugene Stock, the secretary of the Church Missionary Society, declared in retrospect that the most striking feature of the 1860 Revival was the phenomenal prayer meetings: . . . 'I can never forget the 9th January 1860, when at nine o'clock on a bitterly cold morning that hall was densely packed for nothing but simple prayer for the outpouring of the Holy Spirit.'[2]

'That hall' was the huge Islington Agricultural Hall. The second week of January was devoted by multitudes of believers to special united prayer for an outpouring of the Holy Spirit all over the world. This feature of the Revival originated in an appeal issued in 1858 by a group of American missionaries at Ludhiana, a small town in Northwest India, asking all Christians throughout the world to set aside the second week of 1860 for united prayer.[3] The response of leaders and people to this call to prayer was as astonishing as it was spontaneous, for in London alone there were at least two hundred united prayer meetings.[4]

Records of the movement in London are full of examples of the effect of prayer on worship, fellowship and evangelism, all of which revived immeasurably. Awakened Christians in London soon found an opportunity of harnessing the flowing tides of revival to generate sufficient power to carry the Light to the most darkened masses of the metropolis. A prime mover in the matter was that 'Evangelical of the Evangelicals,' the Seventh Earl of Shaftesbury, who helped make possible, by sponsoring a Religious Worship Act, the holding of services by clergy in unconsecrated buildings.[5]

The stage was set for one of the most ambitious efforts in all history to reach the masses of a great metropolis. On New Year's Day 1860, the Britannia, the Garrick and the Sadlers Wells Theatres were thrown open for Sunday evening services for the people, attracting 'overwhelming' and 'immense' audiences to hear sermons by Established clergymen and Dissenting ministers.[6] Another two theatres were opened later that month, and a couple more in February, by which time all seven were accommodating an aggregate attendance nightly of over 20,000.[7] Special services for upper and middle class people were held in St. Paul's Cathedral and Westminster Abbey, and also in St. James's and Exeter Halls in the fashionable West End.

Numerical reports are unavailable regarding aggregates of vast but orderly crowds attending St. Paul's Cathedral for special services, led by the Bishop of London, 'with his usual zeal';[8] nor are estimates given of total attendances at very similar services in Westminster Abbey; but on the basis of sitting space and reports of crowded gatherings, an aggregate of 100,000 is calculated by the writer.

Seasonal aggregate attendances at theatre services of the Shaftesbury United Committee appeared to be in excess of 250,000.[9] Likewise, Free Church theatre services held by Baptist, Congregationalist, Methodist and Presbyterian ministers in St. James's Hall, Piccadilly and the Britannia Theatre in the East End, attracted an aggregate of 250,000 eager auditors.

Independent services were begun in the Victoria Theatre, Waterloo, by Richard Weaver and continued by William Carter. No less than 559 services were held in the first four winters with an aggregate of 865,100 people in attendance, an average seasonal aggregate of over 200,000 in a single theatre.[10] Sunday afternoon meetings for inquirers and converts were arranged, and an observer reported more than 400 present, while the evening meeting was 'crammed to the roof.' It is claimed that, in April 1862, the converts' meetings filled the theatre, hundreds were turned away and there were insufficient workers to deal with the many penitents who sought salvation.

Another committee, known as the Additional Theatre Services Committee, commenced work in four theatres—the Mary-le-bone, Soho, Surrey, and City of London Theatres. Usually hundreds remained for prayer, inquiry or decision. Aggregate attendances numbered 200,000 a season.

Services in Whitechapel's Garrick Theatre were taken up by an East London Special Services Committee that rose from a conference called on 23rd January 1861 by Reginald Radcliffe in the Sussex Hall in Leadenhall Street to discuss the need of the East End of London.[11] To some 200 zealous Christians, Baptist Noel truly prophesied: [12]

> . . . If this work is done, we shall see some unknown Luthers and Whitefields excavated out of this dark mine, to spread the Gospel farther and wider than we have any idea. I believe we are on the eve of a greater work than England ever saw, and the East End of London is the right place to begin.

Out of this East End of London venture grew the Salvation Army, a subject reserved for later treatment. No record of numbers reached by the East London Committee is available, at the City of London or Garrick Theatres, or elsewhere.

In addition to all these organized, committee-controlled activities were 'numberless special services in and around London.' On the basis of known figures alone, it can be safely said that a million aggregate of London's unchurched folk were reached Sundays in theatre services.[13]

Nowhere in the stirring accounts of Revival in London was there any evidence of prostration or hysteria. The work in London seemed to have developed in a different way from what preceded it in Ulster, Wales or Scotland. The London Revival of the early 1860s was one of preaching. All the many evangelistic campaigns which were held throughout the metropolis in the revival years of the 1860s are too numerous to be chronicled here. The results were manifold: in the revival decade, prior to 1865, the Protestant churches of London added 200,000 seats to total accommodation, a 60 per cent increase which outstripped that of the fast-growing population of the metropolis by a small margin.

Into southwest England, the Awakening spread. Bishop Handley Moule in later years recalled rural Dorset days:[14]

> I must not close without a memory, however meagre, of one wonderful epoch in the parish. It was the Revival. The year was 1859, that 'year of the right hand of the Most High' . . . (the year in fact was 1860—editor). Ulster was profoundly and lastingly moved and blessed. Here and there in England, it was the same: Fordington was one of the scenes of Divine Awakening. For surely it was Divine. No artificial means of excitement were dreamt of; my Father's whole genius was against it.

No powerful personality, no Moody or Aitken, came
to us. A city missionary and a London Bible-woman
were the only helpers from a distance. But a power
not of man brought souls to ask the old question:
'What must I do to be saved?' Up and down the village
the pastor, pastoress and faithful helpers, as they went
on their daily rounds, found 'the anxious.' And the
church was thronged to overflowing, and so was the
spacious schoolroom, night by night, throughout the
whole week. The simplest means carried with them
a heavenly power. The plain reading of a chapter often
conveyed the call of God to men and women, and they
came to Jesus as they were.'

The saintly Bishop affirmed that hundreds of people had
been awakened and continued in grace. A great social uplift
followed. Shortly afterward, Moule went up to Trinity College
in Cambridge, where in 1867 he declared his faith.

Though instances of spontaneous revival could be given
in reports from all parts of Cornwall,[15] the most effective
work developed through a visit of William and Catherine
Booth—described as a 'wilderness' experience by General
Booth's biographer, Harold Begbie.[16] Booth was yet to do
a greater work, but the period of these Cornish Revivals
(1861-62) was one of profoundest import in his life.

How did Methodists show their appreciation of the Booths?
In June 1862, the Methodist New Connexion Conference at
Dudley accepted Booth's resignation, disapproving of his
revivalism.[17] Then the Primitive Methodist Conference at
Sheffield aimed a blow at his calling in a resolution urging
all its pastors 'to avoid employing of revivalists, so-called.'
And the Wesleyan Conference in July at Camborne, in spite
of their knowledge that the Booths had added 4247 new members to Cornish Wesleyan churches, directed its superin-
tendents not to sanction the use of their chapels for continuous services by outsiders. It is impossible to reject the
opinion widely held in Cornwall that opposition to William
Booth was caused by ministerial jealousy of a free-lance.
The Booths departed from Cornwall with the jeers of a
Wesleyan President about 'the perambulations of the male
and female' ringing in their ears.[18]

Cornwall and Dorset were not the only parts of the West
country to experience revival in the 1860s. Devonshire and
Somerset enjoyed awakenings also, as did the historic city
of Bristol, where Wesley and Whitefield had sown the seed.

In East Anglia, union prayer meetings began in 1859. In 1860, local awakenings began, and in 1861 the evangelistic phase of the Revival was in full swing. The most outstanding work was accomplished in Lowestoft by Radcliffe and Henry who found no building large enough for the great crowds and hurriedly hired the big railway depot, to which were admitted 3000 of a population of 9000.[19] Hundreds were converted, reclaimed from profanity and immorality. Police arrests for drunkenness dropped from 120 to 20 nightly. An awakening spread throughout the eastern counties, Norfolk, Suffolk, Essex and east and west of the Fens.

In the South Midlands, ever so different from industrial belts to the north, the Awakening was felt in the little towns and historic boroughs. One of the most remarkable movements took place in the town of Wellington in Salop, where Dr. J. Edward Cranage, an educator, became the vehicle of movement after a visit to the Irish Revival.[20]

There was an awakening in the university communities. At that time, Oxford University was anything but an evangelical stronghold. Wadham College matriculated young Hay Aitken in 1861, fresh from a tour of evangelism in the revival areas of northern Scotland. Aitken and his friend Freeman vowed to speak to every last Wadham undergraduate about his spiritual welfare.[21] It seemed likely that the ambitious evangelist extended operations to the whole University, as 'a sort of evangelical Revival among undergraduates had taken place, especially at Wadham, where W. Hay M. H. Aitken, afterwards the famous missioner, had been in residence.'[22]

There was much the same order of prayer meetings in Cambridge University, where an observer informed friends that 'On the Sunday evening, I was in a prayer meeting at Cambridge, nothing but undergraduates . . . crying to God for wholehearted consecration.'[23]

Into the Oxford prayer fellowships was thrust a young undergraduate, Francis James Chavasse, afterwards to be so well-known as the evangelical Bishop of Liverpool. And into the Cambridge prayer fellowships came Handley Carr Glyn Moule, already impressed in the 1860 Dorset Revival, afterwards well-known as the saintly Bishop of Durham.

The Oxford and Cambridge daily prayer meetings during term have continued effectively for a hundred years or so. From their renewal in the twentieth century developed the Inter-Varsity Fellowship of Christian Unions, worldwide.

12

APPRECIATION–AND DEPRECIATION

Unlike the American Awakening of 1858, the British 1859 Revival early became the subject of controversy. Critics found in the movement in the North of Ireland much that was offensive to their sense of propriety. The phenomena known as 'prostrations,' though commonplace in the early years of the Wesleyan movement, excited derision. There was also an attempt to deny the undoubted moral and social benefits. Otherwise, ecclesiastical parties took sides according to their prejudices, which meant in effect that the Evangelical party in the Church of England and the vast majority of the Free Church bodies ardently supported the movement, while traditionalists and rationalists ranged themselves against it.

Some organs of the British press stooped low in their treatment of the 1859 Revival, these attacks being not merely due to misinformation. A Belfast newspaper which disliked the Revival upon religious grounds—for it was of Unitarian background—attacked the movement in the pettiest possible ways.[1] Lest this example be attributed to Irish zeal for combat in the journalistic field, one must point out that the same sort of thing was perpetrated (with as feeble justification) by London's greatest newspaper in attributing to the Revival a propensity for driving people mad, a theme which its editors maintained in spite of all evidence to the contrary.[2]

Throughout the newsworthy period of the Ulster Revival, 'Timesmen' adopted an attitude of opposition to the movement, leaving no possible criticism unsaid.[3] Consistently, they played up all that enemies of the Revival had to say, and consistently ignored or played down or contradicted everything that the friends of the Revival movement claimed. Dr. G. M. Trevelyan commented on the unfortunate influence of London's great newspaper of that very period.[4] Certainly it is easy to paraphrase Trevelyan's assessment and add that, when the great newspaper decided pontifically that the Revival was all fanaticism, and doing harm instead of good, anti-Evangelicals, secular and religious, believed what they read and acted accordingly.

Charles Dickens made reference to the Ulster Awakening in his writings. The novelist proclaimed the outbreak of hysteria and denied the reports of moral improvement by quoting Belfast statistics, 'those fatal figures, those unenthusiastic, disbelieving, obstinate statistics, to destroy all these beautiful assertions.'[5]

The Rev. Franklin Bewley, resident Anglican clergyman in the parish of Tullylish, County Down, retorted:[6]

> I was never so shocked as with the gross falsehood of The Times that the result of the movement has been to fill the streets of Belfast with prostitutes and drunken revellers. Never was there a more manifest distortion of facts.

Nevertheless, the Mayor of Belfast (himself a friend of the Revival) admitted that there was an increase in the number of cases brought before the magistrates in the city of Belfast. In 1858, there were 2539 cases of drunkenness: in 1859, 3112, an increase of 573.[7] About this increase, Professor Gibson stated:

> If it had been asserted by the advocates of the religious movement that every individual of the 120,000 or 130,000 inhabitants of Belfast had been brought under the influence of the Revival, these statistics of drunkenness might be legitimately appealed to in the case. But it is a fact which admits of no dispute that no person has, during the year in question, been brought before the police court of Belfast, on a charge of drunkenness, who has ever been brought under religious influences.

The implication of Prof. Gibson's and others' remarks was that the increased drunkenness occurred among the minority of 40,000 who were forbidden to attend revival services. The London critics again emphasized apparently contradictory statistics on 28th March 1860, but the general religious press retorted that none of the inebriates was a convert of the Revival.[8]

Defenders of the Revival pointed out that in the County of Derry there were 100,000 Presbyterians, but not one drunken person calling himself a Presbyterian, adding that the question did not turn upon the number of cases, but upon their religious profession.[9]

In an attempt to settle this controversy, the following authoritative figures from official records were secured concerning all criminal convictions in the Six Counties for the years 1855-1861:[10]

years	1855	1856	1857	1858	1859	1860	1861
Antrim	254	123	146	129	104	66	79
Armagh	125	119	69	100	84	133	115
Derry	96	90	78	85	60	42	73
Down	163	147	153	130	104	82	111
Fermanagh	70	80	54	101	53	48	119
Tyrone	181	195	128	91	70	85	96
totals	889	754	638	636	475	456	593

These statistics for the Six Counties seem to show that the period of the Revival produced a considerable decrease in crimes committed against society. In the year 1859, a Belfast morning newspaper reported decreased 'drunkenness and depravity' as a result of the Revival, quoting a Belfast police constable who averred that he had not seen a drunken person for weeks; a former average of convictions being twenty-one monthly, but only sixteen occurring in April, four in May and none at all in June or July.[11] This policeman's district was a nominally Protestant one.

At the Ballymena Quarter-Sessions in April 1860, His Worship congratulated the community that there was not a single case of indictment upon the record.[12] At the Quarter-Sessions in Coleraine, April 1860, the judge congratulated the jury that there was only one new case to be considered, a very unimportant one. At the Quarter-Sessions in Belfast, April 1860, there were only three cases, all of them trifling in character. At the Quarter-Sessions in Londonderry, April 1860, there was no criminal business at all, and His Worship was presented with a pair of white gloves. At the Quarter-Sessions in Down, April 1860, there were no prisoners appearing on the calendar for trial—an astounding record!

Another charge was made by local critics against the 1859 movement—that it increased insanity. Both Dr. Gibson and Dr. Weir exploded the figures given by local critics, conclusively.[13] Neither had access to the comprehensive figures based upon the Inspector of Asylums Reports which showed that, in spite of a widening definition in the years 1851-61, the total number of insane in asylums and under restraint in Ireland in 1859 was 11,218 as compared with 14,141 two years earlier, and 16,732 two years later.[14]

So often was the charge reiterated by the enemies of the Revival that it had caused an increase of sexual immorality that the opinion persisted in Ulster till recently. Reference has been made to Belfast and London journalistic opinions but there is plenty of evidence to the contrary.

The Rev. John Baillie was startled to learn of a prayer meeting being held by converted inmates of a house of ill-fame![5] Benjamin Scott, Chamberlain of the City of London, discovered that the Ulster Penitentiary for the Reform of Fallen Women was in great need of funds and space to take care of an influx of converted prostitutes seeking rehabilitation.[16] Dr. Hugh Hanna, noting that Belfast was infected as elsewhere by the great social evil, declared that the movement had entered into the haunts of its worst wickedness, bringing many a Magdalene to the feet of Christ and enabling ministers to get audiences of attentive and tearful listeners. Certain prostitutes confessed that they were first made to consider an amended life by the falling off in business.[17] The Rev. John Venn of Hereford quoted a Belfast policeman who saw a body of fourteen prostitutes making their way to a House of Refuge as the result of a visit to a prayer meeting.

Most of these instances concerned the reform of professional harlots, not the incidence of occasional promiscuity with its outcome of illegitimacy. The only possible checking on the occurrence of non-professional immorality would have been the Registrar-General's summary of illegitimate births. Alas, in Ireland, the compulsory registration of all births and deaths was begun in 1864, too late for reference. Scottish figures indicated that the 1859 Revival diminished noticeably[18] the incidence of illegitimacy in the year 1860! (Records in Ahoghill, for example, noted increased church membership, but fewer charges and fruits of immorality)

There were prostrations in the 1859 Revival in the United Kingdom, rarely but sensationally. The masses of both Ulster and Scotland were largely uneducated in 1859, and subject to the same impulses that moved the frontiersmen of Kentucky and Tennessee in 1800, the leading edge of the westward movement in North America being Scotch-Irish.

Regarding the 1859 'physical effects,' among constructive critics there were three opinions: first, that of attributing the physical phenomena to hysteria; and second, that of ascribing them to epidemic agency; and third, that of imputing them to sympathetic action, the latter being the theory of Prof. James McCosh of Queen's University, Belfast— with which he opened his discourse to the 1859 Evangelical Alliance meetings.[19] Time past he had watched a shipwreck on the east coast of Scotland, seeing a distraught mother agonize for her sailor son in the rebounding ship, but when at last the ship struck the rocks and went to pieces, the poor mother fell down convulsed and prostrate, and remained so until they brought to her her rescued son, after which she rejoiced with abandon. Professor McCosh concluded that conviction of a sinner by the Holy Spirit might cause prostration in the same manner, and that the physical manifestation was determined by the temperament of the individual. It was admitted that for every case of conviction in spirit followed by reaction in body there might be another one stirred to physical reaction by sympathetic suggestion. Dr. McCosh refused to regard bodily manifestation as a test of Divine working, but considered it a physiological accident.[20]

Dr. Merle D'Aubigne', historian of the Reformation, delivered an address on 3rd October 1859 at the Geneva School of Theology and asked the critics of the Ulster movement, 'Is it surprising that a strong emotion of the mind should also act upon the body?' He himself recalled, perhaps forty years earlier, having witnessed a similar movement in Schaffhausen under the preaching of Pfarrer Spliess, and although there were strange physical phenomena, the good work was still continuing. 'Bodily affections only prove one thing—existence in the soul of a deep and powerful feeling.'[21]

In discussing the present writer's observation of prostration under conviction of sin in Latvia in 1935, the Indian scholar, Bishop A. J. Appasamy, observed:[22]

> One may recall that when the Methodist Revival began in England in 1738 there were many such instances. People fell to the ground as though they had been given a sudden blow; they shouted in much agony; their bodies passed through many cruel and unseemly convulsions.
>
> Sometimes they continued thus for a number of hours. Their misery was followed by an immense joy that their burden of sin had been lifted and that they had found peace in God.
>
> There was much controversy about the value of such experiences. John Wesley studied the many instances which came under his observation with genuine sympathy and careful criticism. After twenty years' observation and reflection, he wrote (Journal of 25th November 1759)
>
> . . . 'The danger was to regard extraordinary circumstances too much . . . as if these were essential to the inward work, so that it could not go on without them. Perhaps the danger (now) is to regard them too little, to condemn them altogether, to imagine they had nothing of God in them, and were a hindrance to His work.

Whereas the truth is (1) God suddenly and strongly convinced many . . . the natural consequence whereof were sudden outcries and strong bodily convulsions; (2) to strengthen and encourage them that believed, He favoured several of them with divine dreams . . . (3) in some of these instances, after a time, nature mixed with grace; (4) Satan likewise mimicked this work of God, in order to discredit the whole work . . .

At first, it was doubtless wholly from God. It is partly so at this day. And He will enable us to discern how far, in every case, the work is pure, and where it mixes or degenerates.'

This sound and judicious summary holds true of Edwin Orr's experience in Riga and elsewhere, and is in keeping with his conclusions as a critical historian regarding such manifestations during the great Revival of 1859 in his native Ireland.

The Anglican establishment in England, Wales and Ireland together with the Nonconformist Episcopalians in Scotland, formed the largest ecclesiastical organization in the British Isles. Establishment enhanced the Church's position.

Anglicans encountered the Awakening in Ulster in 1859. The Church of Ireland (later disestablished) had usually been predominantly evangelical, but a minority of its leaders had been somewhat exclusive in attitude towards non-Anglican evangelicalism.[23] As a consequence, most Churchmen in all Ireland welcomed the 1859 Revival, but some were critical of its occasional excesses or its interdenominational comity. Critics hinted that the order of the Established Church was incompatible with the exuberance of the awakened, but converts spoke of the liturgy with joy as fitly expressing faith.

The background of Scotland was as fiercely Reformed as that of Ireland was Roman Catholic. Nonconformist Anglicans represented a more traditionalist and less evangelical reaction, hence Scottish Episcopalians were lukewarm to the 1859 Revival.[24] In Wales, four-fifths of the population adhered to a strongly evangelical Dissent, but Welsh Episcopalians gained 20,000,[25] indicating enthusiasm little less than other denominational elation.

In England, the Church of England was, in every way, the largest ecclesiastical body. The attitude of its leaders to the 1859 Revival was as varied as their schools of thought, and their Bishops, like the children of Israel in the days of the Judges, did every man that which was right in his own eyes.

The Bishop of Hereford (Hampden) attacked the movement in Ulster as 'savouring of John Wesley,' but the Bishop of Carlisle (Waldegrave) cooperated wholeheartedly. The Bishop of London (Tait) gave his clergy freedom of action, and 28 of them declared the Revival 'the wonderful work of God.'[26] The Bishop of Ripon (Bickersteth) cordially approved an Anglican project for revival services in Bradford, but disapproved of interdenominational cooperation in them.[27] So the cooperating Anglican clergy and Free Church ministers arranged Sunday evening services, alternating in sponsorship, with the result that on some Sundays the preachers enjoyed the Episcopal blessing as well as the Divine benediction, but on others only the Divine benediction. The Broad Churchmen, or Liberal-Evangelicals, supported or opposed according to emphasis.

A standard work on the Evangelical Party in the Church of England outlined the permanent good accruing to sympathetic Anglicans from the revival movement.[28] This included the opening of the London College of Divinity in 1861; and the foundation of the Anglican Deaconesses movement in 1860; the establishment of many Evangelical Associations of Clergy and Laity; also the informal enterprise of open-air preaching by Evangelical clergy, which became quite general. The Evangelical Bishop Baring of Durham helped build 119 new churches in the diocese, helped enlarge 130 others, founded 102 new parishes and increased the number of clergy by 189, from 1861 onwards.

There were regrets by Evangelical Anglicans. Dr. Eugene Stock, Church Missionary Society director, wrote in recall: . . . 'I have always felt that if our clergy had more heartily welcomed the (1859) Revival, its effects within the Church of England would have been much greater.'[29]

The church historian, Elliott Binns, recorded his opinion tersely that 'When the revival movement began in 1859, the Evangelicals stood apart, and for this reason largely failed to reap any fruit from it.'[30]

Nevertheless, the claim has been made and not contradicted that a quarter of a million converts were gathered by Anglican Evangelicals in England. There would have been many more but for the bitter opposition of Anglo-Catholic exclusivists, who (in those days) were so opposed to interdenominational cooperation that one protested the attendance of Anglican clergy at the funeral of the saintly Congregational preacher, John Angell James, a protest sustained by editors, reflecting the Anglo-Catholic constituency.

In contrast with the Anglicans, the Baptists cooperated with the 1859 Revival movement in Ireland, Scotland, Wales and England. No opposition was in evidence. Baptist editors discussed the peculiarities of the Revival, the attacks of its critics, the praises of its friends, all the while endorsing it.

The Baptist Union supported the movement.[31] Spurgeon claimed that his congregation had been experiencing revival for a decade, but he warmly supported the 1859 movement, and he built his Metropolitan Tabernacle on the crest of it. This was not an isolated event, for the number of Baptist churches built from 1860 to 1870 (and surviving) in London was unmatched before or after. Baptist church sittings in London increased by 33,325, or 60%, in the Revival decade. Of the quarter of a million Baptist church members in all of Britain in 1865, 100,000 represented the fruits of Revival.[32]

The Congregational Union devoted a session of its assembly in 1858 to discussion of the American Awakening.[33] It met at Aberdare in Wales at the height of the Welsh Revival, and there 15,000 gathered for an open-air service. In Ireland in 1859, the Congregational Union of Ireland was formed. When it reached England, the Revival added 90,000 members to the English congregations, 135,000 in all of Britain.[34]

The Irish Methodists added 5000 to their 20,000 members in a single year, with 'holy enthusiasm.' In Great Britain, the Wesleyans added 75,000 in seven years of awakening. In all the Methodist constituencies, Wesleyan, Primitive, New Connexion, Free Churches, and Bible Christian, additions surpassed 200,000. A careful reading of the records showed that restrictions against revivalists by Methodist Conferences were aimed at itinerants outside denominational control. In Methodism, the more evangelistic Conferences gained much more benefit than the cautious Wesleyan body.[35]

Contrary to historical misinterpretation, the Presbyterian Churches of Scotland—all three Assemblies—supported the Revival of 1859, as did the Irish Presbyterian Church fully. Scotland had an unusually high church adherence, 2,500,000 in a population of 3,000,000. Approximately a tenth of the population professed conversion in the 1859 Revival period, the great majority in the Presbyterian constituency, though nominal church membership failed to show such additions. In Ireland, there were 60,000 converts in the Presbyterian fold. In Wales, there were 40,000. In England, Presbyterians greatly increased their seating capacities. The number of Irish students for the ministry doubled in three years.[36]

The Christian Brethren made striking gains in the Revival of 1859, as their biographical literature indicated.[37] Quakers (down to 15,000 members) also gained, and from 1860 onward evidenced a changing outlook and altered emphasis.[38]

The Unitarians in Ulster deplored the effects of the 1859 Revival, one of their ministers actually closing down Sunday evening services when other churches were packed. Unitarian ministers were already critical of the theology of the Revival, but their antagonism was sharpened further by the intolerant attitude of the Trinitarian Protestant majority, who detested Unitarianism as much as Roman Catholicism. Approval of the Revival was voiced in the London Unitarian Quarterly Meeting, not attributing it to the triumph of orthodoxy; but it also expressed incredulity that the Revival had occurred in the most educated and advanced part of Ireland.[39]

In Ireland, the Roman Catholic majority attributed the Revival to the agency of the Devil.[40] In certain areas, numbers of Roman Catholics were converted, and violence resulted, Evangelical ministers and people being attacked on the street. Priests warned their flocks against the alarming contagion, a Bishop lamenting the success of the Devil destroying souls through people incarnate of Satan, carrying Bibles.[41] A Dublin newspaper proposed testing the Divine origin of the Revival: if party strife ceased on the 12th July, the date of the Orange celebration, it would be a miracle. Instead of provocative marches, Orangemen quietly attended services of prayer. From 1860, the Roman Church began to promote the services of Passionist priests, a society of Roman evangelists.

There is no doubt that the accession of converts in Wales exceeded 100,000, as did the Irish figure. In Scotland, about 300,000 were converted. The Free Churches of England won about 400,000, the Church of England 250,000. Thus the total of converts in the United Kingdom exceeded a million, out of a population of 27,000,000, much as in the United States.

Geographically, the Awakening affected Christian people in every county of England, Scotland, Wales and Ulster. It reached a mass of people far more numerous than did the Evangelical Revival of the eighteenth century. Unlike earlier movements, it produced no cleavages among Christian denominations, invalidating the notion that Revival is necessarily schismatic. It presented the Churches with a host of new auxiliary organizations, missionary, evangelistic, social and philanthropic, not least the Salvation Army in the home field, and the China Inland Mission in the foreign.

13

MID-CENTURY IN EUROPE

The Scandinavian countries had experienced great awakenings at the turn of the nineteenth century, awakenings more thorough and effective than the movements initiated by the Reformers and the Pietists. The transformation of Norway under Hans Nielsen Hauge was unmatched in the history of the country, and there were similar movements in Denmark and in Sweden, generally described as 'the readers,' while Paavo Ruotsalainen, of humble birth, led a Finnish revival.

In succeeding generations, there was renewed awakening. In Norway, a movement at the mid-century raised up Prof. Gisle Johnson of Oslo within the State Church itself. In the 1830s, a British chaplain named George Scott began a work in Sweden which profoundly changed the life of the nation. Expelled, Scott was succeeded by Carl Olof Rosenius.

In the general revival throughout Sweden, the less stable leaders of the unorganized movement of the revival 'readers' faded from sight and left Rosenius the undisputed director of the movement. News of the American Awakening of 1857-58 and of the British Revival of 1859-60 added strength to Swedish Evangelicals.[1] The National Evangelical Foundation (Evangeliska Fosterlands Stiftelsen) was expanded. In 1858, Paul Peter Waldenström was converted, began preaching in Uppsala in 1859, and within three years church pulpits had opened up to him everywhere.[2] He rose to succeed Rosenius as the outstanding leader of the revival movement.

Professor Gisle Johnson was a worn-out man by the year 1860, but the mid-century revival in Norway continued in strength and received invigoration from another invasion of Rosenius evangelists from Sweden. These two forces combined to give Norway one of its most fruitful periods of Christian growth.[3]

Denmark was involved in political troubles at the mid-century, more particularly in Schleswig-Holstein, opposing in 1864 the rising nationalism of Germany, when Prussia and Austria attacked Denmark, soon defeating the Danes despite their spirited defensive action.

Meanwhile, religious awakening had begun on the isolated Danish island of Bornholm, far to the east in the Baltic Sea. It was led by P. C. Trandberg, a powerful preacher of repentance and conversion.[4] By 1863, Trandberg had an eager following of a thousand awakened believers. In 1865, Vilhelm Beck and Johannes Clausen engaged in a wider ministry of evangelism and revival and enrolled their following in the Church-related Indremission.[5] From Bornholm, closer to South Sweden than to the metropolitan parts of Denmark, the Trandberg revival spread to the city of Copenhagen and through Zealand, Lolland and Jutland. In its outreach, this Awakening stirred up the strong opposition of Lutheran High Churchmen, but (known as the Luther Mission) it remained within the national Church. The leader of the High Church party was a brilliant, many-talented clergyman, N. F. S. Grundtvig, who made a lasting contribution to Danish schools, and became famed as one of Denmark's greatest figures.[6]

As in Sweden and Norway, at that time united under a single monarchy, the resurgence of the evangelical spirit created new movements within the predominant Lutheranism of the community, rather than creating new denominations outside the State Churches. This was true in Finland also, as the Awakening in the Scandinavian countries flowed over the Gulf of Bothnia to Swedish-speaking folk and Finns.

Pioneers of the Baptists and the Methodists entered the Scandinavian countries about this time, through the conversion of individual persons, but their total strength remained small, and the national life continued to be overwhelmingly Lutheran in theory and practice.

The Ulster Awakening created great interest in Geneva, and stirred up revival movements in the French-speaking Reformed Churches in Switzerland, France and Belgium. Shortly afterwards, a revived English Baptist pastor, R. W. McCall, opened a preaching hall in Paris to reach spiritually destitute working men.[7] It had a profound influence.

There had also been a widespread awakening in Germany that followed the Napoleonic Wars. This awakening lasted a whole generation, deepening its impression upon the life of the nation through extensive home missions, and exporting its most dedicated products to the far corners of the earth as missionaries. The Germans often served in the British missionary societies. But the mid-century brought about a spiritual decline in the land of Luther, for reasons political as well as spiritual.

Contact with British and American leadership served to give to German Evangelical Christianity a new lease on life after the 1858-1859 Awakenings. Theodor Christlieb had served in a Lutheran Church during the Revival in London and returned to Germany to promote evangelism.[8] Robert Pearsall Smith, an erratic convert of the Awakening in America in 1858, visited Germany and revived the circles of Pietists there. The zeal building up broke out in great evangelistic operations following Moody's great campaigns in Great Britain.

Revival in 1858-59 in America, Britain and Europe also provided converts who became famous German evangelists, among them Carl Heinrich Rappard, Otto Stockmayer and Friedrich von Schlümbach, Anna von Weling and Friedrich Wilhelm Baedeker, all of them active in Germany for years. Twenty years passed before the full impact of the 1858-59 Awakenings was felt in Germany, but it was obvious that the leading evangelists traced their motivation back to the Revival directly, and as renewed through D. L. Moody.[9]

But there were local awakenings throughout the German lands in the wake of the 1859 British Revival. From 1860 on, the Evangelical Alliance promoted evangelistic conferences as well as annual weeks of prayer. Local revivals ensued. At Eberfeld, in Germany, a week of prayer brought about an extraordinary revival in the municipal orphanage which provoked reaction and controversy.[10] The municipal council dismissed the godly director of the orphanage, whereupon the provincial synod protested. In the court case which followed, fourteen of the three hundred orphans yielded to persuasion by inquisitors to say that they had dissimulated. The judgment was appealed to the Supreme Court in Berlin, which reversed the dismissal and ordered the council to pay.

Samuel Hebich, under whom a remarkable awakening had occurred on the Malabar coast of India, returned to his native Germany at the time of the mid-century awakening. Although broken in health, he preached for another nine years in Wurttemberg, Baden, and Switzerland. Hebich in his utterance was often crude, but he gained a tremendous local following, preaching three times a day, in churches and in public bars. His dynamic was revival, and his method was evangelism in its simplest, most straightforward forms.[11]

In due course, the organizations raised up by the 1858-59 Awakenings, or expanded therein, invaded Germany and set up their German counterparts in thorough Teutonic style.

In the Russian Ukraine, German settlers (both Mennonite and Pietist) had experienced great awakenings at the mid-century. Their zealous outreach resulted in their Russian compatriots engaging in prayer, the movement taking on it the name Stundist, from its hour of prayer.

The same tide of revival reaching the western world had its effect among the German-speaking settlers in the Volga region of Russia and other parts of the Ukraine. Edward Wuest, the Pietist pastor of Neu Hoffnung, under whom the revival among the Lutherans began, died in 1859. At that time, there were 30,000 Mennonites in the settlements of Molotschna and Choritza. Numerous conversions were then occurring among Mennonites, provoking a call for a church of regenerate people. The first Mennonite Brethren Church was formed in Elizabethtal in January 1860, and thereafter adopted baptism by immersion as its practice.[12]

Soon enterprising German Baptists entered the Russian Empire with an evangelical and evangelistic message.[13] Not only was there revival in fullest measure in the 1860s in the Ukraine, but other movements of an evangelical type began, such as the remarkable ministry of a British peer, Lord Radstock, converted in the 1860 Awakening in Britain and called to a ministry of evangelism among the Russian aristocracy.[14] Radstock was followed by Friedrick Wilhelm Baedeker, a British subject, who evangelized throughout all of the Russian provinces and territories.[15]

Evangelical Christianity in the Russias flowed in several streams—German-speaking Lutherans and Mennonites and the Russian Stundists influenced by them; the Baptists of the Ukraine, generally of peasant stock; and the Evangelical Christians, converts of Lord Radstock and Dr. Bædeker, of upper class background and residents of the great cities of Great Russia. These streams and others converged into a flowing river, but they each owed something to the Revival of around 1860.

The Russian Orthodox Church remained comparatively uninfluenced by the movements of evangelical awakening. Attempts were made to win over the non-Orthodox by every means; in fifty years, 35,000 Protestants wavered.[16]

In spite of ruthless repression by Church and State, the Evangelicals of Russia continued to multiply, the Baptist influence becoming predominant and leading to a Union of various evangelical bodies in the century following.

*   *   *   *

The revolution of 1868 brought a measure of religious liberty to Spain, encouraging the growth of a number of Protestant gatherings and the entrance of missionaries from Great Britain, Germany and the United States. There was little opening for evangelism in Portugal, the converts of an awakening in Madeira being forced to emigrate to Brazil and the United States. In Italy, the Waldensians were encouraged by the tolerance displayed by the new united Italy, and an invasion of Protestant missionaries occurred. In the Balkans, the American Congregational and Methodist boards opened up work at the time of the 1858 Revival, and in Greece a Greek Evangelical Church came into being.

In Mediterranean Europe, however, the number of the Evangelicals remained an infinitesimal proportion of the general population which followed Roman Catholic or Greek Orthodox traditional ways.

14

REVIVALS IN THE SOUTH SEAS

At the mid-century, gold was discovered in Australia, chiefly in Victoria. A gold rush set in, drawing population from overseas and from other parts of Australia. Church attendance in Victoria increased 50% in 1852, but membership in South Australia and Tasmania showed corresponding declines, all-Australia membership remaining the same.[1]

Pastoral evangelists followed the gold rush and reported that people of all denominations were attending their regular services, with certain very satisfactory conversions as a result.[2] In the Ballarat and Bendigo goldfield, missionaries were busy in 1853, but observers deplored its moral state.

Fifty thousand people were busy wresting gold from the earth—three million ounces in six years. So the floating population of the goldfields provided a welcome opportunity for evangelists, and rapid gains were made. Membership in the Methodist churches of Victoria had remained stationary in 1853, but increased 25% in 1854.[3] After six years, the Ballarat circuits reported a membership of three hundred, with ten times as many auditors, meeting in ten chapels.[4]

A conference of ministers meeting in mid-1857 resolved to pray for general revival and for themselves,[5] seeking a richer baptism of the Holy Spirit, promising to pray for each other and to promote Saturday evening meetings for prayer. Not a few of these gold miners were men from Cornwall and Yorkshire, who could recollect the revivals long past. It was reported annually that the work in Victoria was quietly advancing, the increase averaging about ten per cent.[6]

The population of Australia in 1860 was about a million, with few concentrations of population, Sydney and Melbourne competing in size. Towns were small, churches likewise. News of the extraordinary awakening in the United States of America in 1858 captured the attention of the Christian public in both New South Wales and Victoria in 1858 and 1859. Not everyone was pleased, for a news editor stated:[7] 'We fear that we are going to have in this colony a repetition of evils arising from revivals such as have taken place in America.'

In view of the fact that the 1858 Awakening in the United States had received an almost universal commendation as a movement free from fanaticism, a Methodist journal justly complained that its secular contemporary had not told its readers what the evils complained of were, and tartly attributed the editorial remarks to a recognized hatred of religion.

Reports of the American Awakening had raised hopeful desires in many a heart. There were soon to be evidences of an awakening in Australia also, even before the news of the Revivals of 1859 in Britain had been received.

By mid-1859, Christians in Melbourne and Sydney were encouraged to read the news of the Revivals in Ulster, Wales, Scotland and England.[8] Sydney religious editors published a 'call for prayer' in which it was said: 'It will be a happy day for Sydney and New South Wales when a similar influence visits us here.'[9] This was followed by a serialized account of 'The Great Awakening in Ireland,' and in 1860 a supplement was published, containing a five-column lecture on the subject of Revivals.[10] Similar reports were circulated in Melbourne and other towns.

The immediate effect of these reports of the American Awakening was the organization of many prayer meetings of the united type in Australia. Union prayer meetings began in 1859.[11] 'Even in Australia,' reported the Wesleyans, 'we see our signs.' As in Victoria, so also in New South Wales, where in the New Year of 1860 a religious editorial noted:[12]

> It is said that in some of the places of worship in Sydney, the prayer meetings have become so thronged with an attendance so unwontedly large as to indicate a movement prefatory to some great design of God.

Crowded prayer meetings were held in Geelong in 1859, fully interdenominational in character, but with the goodwill of the Bishop of Melbourne,[13] who occasionally presided. United prayer meetings were organized on Fridays in the Anglican, Baptist, Congregational, Methodist and Presbyterian churches of Sydney, and in the Y.M.C.A.[14] Similar united prayer meetings sprang up also in New South Wales, Queensland, Victoria and Tasmania, and in South Australia and Western Australia.[15] They were followed by united evangelistic services in city theatres, following a London pattern. The Theatre Royal in Melbourne was crowded out Sunday by Sunday in June of 1860, with fifty thousand attending a dozen services.[16] The congregations were 'very large and attentive,' yet regular worship services were not at all diminished.

Besides Geelong, similar services were held in Bendigo and Ballarat,[17] and in the other big towns of the Australian colonies. In smaller places, wherever an evangelical church was found, there were meetings for prayer. Local revivals of the phenomenal sort began to occur in various parts of the colonies. Though not as extraordinary as those reported from the United States or the United Kingdom, they were sensational for Australia. The Rev. J. D. Wittaker, pastor in Kooringa, South Australia, announced five hundred conversions in three months in 'a most glorious revival of religion . . . never such a one in this colony before.'[18]

An awakening occurred among the Aborigines in Victoria, of such intensity and extent that two Moravian missionaries involved called for, and received, the support of interested people in the various denominations.[19]

In the Victorian goldfield, 'revival services, full of holy zeal and fire' were reported from Golden Square Methodist Church in Bendigo.[20] There the ministry of the Rev. Richard Hart, which had made a good start in 1860, was marked by 'glorious revivals' which continued long in the Bendigo area. 'A great and solemn interest' characterized the movement.[21]

As early as 1859, there was an awakening in Ballarat. The Rev. James Bickford reported on the 'deep searchings before God' in the Wesley and Mount Pleasant Churches, where 'a revival of God's work had broken out.'[22]

In October 1860, an awakening commenced at Geelong, with two hundred instances of outright conversion, some of them very striking.[23] These Victorian revivals followed the pattern of the Irish Revival, with prayer meetings every night in the churches, with all the phenomena of the Ulster movement, except prostrations.[24]

In the vicinity of the capital of Victoria, an awakening was reported in Brighton as early as 22nd May 1859. The extraordinary movement began with testimony, and before long 'the cry of distressed souls' marked the meetings.[25] Special services were held daily. Before the end of 1859, the same movement had spread. 'Recently there has been in Melbourne and neighbourhood an extensive revival in our churches.'

When the great Wesley Church was opened in Melbourne in 1858, its 1700 seats were seldom more than half occupied, but by 1860 the church was crowded.[26] In 1861, the enterprising James Taylor, pastor of the Collins Street Baptist Church in Melbourne, carried on Theatre Royal services with thousands attending.[27]

Similar revival was reported in New South Wales in packed prayer meetings, while in South Australia an Adelaide pastor rejoiced that 'the whole place is turned upside down.'[28]

By the end of 1860, those indefatigable statisticians, the Methodists, were reporting gratifying gains in every department of their work—171 chapels, an increase of 29; 169 Sunday Schools, an increase of 28, making a total of 1577 Sunday School teachers which represented a 20% increase, and 12,249 pupils, a 30% gain. Church attendance reached a total of 38,932, of whom one in eight was a newcomer.[29]

The movement of prayer and revival passed its peak in 1861, and reports of the two years following suggested a decline in spiritual enthusiasm. But, in 1864, a 'gracious revival' occurred in the Tasmanian capital, Hobart, arising from a week of prayer conducted by Spencer Williams. This was followed by a 50% increase in membership among the Tasmanian Methodists alone in a single year.[30]

The mid-century Awakening in Australia entered a new phase in 1863, one of organized evangelism with revival. The 1858 Awakening was being extended to all six continents by the remarkable ministry of a very unusual Methodist— William Taylor, who proved to be one of the most versatile evangelists of all time, a follower of John Wesley who made the world his parish in a way that few Christians ever did.

Taylor was born in Virginia in 1821,[31] converted in 1841, and a year or so later began to work with the Baltimore Conference of the Methodist Episcopal Church. He served as an itinerant preacher till 1848. In 1849, Taylor followed the Gold Rush to California. Lacking either church or hall, he used a wooden box for his platform on the wharf at San Francisco, soon gathering his congregation. Taylor became known up and down California as 'the street preacher.'[32] He was known overseas as California Taylor.

He returned to the Eastern States and Canada to engage in the happy opportunities of the 1858 Revival, and a few years later heard a call to a world wide ministry. Taylor thus had experience of pioneering and of dynamic revival.

In 1863, William Taylor of California reached Australia, and commenced evangelizing in the Methodist circuits, and an impact was felt in other denominations also. Most of 1863 he gave to ministry in Victoria and Tasmania; 1864 to New South Wales and Queensland, with a side trip to New Zealand; and 1865 to South Australia. His evangelism was very fruitful, for more than 6000 converts were received thereby.

The population of Victoria in those seven fruitful years owed allegiance to Protestant denominations us follows:[33]

years	1857	1864	% growth
Anglican	173,374	212,068	22
Presbyterian	65,172	87,103	25
Methodist	27,196	46,511	72
Congregational	10,736	12,777	20
Baptist	6,412	9,001	40
Lutheran	6,488	10,043	55

German immigration into the British Colonies was heavy after the Crimean War. The Baptist rate of increase showed its debt to the Revival, but the vast increase in Methodism seemed due to both the Revival and evangelistic campaigns.

The ubiquitous William Taylor of California arrived in Tasmania and gave further impetus to the work there.[34] The Hon. Isaac Sherwin announced that the local Launceston Christians were 'rejoicing in an outpouring of the Holy Spirit and in an extension of borders.' Hundreds were converted, membership doubling among Launceston Methodists alone.

Membership at Wesley Church in Melbourne was at its greatest for many years just after the visit of California Taylor to Victoria. Even in the faroff Echuca circuit, the believers were quickened and a considerable interest among outsiders was engendered through Taylor's visit.[35]

The Methodist statistics showed an active membership of five thousand in 1852, but in 1867 the number exceeded twenty thousand, an increase of 300% in fifteen years.[36] The greatest gainer was Victoria, where membership increased ninefold, while in South Australia there was a fourfold increase, New South Wales with Queensland a 250% increase, Tasmania doubling its membership, and the tiny Western Australian membership growing from 60 to 160.

The revivals of 1859 onwards established a pattern of spiritual renewal, especially among Victorian Methodists. In 1873 a great revival was reported from Geelong, while 'a tremendous revival swept across the Methodist churches of the Bendigo district.' Later, Thomas Cook reaped a harvest in Geelong, 375 inquirers receiving counsel. There was a continuous revival in Kentishbury circuit in Tasmania.[37]

It can be clearly seen that Australia—contrary to public opinion which seems convinced that widespread revivals of religion are alien to Australian experience—was neither insulated nor isolated from the movements of the Spirit which touched the English-speaking world elsewhere.

The decade following the 'times of refreshing' proved less prosperous in some ways in New Zealand, treated as part of Australasia by several denominations, as one set of figures for communicant and trial membership shows:

1860	1861	1862	1863
32,180	33,964	36,307	38,075
6,897	7,657	6,514	7,527

In New Zealand, a decrease was noted of 464 during 1860, and of 55 in 1861, doubtless due to the Maori wars, but in 1862 membership began to increase once more.[38]

In New Zealand, the 1860s were marked by bloody wars with Maoris: unprecedented warning was given the Governor of New Zealand by the Governor-General of Australia, Sir William Denison, regarding the unjust treatment of the Maoris by the New Zealand authorities.[39]

New Zealand Methodists more than trebled their white membership in the twelve years between 1854 and 1866, from 508 to 1826. But during the same period, the Maori membership decreased tragically, from 3060 to 454. The bitterness of the Polynesian population against the land-grabbing of the settlers was a major factor, together with a resultant growth in syncretistic sects.

The ten years between 1854 and 1864 indicated a steady growth in both the Polynesian kingdom of Tonga and the Melanesian kingdom of Fiji, according to Methodist data:[40]

year	Tonga	(trial)	Fiji	(trial)
1854	6,687	80	2,954	1,085
1855	6,476	110	3,600	1,456
1856	6,275	140	4,251	1,836
1857	6,615	377	6,049	2,690
1858	6,646	258	8,345	3,452
1859	7,874	851	9,715	4,001
1860	8,230	539	10,342	5,308
1861	8,564	461	11,251	4,798
1862	7,954	897	13,101	5,216
1863	7,423	897	14,273	4,658
1864	7,482	348	14,380	4,412

At the crest of the Revival, 1859-61, Tongan Methodists added 30% to their membership. In 1862, King Taufa'ahau granted a constitution to his kingdom. In Fiji, Thakombau as king had embraced Christianity in 1854, leading a people's movement in the Church which increased communicant and trial membership by more than 5000. The next five years, the period of the Revival, brought in more than 5000 also.

In Hawaii, during the American movement of 1858, the various stations of the Hawaiian Evangelical Association reported earnest prayer here and there, little increase in some districts, decrease in others, few conversions in one place, universal stupor in another, the 'heavens as brass.' A year later, some were reporting temporal improvements. In 1860, Hilo announced a 'gentle and precious revival of religion,' and Wailuku reported unusual quickening, while at Kaneohe unusual interest was seen, church members revived, backsliders restored, and sinners converted. Lahaina's leaders' hearts were 'singing with joy' over crowded and solemn meetings which produced hundreds of converts. In Honolulu, the revival of religion was compared with the great awakening of a quarter century before. Throughout 1861, the American Board reported the Awakening as a new baptism of the Holy Spirit, nearly universal throughout the islands of Hawaii, the most fruitful time for twenty years, gaining 1500 inquirers and adding 750 to the churches that year.[41]

The awakening in Hawaii affected the Hawaiian missions in Micronesia within a year, all nights of prayer being held at Ponape, where the presence of the Holy Spirit was manifested with remarkable power for two years following.[42]

In Indonesia, during the period of the Awakening, there was rapid growth of the Christian churches in the Great East cluster of islands, involving revivals of the congregations of believers and folk movements of interested communities on Celebes, Ceram, Amboina and nearby settlements where national Christians began to extend the boundaries of the faith.[43] There was pioneering in other Muslim and pagan parts. In 1861, the Rhenish missionaries opened up a great work among the Bataks of Sumatra, and shortly after effected an entrance to the island of Nias—both followed by revivals.

In spite of the tight control of the Spanish government, what resembled both an evangelical awakening and a folk movement occurred on the island of Panay, where a Filipino priest, Padre Juan, preached from town to town a simple gospel based upon the Scriptures.[44] His message was truly reinforced by his spotless character, ascetic habits, and powerful ministry. Padre Juan was hunted by the Spanish authorities, captured, and shipped to Manila, where he was adjudged insane and incarcerated until his death. During the next great awakening, in the early 1900s half a century later, the descendants of his converts eagerly petitioned American Baptist missionaries to instruct them.

15

REVIVAL IN SOUTHERN AFRICA

South Africa and United States are separated by 6000 miles of ocean. Communications were difficult in those days, but a direct link was forged by American Board missionaries returning from Boston to Natal in 1858.[1] In answer to the prayers of revived multitudes in Boston, a general reviving began at the American mission stations among the Zulus in 1858, and spread to the British Wesleyan stations in the same area, within a year. Wrote the Rev. Joseph Jackson:[2]

> I rose early this morning to preach to the people, but soon found by their sleepy countenances that they had had but little rest during the night. After the service, I was informed that just as they had been about to separate, while singing the concluding hymn, the Spirit fell upon them in such an overpowering manner that they could not depart, but continued in prayer till break of day.

Throughout 1859, one full year before the extraordinary awakening among Dutch South Africans, the Zulu awakening continued in power.[3] Far to the west, an awakening began in Botswana among people of different background and speech. In 1860, when European churches at the Cape had begun to feel the movement of the Spirit, the Americans reported from Zulu parts of Natal:[4]

> Christians at some of the stations became so much revived that they were unwilling that the meetings should cease . . . the daily prayer meetings were continued morning and afternoon through succeeding weeks.

Seven years after the original outbreak of revival, 'very considerable prosperity' in all things spiritual was enjoyed. Statistics indicated more than a doubling of Zulu members, before a second wave reached Natal Zulus through Pamla, a Fingo chief become evangelist.[5]

The Bantu Awakenings of 1858 onward evidenced nothing resembling the phenomena of the Revivals in Ulster and the Cape occurring among well-taught Christian people, being directly related to the 1858 Awakening in the United States. They stirred up missionary enthusiasm among Africans.

Very different from Australia were conditions prevailing in South Africa, the other southern commonwealth. Here the people were of Dutch extraction, mixed with British strains, confronting a mass of people of another race and way of life. The deep piety of the Dutch farmer had set the standard for religious life in the sub-continent, and there the Dutch Reformed ministry at mid-century was strongly evangelical in content and personnel.

It is curious to note that a revival began at Grahamstown in South Africa simultaneously with the outbreak of the 1857 Revival in the United States. It affected the Europeans and Bantu alike.[6] There was no possible link of communications between the two communities to account for it.

In Capetown, the organ of the Dutch Reformed Church presented its readers regular news of the 1858 Revival in the United States of America.[7] Persistently, the details of that great awakening were carried into the homes of the Christians far and wide in South Africa.

Interest was building up among Dutch and English folk, so a conference of missionaries and ministers was held at Worcester, in the Cape Province of South Africa, during the month of April 1860, to hear some first-hand reports of the Awakening in the United States and the United Kingdom given by South African ministers or overseas missionaries. Three hundred and seventy-four attended this conference, coming from as far away as Fauresmith and Bloemfontein in the Orange Free State.[8] Twenty congregations were represented by some sixteen Dutch Reformed ministers and other Methodist and Presbyterian leaders.

Seven weeks later, at Whitsuntide, the outbreak came. The new minister at Worcester was Andrew Murray.[9] One Sunday evening, sixty young people were gathered in a hall, led in intercession by J. C. de Vries, an assistant of Andrew Murray.[10] Several had risen to announce the singing of a hymn and to offer prayer, when a Fingo girl in the employ of a farmer asked if she might do the same. Permission granted after hesitation, the girl poured out a moving prayer.

De Vries reported that while she was praying, a roll of noise like that of approaching thunder was heard, coming closer and closer until it enveloped the hall, shaking the place. The company burst into prayer, a majority audibly, a minority in murmuring tones. An unusual outpouring of the Holy Spirit appeared to be taking place.[11] Long afterwards, J. C. de Vries recalled his emotions:[12]

A feeling that I cannot describe took possession of me. Even now, forty-three years after these occurrences, the events of that never-to-be-forgotten night pass before my mind's eye like a soul-stirring panorama. I feel again, as then I felt, I cannot refrain from pushing my chair backwards and thanking the Lord fervently for His mighty deeds.

Meanwhile the Worcester congregation had engaged in its regular Sunday evening worship, Andrew Murray having preached. Notified, the minister hurried over to the hall and found the whole company still engaged in the simultaneous prayer, with de Vries kneeling at a table instead of trying to control the unusual manifestation.

Asked for an explanation of the extraordinary conduct of the people, de Vries explained, if explanation it could be called. Andrew Murray was far from satisfied, and walked among the distressed people calling for silence, 'Mense, bly stil! Mense, bly stil!'

No one took the slightest notice of their new, revered minister, and even de Vries kneeled at the table in holy awe of the Divine visitation. In a loud voice, Andrew Murray called again: 'I am your minister, sent from God. Silence!' Again, no one responded and the prayer continued.[13] Each seemed more concerned with calling on God for forgiveness of an intolerable weight of sin and shame.

Andrew Murray went back to his assistant and requested him to start singing the hymn in Dutch, 'Help the soul that helpless cries!' but the simultaneous intercession continued. So the bewildered Andrew Murray departed, exclaiming 'God is a God of order, and here everything is in confusion!' It was some time before Andrew Murray was convinced of the Divine nature of the visitation. De Vries, who had experienced the phenomena from the beginning, was not only convinced but overwhelmed. He remained in prayer.

Prayer meetings were held in the little hall, evening by evening; each meeting generally began in a period of profound silence, but, as soon as several prayers had risen, the place was shaken as before and the whole company of people engaged in simultaneous petition of the throne of Grace. The meetings often went on until three in the morning, and even then the people were reluctant to disperse, singing their praises on the way home through the sleeping streets. The town of Worcester was stirred, and prayer meetings multiplied in the valley.

Crowded attendances moved the meetings to the larger school building, which soon filled up. On the first Saturday evening in the school, Andrew Murray took a lead by reading a passage of Scripture and giving his pastoral commentary. Then he engaged in prayer and invited others so to do. Again the mysterious roll of approaching thunder was heard in the distance, coming nearer and nearer, until it enveloped the building, and all were engaged in prayer again.[14] Andrew Murray tried to quieten the people, walking up and down among them, but a stranger tiptoed to him and whispered: 'I think that you are minister of this congregation. Be careful what you do, for it is the Spirit of God that is at work here.' He said that he had recently arrived from America.

The movement of 1860 stirred every part of the community of Worcester, the old and young, rich and poor, white and Coloured.[15] Many of the younger generation were converted. And besides Worcester, Montagu, Wellington and Calvinia experienced similar movements; while in Murraysburg also there was a 'shaking awake' followed by hundreds of wonderful conversions, Ds. Hofmeyr averring that there were not fifty unconverted people left in the district. The revival reached Richmond at the end of 1861, as it did Graaff-Reinet, where the elder Murray prayed. There are records of awakenings in Franschoek, Stellenbosch, Paarl, Tulbagh, Villiersdorp, Robertson, Swellendam, Aberdeen, Beaufort West and Prins Albert.[16] These were outstanding. In not only the remoter towns, but in remotest farms far from communications the Awakening was felt, as far away as Kroonstad in the Orange Free State, Hartebeesfontein in the Transvaaler Republic and Ladysmith in Natal. It was country-wide.[17]

Professor Nicholas Hofmeyr of Stellenbosch reported to the South African Evangelical Alliance that the vast changes wrought by the Awakening were little short of revolutionary. Indeed fifty young men in the Worcester congregation in 1860 offered themselves for the ministry,[18] and the Stellenbosch Theological Seminary, commenced a year before by the godly John Murray and Nicholas Hofmeyr, was set on its course.

G. W. A. van der Lingen, the scholarly pastor of Paarl, enjoying 'the glory of the Church in the first century,' said:[19]

> The attendance has never been so good as in the year that has just passed. On many occasions, not only were all the seats and benches fully occupied, but people sat in the aisles and on the steps. Often many people were turned away because they could not get a place.

The movement in Paarl revived family prayers, drew a multitude to Holy Communion, multiplied prayer groups, increased Christian giving, and developed a missionary sense of responsibility for the needs of the heathen. This may be taken as typical of the great majority of the rural churches of South Africa. There was comparatively little reviving in the English-speaking churches during the period of the Awakenings in United States and Great Britain.

At that time, the spiritual life of the Methodist churches was declining. The European circuits had settled down to a life of formality, and there were few conversions. The 1860 awakenings in Dutch Reformed churches, together with news of revivals in the United States and the United Kingdom, encouraged many Methodists to pray for similar blessing in the Eastern Province and Natal. The answer to prayer came through the visit of William Taylor of California.[20]

Taylor arrived in Cape Town and began preaching in the Wesleyan chapel, and at Wynberg. He was dismayed by the smallness of the chapels and the even tinier congregations filling a third of their seats. He made his way around the coast to Port Elizabeth and preached there and at Uitenhage and Grahamstown. His meetings were blessed with numbers of conversions, but as yet no real break had occurred.[21]

After stirring times in America and Australia, Taylor found it hard to appreciate the pessimism of his South African Methodist hosts. He told a superintendent in Port Elizabeth that his proposed meetings would be orderly and terminate by ten o'clock each night. This simple remark provoked his host to a burst of laughter, for he averred that the local Methodists could not tolerate any service continuing after eight o'clock. Nevertheless, local people tarried and there were from a dozen to a score of seekers each evening. This was the beginning of a movement among the English-speaking churches, which gained strength in the following months.

The first outbreak of revival enthusiasm came among Xhosa folk, at a place called Annshaw, some twenty-five miles from Kingwilliamstown. Taylor's interpreter was a young African chief, Charles Pamla.[22] Six hundred people had crowded the mission chapel, mission natives in quasi-European dress, heathen tribesmen in red blankets. Taylor preached to believers on 'Ye shall receive power after that the Holy Ghost is come upon you.' That evening he preached to outsiders on 'Turn ye from your evil ways, for why will ye die?' He enjoyed rapt attention.[23]

Pamla had such a genius for interpretation that he sang a hymn in Xhosa alternately, line by line, with Taylor's English words, though he had never heard the hymn before. A profound stillness fell upon the people, and, when Taylor announced an aftermeeting, two hundred penitents came forward to the front seats, kneeling in contrition.

There were no wild scenes of confusion, but there was simultaneous audible prayer— sighs and groans and floods of tears. William Taylor insisted upon dealing with these inquirers on the spot, and continued with his helpers until midnight. Then Taylor dismissed them, but they were back at sunrise for praise and prayer. Next day, the work continued, Taylor systematically dealing with the inquirers and enrolling them. After his departure, another 165 professed faith, an unprecedented 300 in five days of evangelism.

At Healdtown, a thousand natives crowded the Wesleyan chapel seating 800, and an extraordinary power of the Holy Spirit moved the audience. A strange stillness preceded the rush of the three hundred inquirers to the front, and the service lasted from eleven a.m. until four p.m. Numbers of Europeans professed conversion in the meetings.[24]

While continuing his ministry to the Europeans in nearby Fort Beaufort, Taylor reaped a greater harvest among the Xhosa-speaking people. 'The awful presence and melting power of the Holy Spirit on this occasion surpassed anything I had ever witnessed before,' said Taylor. On another occasion, Taylor preached strongly on the Commandments, and a couple of hundred in the Healdtown chapel fell on their knees, crying, sobbing and groaning. The number of converts in two days exceeded three hundred.

Taylor was concerned that perhaps the cultured lady of the Rev. Thomas Guard might be offended by what she had seen. But she assured him that, although she had seen the pageants of royalty in Europe, and the opening of the great Exhibition of 1851, she had never seen anything to stir her soul as much as the revival among these simple Africans.

Now William Taylor found the doors open for a very wide ministry in South Africa.[25] He journeyed round the circuits, seldom staying more than a week in a place. His successes with the natives impressed the Europeans; at Fort Beaufort, some eighty-five Europeans were converted, a hundred at Queenstown, and many in Cradock, where he preached with two interpreters, one into Dutch and the other into Xhosa. Among the Europeans converted was the Dutch interpreter.

6 0 2 2 6

The converts at Queenstown (according to the Rev. H. H. Dugmore) were of every age from ten to sixty, married and unmarried, fathers and mothers of families, people phlegmatic or excitable in temperament, enthusiasts and scoffers, persons of varied social rank.[26] By October, the Queenstown circuits were reporting six hundred additions.

At Kamastone, Xhosa people were moved as at Annshaw, and at Healdtown, and a number of the Hottentots besides. Simultaneous audible prayer followed the preaching, no one voice being raised above the others. William Taylor held five prayer meetings and preached six times.[27] The Rev. William Shepstone, the father of a famous son, reported the addition of 250 to the Wesleyan society, and by the end of the year another hundred had been won. This revival spread to the London Missionary Society's stations at Hankey and Kat River, with hundreds of converts registered.[28]

The Clarkesbury Circuit[29] increased from a hundred to more than four hundred and sixty in membership. Shepstone reported from Queenstown Circuits that more were added after the departure of Taylor than during his visit there. At Butterworth, there were one hundred and forty-seven, at Clarkesbury, one hundred and eighty-five converts; at Morley one hundred and fifty, at Osborn, one hundred and fifty-seven converts; at other places hundreds more.[30]

William Taylor continued through the Transkei, preaching with Charles Pamla.[31] The Xhosa people gave Taylor the name of Isikuni Sivutayo, the Blazing Firebrand. He was six feet tall, broad-shouldered, with a long, flowing beard. In Natal, Taylor preached in the towns to the Europeans and Pamla preached at the stations to the Zulus.[32] In five weeks, more than three hundred Europeans had been converted, and more than seven hundred Zulus.

During William Taylor's journey through the Cape Colony, Kaffraria and Natal, the ministers recorded the names of more than four thousand people converted to God, but in the weeks that followed and in the places afterwards moved, in Methodist churches and in other denominations, 7937 made profession of faith in seven months.[33] A lasting impression was made on British settlers and Bantu tribesmen:

> After the lapse of more than half a century since the Wesleyan missions were commenced in South Africa, a great and favourable change has taken place in the native work . . . there has been a glorious revival of religion in South Africa in the European and Native population.

16

THE IMPACT ON INDIA

Apart from India, there were not many Evangelicals in Asia at the mid-century. Did the 1858-59 Revival affect them in any way? The reports were as scattered as the churches.

Before 1860, there were neither Evangelical missionaries nor Evangelical churches in either Japan or Korea. There were both—but in very limited numbers— in the Empire of China which constituted at that time the greatest missionary challenge and opportunity in the world. There were only 115 Protestant missionaries in the whole country, chiefly concentrated in the coastal cities and river ports.[1]

In 1860, a revival began among the missionaries in the port of Shanghai.[2] At the same time, there were stirrings in the tiny Christian assemblies of Chinese, as (for example) the remarkable work of grace at Lauling, near Tientsin, in the 1860's, described as 'wholly a work of God,' in which seventy men, fifty women and twenty young people requested baptism, an unheard-of thing in those days of antagonism.[3]

At the opposite end of Asia, American missionaries were reporting a religious awakening in Beirut, in the Lebanon, in the 1860s.[4] There was also an awakening in 1861 among Armenians in Central Turkey, beginning at Marash, where in private homes prayer meetings multiplied, attended by Roman Catholics and Gregorians until crowds of a thousand to fifteen hundred gathered.[5] An evangelical church that had six members in 1855 increased from 182 to 275 in 1862.

In the 1840s, there had been a remarkable awakening of Nestorian Christians in Iran, marked by its suddenness. A dozen years later, in 1859, revivals began among them again. It was said: 'The effects of these revivals are by no means limited to the souls converted. An enlightening, softening, and elevating influence of unwonted power has gone forth from them, affecting large masses of people.'[6]

At the middle of the nineteenth century, the population of India was approximately one hundred and fifty million people. Of these, there were 91,092 Evangelical Christians, of whom fifty-one thousand were living at the tip of India, in the Anglican mission-field around Tirunelveli and the Congregational mission-field in South Travancore,[7] where awakenings had occurred on either side of the Ghats at the beginning of the century. Less than forty thousand Christians were scattered over the rest of the huge sub-continent.

Throughout India, there were perhaps about six hundred missionaries, mostly ordained men and their wives. But these missionaries were overwhelmingly evangelical and evangelistic. It is certain that they had a burden for the rapid evangelization of India.

In the field of the Lutheran Mission, at Chota Nagpur, there was fierce persecution during the period of the Mutiny, but, in tribute to the depth of the work of grace among these people, it was said that 'During the persecution, not a single Christian denied the Lord Jesus, nor did anyone renounce Christianity.'[8] Although the Mutiny and its sad antagonisms poisoned Indian-British relationships, it was no more than a slap to Christianity.

While the phenomena of evangelical revival were being reported from over the United States in 1858, a company of American missionaries in Ludhiana (Northwest India) asked all Christians to set aside the second week of January 1860, for united prayer for Divine blessing.[9] The response all over the world, as in India, was phenomenal.

News of the 1858-59 Awakenings in America and Ireland caused excitement in all the Evangelical communities in India.[10] An outstanding leader in the resultant movement of prayer was Alexander Duff, who declared his support of the worldwide Awakening in unmistakable language:[11]

> In the face of the myriads instantaneously saved under the mighty outpourings of the Spirit of grace, I feel no disposition to enter into argument, discussion or controversy with anyone.

In Calcutta, Dr. Alexander Duff sponsored united prayer meetings, supported by Anglicans, Baptists, Congregationalists and Presbyterians.[12] Similar prayer meetings were begun in Madras, Bombay, and other cities. A great and increasing spirit of prayer prevailed among the Christians, but no one was sure how these prayers would be answered. 'Something like a Revival movement seems to be springing-up in Bombay and Poona,' it was reported, and a call to prayer was issued urgently by the Bishop of Bombay.[13]

One of the greatest missionaries in the middle of the nineteenth century to serve India was George Bowen of Bombay.

After describing Bowen's calm, phlegmatic temperament,
his biographer, Robert E. Speer, stated illuminatingly:[14]

> Once however in 1859, on the day the news came of the
> great Revival in the North of Ireland, he was greatly
> moved and seemed almost beside himself. The possi-
> bility of such a work in India seemed for the first time
> to fill all his thoughts.

George Bowen spent upon occasion most of the night in
prayer for revival in India. There were many others like
him, not only among the missionaries, but in the European
military and civilian population of the British cantonments.
India had just emerged from the trying days of the great
Indian Mutiny. Among the British garrisons were many outstanding Christians, and, thanks to the humanitarian but
imperialist zeal of the Clapham Sect in London, there were
also many ardent Christian men in the Indian Civil Service.
So the general movement to prayer in 1860 helped to bring
about local revivals among Europeans, as at Sialkot, where
occurred the conversion of officers and men, and civilian
residents of the cantonment.[15]

But the significant thing about the impact of the 1858-59
Awakening upon India was not the stirring among European
missionaries and civilians, rather the outbreak of revivals
among indigenous Christians, and the folk movements of
Indian communities to Christianity that resulted therefrom.

In far-off Assam, the period following 1861 saw a revival
among the churches of the Brahmaputra towns, Gauhati,
Nowgong and Sibsagor, besides tremendous growth in both
the Garo Hills and Upper Assam. From this movement came
the pioneer evangelists who initiated work among the other
head-hunting hill tribes.

The mid-nineteenth century awakening in the Tirunelveli
district of Tamilnad commenced in the ministry of a national
evangelist, one who had been influenced by the best among
the Christian Brethren as well as the Anglicans.

John Christian Arulappan was born near Tirunelveli in
the year 1810. He entered mission work in 1825 and was
influenced both by Anthony Norris Groves and the German
Rhenius.[16] Of him it could be said that he was found faithful.

In 1859, Arulappan read how God had visited both America
and Great Britain in reviving power. He began to pray soon
for a movement of the Spirit in India, a movement which
anyone in his right mind would have judged as likely as snow
in summer. The burden became an obsession with him.

In the same locality, a poor woman suffered a very vivid dream about an awe-inspiring man who severely questioned her: 'What has Christ done for you? What love has He shown you?' She shared her concern with another woman, and both were so distressed that they came to Arulappan for his counsel. They could not eat, and they trembled and cried. Arulappan requested the women to read the First Epistle of John, which concerns confession of sin.[17]

A 'wonderful work of the Spirit' began on the 4th March 1860, and in May the Spirit was poured out openly upon the congregations. Some there were who prophesied and rebuked the people and others beat their breasts in contrition, and some fell down, wept bitterly and confessed their sins.[18]

> Old and young, men and women and children, suddenly seemed crushed by the agony of a deep conviction of sin, and then, as suddenly, seemed to believe in the forgiveness of sins.

What was startling about this outburst of the phenomena of revival was that it was occurring among people who never expected it, nor did the missionaries who had brought them the Gospel. There were tongues, visions, and prophecies, none of which were familiar to the godly clergy of the Church of England. Some reacted against the movement immediately: 'I wrote disparagingly in my last letter,' said one, but added: 'The effect of their proceeding has been extraordinary. The heathen listen to them attentively. Their doctrine is sound and pertinent, exhibiting a right understanding of Law and Gospel.' The Anglicans reporting were astounded, for the movement among the nominal Christians and unevangelized villagers produced the same sort of prostrations and outcries noticed within the year in the 1859 Revival in Ireland. There were thousands of lasting conversions.[19]

Prayer meetings were continuing throughout South India from the 1860s into the 1870s. The Archbishop of Canterbury had appointed 3rd December as a worldwide Day of Prayer. Church of England missionary editors in Madras announced late in 1873 'Signs of a Religious Awakening in Travancore' —the report apparently from the pen of David Fenn, veteran Anglican missionary.[20] Revival began in the Mavelikara and Tiruvalla sections, in districts where missionary efforts had been most concentrated and the work of the reformation most marked and active in the Syrian Church. A visit of followers of the Tamil teacher, Arulappan, was the more immediate cause of the developing excitement:[21]

> . . . In July last, in Mankuzhi, a woman of our congre-
> gation had a remarkable dream. A dark cloud seemed
> to come down . . . and at the same time she heard a
> voice saying to her 'Except you repent, you will perish.'

> About the same time, the wife of an evangelist, a truly
> Christian woman, had a similar vision. The two women
> began to speak and pray with others earnestly. Soon
> after this, a C.M.S. schoolmaster in Kattanam was
> struck down, his body trembling and his mind over-
> powered with a sense of his sins. Others in Kattanam
> were similarly affected . . . The movement spread till
> it reached into all nine congregations of the C. M. S.,
> and into thirteen of the Syrian Church.

The Metran, Mar Athanasius, acted towards the movement judiciously and sympathetically,[22] and gave leave for
special services and prayer meetings in Syrian churches.

At Chengannur, in a Syrian Reform Church, Fenn found
a congregation of two hundred, all on their knees and in a
state of excitement.[23] There were violent outbursts of grief
over the sufferings of the Saviour and over their sins which
had caused them. This was followed by 'united' prayer, no
doubt, simultaneous and audible prayer.

At Puwattur, in an Anglican parish, the local Anglican
missionary, J. M. Speechly, declared that the whole community had been quickened into renewed earnestness after
Divine things. Prayer meetings were being held in churches
and prayer houses for months on end. Suitable buildings for
prayer had been erected, and in several of them there were
daily meetings for prayer. 'The people could hardly bear to
leave the churches and came to them day after day.'

A family of Kerala Brahmins had been converted in 1861.
Justus Joseph and his brothers became very active in the
great awakening.[24] Other Anglicans took advantage of this
revival. There were very successful meetings in Kottayam
directed by the Rev. Henry Baker of the Church Missionary
Society, wherein 589 converts were baptized in one day in
January of 1875. Nevertheless, the Anglican missionaries
were much concerned about 'the strange physical manifestations,' such as prostrations similar to those occurring in
Tirunelveli in 1860.

It is more than significant that the thirteen congregations
of the Syrian Church moved by the Awakening formed the
nucleus of the Mar Thoma denomination, the evangelical and
reformed sector of the historic Syrian Church.

The Kerala Awakening was marked by intense sorrow for sin. It reformed the lives of drunkards, of deceivers and extortioners, and brought about a restitution of property wrongly acquired. It increased the sale of Scriptures, a 70% increase in 1874, and promoted the earnest evangelization of the heathen, as well as diligence in attending the services of Divine worship and prayer meetings.[25] The most stirring lyrics of Malayali Christians had their origin in the 1873 Kerala Awakenings. It was this Awakening which enabled the Syrian Mar Thoma Church, about to lose its property, to build and to fill its parish churches. It also expanded the work of the Anglicans.

The major proportion of the fruits of revival were conserved in the fellowship of the Syrian Mar Thoma Church and that of the Anglicans in Kerala. But a minor part became schismatic—3000 Syrians and 200 Anglicans led astray.[26]

As one of the leaders in the Kerala Revival, Justus Joseph aimed to conserve and perpetuate the blessings of the work, but he made the usual mistake of confusing the human response to the Spirit's working with the working of the Holy Spirit Himself.[27] There had been emotional outbursts in some of the meetings, so he tried ardently to conserve all the emotional patterns. This led to sheerest emotionalism, which meant the manipulation of emotional response. And there had been cathartic confession of sins also. Justus Joseph sought to perpetuate the confession of sins in detail. This led to shocking exhibitionism which disgusted saner worshippers and brought ridicule.

Another leader, Kudarapallil Thommen of the Chengalam parish, professed to receive a divine revelation of the Second Coming of Christ within six years. The prophet of the Six Years' Advent predicted days of darkness between 10th and 12th August 1876; and there was a merciful falling away from the fanaticism through the non-fulfilment of prophecy.[28]

It was unfortunate that the minor movement called itself 'the Revival Church,' which served to discredit the major movement in the memory of some churchmen. Proper perspective is seen in the fact that the strength of the Revival Church dwindled down to 1051 by the year 1901, while the Mar Thoma Church and the Anglicans continued to build the converts and their succeeding young people into their parishes. Walker of Tinnevelly not only redeemed the good name of evangelism but influenced hundreds of the Six Years' Advent people to re-enter the major Evangelical Churches.

That the Anglicans gained from the 1873 Awakening is seen in the fact that adult baptism was given 4632 people in the 1870s, 2497 in the next decade.[29] In the confused state of Mar Thoma affairs, statistical records are lacking, but it is well-known that their numbers increased by the thousands annually, in spite of the vicissitudes of reformation.

News of the 1858-59 Revivals in America and Ireland caused reactions in Andhra also, with united weekly prayer meetings resulting.[30] Word of the revival farther south in Tirunelveli under Arulappan reached the Godaveri delta and stirred hearts afresh. In December, a scholar was reading a portion of Scripture when taken with great trembling and so was thought to be dying. He revived and testified to all his students that they were sinners and needed to repent and to believe in Christ. A little later, a young man was struck down in the open field and bore testimony without fear to all around. A notable feature of this revival in 1861 was its effect on Brahmins. A Brahmin convert preached in Palakol market place to large audiences.

It was the influence of these 1860 prayer meetings that produced the destined leaders of a far greater movement, according to John Clough, an American Baptist missionary whose own conversion took place during the 1858 Awakening in Iowa, and who later baptized 9606 believers in a matter of a few days in Andhra.

The circumstances were these.[31] Cattle disease in the Rajahmundry and Machilipatnam districts in the north of Andhradesa brought an influx of shrewd Madiga merchants and leather workers. One, Vongulu Abraham, was baptized. Periah, a relative, was converted in turn, and became an ardent evangelist through whose influence John Clough began his ministry in Ongole, organizing a church on New Year's Day 1867.[32]

'We began 1869,' reported John Clough to the American Baptist Telugu Mission, 'with a week of prayer.'[33] There followed a spontaneous revival that year, the beginning of a folk movement. And the year 1869 became a great year in their history. The converts had been coming in by tens; they now began to come in by hundreds.

There came the great famine of 1877-78 in which five million people perished. Clough was a trained engineer, so he offered to help British engineers construct a section of the Buckingham Canal paralleling the coast. He organized working gangs and paid them.

To avoid the charge of using famine relief to make pros-
elytes, Clough and his friends for fully fifteen months—
from 11th March 1877 till 16th June 1878—had not baptized
a single person.[34] An earnest Roman Catholic missionary
announced, in fraternal concern, that if the Baptists soon
did not baptize their converts, he would baptize them. At
last, when believers' baptism was administered, converts
baptized in one day numbered 2222, in three days 3536, in
thirty-nine days 8691, in all 9606 before the end of 1878.[35]

In the decades after 1860, there were many folk movements of tribes or castes in India, and often the initiatory
conversions could be traced back to 1860 or thereabouts,
when revived missionaries were praying for opportunities
to reach the unreached.

During this period, the Lutheran Mission at Chota Nagpur
working among a primitive people enjoyed a folk movement,
and by 1868 they had baptized ten thousand converts, who in
sixty years increased to 400,000.[36]

There was a similar movement in the Punjab among the
Chuhras that added multitudes to the churches in the 1870s.
Before 1860, there was an attempt to evangelize the Mazhabi
Sikhs, a tribe of professional thieves. Within twenty years,
these folk had been Christianized and turned into useful
citizenry.[37] In 1871, a folk movement began among the caste
of the Sweepers, which added a quarter of a million to the
churches. The first convert was won in the year of grace,
1860. Around Moradabad, a folk movement began among the
Chamars in 1864. There was a similar movement in the
field of the Leipzig Lutheran Mission in South India, where
4,846 converts were won in 1860, but 13,720 in 1885.[38] The
Lutheran Gossner Mission had much the same experience
in the highlands of Bihar, a thousand converts becoming
12,732 communicants in a generation.[39] Boerresen (a Dane)
and Skrefsrud (a Norwegian) were converted in the Revival
in Scandinavia, came to the Hills in 1863, and founded their
own mission among the Santals, a folk movement resulting.

A folk movement, of course, is not a revival in the usual
sense of the word. It evidences none of the intense reactions
of historic awakening, such as conviction of sin and instant
conversion. It is rather a movement of unindoctrinated folk
seeking a better way of life in Christianity, with group or
multi-individual decisions resulting. It is often followed by
a revival or an awakening, as soon as the truths of Scripture
have become known to the newly Christianized community.

Even so, there appears to be some connection between the ingatherings in folk movements and antecedent phenomenal revivals. Many of the folk movements cited by Bishop J. W. Pickett in his study of Christian mass movements in India occurred shortly after the 1860 Awakening. Often the 'first' missionary and 'first' convert were products of revival.

One of Methodism's greatest missionaries, J. M. Thoburn, was called of God in the year of Revival in the United States in 1858,[40] during which he received an infilling of the Spirit. Although many cities of India had shared in the prayer movement of 1860, Thoburn found the work discouraging:[41]

> Revivals and all forms of revival work were unknown in India. The great cities were well supplied with Christian churches but nothing like revival had ever been witnessed in any city of the Empire. A growing feeling of despondency had taken possession of many missionaries, and not a few of those who had witnessed revivals at home were inclined to think it would be too much to expect a time of refreshing in India.

In 1870, word came that 'a great evangelist named William Taylor,' who had won great fame in Australia and South Africa, was on his way to India, and would probably begin his work in the city of Lucknow.[42] On November 25, Taylor began preaching there, and in a few weeks had won a hundred converts in a movement surpassing anything seen by Thoburn in a lifetime. Taylor continued the work in Kanpur, Bareilly, Shahjahanpur, Meerut and Delhi.[43] In Bombay, in December 1871, he followed up his successful ministry by forming fellowship bands.[44] He continued in Bombay presidency for a full year, then commenced in Calcutta in January 1873.[45] In 1874, Taylor sailed for Madras, packed out a hall seating 300, moved to Memorial Hall seating 600, referring converts to Methodist and Baptist congregations. He hired Clarendon Hall in Bangalore, filled its 300 seats, won 140 converts and formed a church of a hundred of them.[46] Of Taylor, it was said: 'What a flame of revival he had become! The living God was with him, and pentecostal fire fell upon the people wherever he went.'[47]

George Bowen commented that the awakenings in India under Taylor's ministry exposed certain preachers of great reputation as utterly useless in leading souls to Christ.[48] And Bishop Thoburn averred in long retrospect that the revival influence, widely felt, really marked the beginning of a new day in the mission fields of India.

17

EMPOWERED PREACHERS

Although prayer meetings proved the greatest vehicle of blessing in the Awakening of 1858-59, preaching was by no means as neglected or discarded as some writers insisted. Beardsley stated that, in some instances,[1]

> Preaching was employed to promote the revival after it had commenced, but this was exceptional and in most cases there was but little preaching aside from that of the regular Sabbath services. The principal means relied upon were the daily union prayer meetings.

And he again supported his position by quoting Finney:

> There was such a general confidence in the prevalence of prayer, that the people very extensively seemed to prefer meetings for prayer to meetings for preaching. The general impression seemed to be 'We have had instruction until we are hardened; it is time for us to pray.'

It is undoubtedly true that reliance upon prayer overshadowed dependence upon preaching, but this conclusion is liable to be misunderstood. Preaching played a secondary part to prayer in the Revival, but it played a very good second. Compared with the quantity and quality of the preaching that had preceded 'the year of grace,' there was truly a great revival of the ministry of preaching. The great focus of interest was the noon prayer meeting, but the interest there was immediately captured and used by the evening preaching services. The Revival of 1858-59 was a revival of preaching, as a careful examination of the foregoing chapters of the narrative shows. The writer is well convinced in his own mind, through reading endless accounts of local situations in the Revival, that fully as many people attended the preaching services as the prayer meetings. There were crowded services every night of the week, and most churches were compelled to hold three or four services on Sunday. With this fact in mind, let us examine the effect of the Awakening upon preaching and preachers.

The ministry of Horace Bushnell was transformed by the 1858 Awakening, according to his biographer-daughter: [2]

The financial crisis was, as every one will remember, followed by a great and unexampled religious Revival that overspread the country and moved society to its very foundations. The excitement of it lasted through the whole winter and late into the spring.

Ministers and all those who took an active part in the direction of the great and frequent meetings of the people were asked to make unwonted exertions and were themselves kept at sustained pitch or strain of feeling that was more exhausting than the work itself.

Dr. Bushnell did not spare himself in the services held at his own church or in the daily union prayer meetings of the city. Under the pressure of work, and by the aid of sympathy prepared for him in his audiences, he resorted for the first time to extempore preaching. He achieved in this a success unlooked-for, as he had always doubted his ability for off-hand speech. Some of these sermons were very remarkable and impressive, and commanded the fixed attention of several intellectual and not hitherto religious men.

One day his good friend, Deacon Collins, who had listened to his preaching ever since he had come to Hartford, said as he walked down the aisle: 'Dr Bushnell must never preach any more written sermons. He may write to print, but not to preach.'

Alas, by May of 1858, Horace Bushnell was obliged to confess that he was utterly broken down in health through the overstrain of preaching and leading prayer meetings.

It was reported, not unnaturally, that Horace Bushnell's tremendous evangelism indicated a return to orthodoxy regarding his modified view of the Trinity, but this was not so. Nevertheless, the Awakening caught him up and transformed his ministry for a few short months before his retirement and subsequent decease.

If the Awakening was able thus to transform the ministry of men who were viewed with suspicion by Evangelicals, what would it not have done for orthodox evangelists?

Theodore Ledyard Cuyler gave an introspective picture of the effect of the Awakening: [3]

The next stage of my life's work was a seven years' pastorate of Market Street Church in the City of New York. To those seven years of hard and happy labor I look back with joy . . . During the year 1858 occurred the great revival, when a mighty wind from Heaven filled every house where the people of God were sitting, and the glorious work of that revival kept many of us busy for six months, night and day.

Dr. Cuyler was born in 1822, in the Finger Lakes district of Western New York, the region of great revivals of the early nineteenth century, the habitat of Finney. His widowed mother dedicated him to the service of God. The success of a few impromptu remarks of his at a cottage meeting decided him to prepare for the ministry, leading to graduation from Princeton Seminary in the year 1846.

Theodore Cuyler's first pastorate was in Burlingham, New Jersey. A remarkable local revival broke out in his church, doubling his membership and shaping his ministry toward evangelism. In 1853, Cuyler moved to New York City, into the Market Street Dutch Reformed Church, where another local revival attended his ministry. One of his helpers in this church was a quiet-spoken businessman named Jeremiah Lanphier who, with the help of M. T. Hewitt, an elder of the church, inaugurated a little prayer meeting in Fulton Street in 1857, with far-reaching results.

A smaller church in Brooklyn next called the young divine, and in 1860 his ministry began to stir that city. With an original 140 members, Cuyler built up the work to 1600 members, then the largest Presbyterian Church in America. In 1866 began a wonderful six months' revival that brought three hundred into the church. Cuyler participated with Moody in the latter's meetings in London in 1873, at the beginning of the great awakening in Great Britain.

Another preacher unusually busy in the 1858 Revival was Henry Ward Beecher.[4] Like Theodore Cuyler, Beecher was already a noted preacher when the revival of religion gave him unbounded opportunity for his talents, besides which gifts, Henry Ward Beecher was helped by his parentage, being a talented son of the famous Lyman Beecher.

Henry Ward Beecher became an immediate friend of the 1858 Awakening.[5] On 20th March, Beecher led three thousand people in the prayer service in Burton's Theatre in New York, and from that time on abounded in the work.

Very different from Beecher in many respects, but with an unsullied fame which outshone him in succeeding generations, was Charles Grandison Finney, who contributed much to the 1858-1859 Revival. The movement taught Finney little about revivals, for he had been the main figure in revivals for a generation previously.[6] Indeed, the Revival of 1858-59 seemed to be a justification of much—but not all—of what Finney had taught in his lectures. The Revival of 1858-59 was certainly not planned and promoted.

Charles Grandison Finney's preaching was of a type to suit the age in which he lived. At that time such strong Calvinistic doctrines as God's sovereignty, man's inability, election, reprobation, and the like, had been taught to extremes, bringing about paralysis among the people in matters of responsibility and decision. Finney on the other hand taught that men were responsible for their sins, and that they were sinners because they chose to be, and that they ought to repent, as the Lord has so commanded them. It was also noteworthy that Finney always preached for immediate decision, trying to make the individual choose then and there to do something. He was a most direct preacher.[7]

The 1858 Revival found Finney in the Boston metropolis. Where before the revival had focussed on his own ministry, now every church was experiencing blessing. Finney worked hard until he left for England that same year.

Another preacher who excelled in the 1858-59 Awakening was Alexander Reed, a Presbyterian whose honorary doctorate was conferred by Princeton. Born in 1832, he was in his energetic twenties when the extraordinary revival reached his community, 186 being added to his church in Chester, Pennsylvania, during the actual Awakening.[8]

Among the Baptists who excelled as evangelists in the wake of the outpouring of the Spirit in 1858 was Jacob Knapp, who had been busy in evangelism since the 1830s, chiefly in rural campaigns but also with cooperating Baptist churches in several cities. For fifteen years, Elder Knapp ministered under a cloud, having been charged (but cleared) with wearing old clothes in the pulpit in order to enhance the offerings! He was a popular, folksy preacher, to judge from his printed sermons, but he had a habit of attacking individuals by name, which often landed him in trouble.[9]

The 1858 Awakening brought Jacob Knapp a renewal of heart and a wider usefulness.[10] In 1860, Knapp returned to Boston and preached for more than four months in three churches, culminating in a series in Tremont Temple. He was one among many anti-slavery evangelists. A Chicago pastor spoke of a month long meeting with Knapp in 1862:[11]

> His preaching was with power. More pointed and stirring appeals to the conscience I never heard. Some of his sermons are full of gospel truth and some present the law in all its terrors; sometimes he says odd and laughable things which are a hindrance rather than a help to his usefulness.

Quite a different sort of man was Absalom B. Earle, who (although a convinced Baptist) usually operated in united efforts with other denominational churches as well. He was committed to presenting higher standards to believers, and he used entreaty rather than fulmination to win converts. It was not unusual to find Earle's campaigns developing into thorough awakenings in whole districts.[12] His winsomeness did not spare him bitter criticism [13] from anti-evangelistic radicals. After successful series in Massachusetts and New York communities, and exceptional campaigns in Boston, Earle accepted an invitation from the ministerial union in San Francisco to campaign in California, and remained out west for a considerable time, preaching to crowds of great size in the infant communities of the Pacific shore.[14] Earle, unlike Knapp, was a direct product of the cordial ecumenism of the 1858 Revival, and his blend of winsomeness, holiness and interdenominational cooperation continued in Moody.

Besides these outstanding men, there were hundreds of others who were given their life's greatest opportunity in the Awakening. The records of the day show that most pastors were busy from morning to night preaching and presiding at meetings. As to what they preached, it is clear from the fragments of sermons and addresses appearing in newspapers that the doctrine was evangelical and the method evangelistic.

Among American contributions to the ranks of British evangelists in the Revival was a devout Methodist, James Caughey, through whom William Booth had been challenged. Some Wesleyan leaders in control of societies boycotted the American's ministry altogether, but he continued ministering in the pulpits that remained open in several Methodist bodies. Caughey had been in Britain several times before— to win more than twenty thousand converts.[15]

In the 1830s, Phœbe Palmer, the wife of a physician, Walter Palmer, became a leader in devotional meetings for women in New York City.[16] For four years in the 1860s, the Palmers visited Caughey's contacts in Britain, carrying with them a spirit of revival to the Methodists. It was Walter and Phœbe Palmer, as a husband-and-wife preaching team, who had inspired William and Catherine Booth to follow suit.

Apart from a steady stream of reports of successful campaigns, there is very little material available in Britain on the ministry of Walter C. Palmer and his wife Phœbe. They evangelized in Britain for five years, excluded from a number of Methodist pulpits by conference regulations.

Edward Payson Hammond was born in the Connecticut Valley in 1831.[17] He was converted seventeen years later, and participated in the American Revival of 1858. Visiting Scotland for purposes of self-improvement, Hammond was asked to preach in Musselburgh in 1860, during the Scottish Awakening. Having left his greatcoat in the vestry, he went there but found the door bolted. A tiny little girl opened it and explained that 'a wheen o'us lassies' were praying there. Hammond overheard a tiny tot offer so touching a prayer that tears sprang to his eyes. His ideas were revolutionized. He became the children's evangelist, and foster-father of the Children's Special Service Mission. Hammond accomplished his greatest work in revival services in the Vale of Dumfries and in the city of Glasgow. His success prepared the way for a fruitful campaign in Boston, followed by great awakenings in the state of Maine, which made him a sought-after missioner from Philadelphia to San Francisco.[18] E. P. Hammond revisited Britain, and maintained a transatlantic usefulness at a time when the exchange of talent was lively both ways. He campaigned also in Canada.

But Hammond's lasting work was as a winner of children to Christ. In the late 1860s, Spurgeon filled the Metropolitan Tabernacle with 8000 children to hear Hammond preach. Seventeen years later, Payson Hammond returned to find that many of the child converts had become Spurgeon's most valued congregational officers and workers.[19]

An American observer, commenting on the spread of the Revival in America and Britain, noted the influence of the prayer meeting movement in both countries, then observed a difference of the spiritual gifts that were manifested in the United Kingdom and the United States during the Revival and the years immediately following: [20]

> As the work spread into Great Britain, new features appeared. Gifts which seemed to exist (in America) in a sort of general diffusion among Christian people were there vouchsafed in greater intensity to individuals. Men appeared as chosen instruments of conveying God's truth to the aroused and interested masses. Lay and clerical evangelists, conspicuous for zeal, enjoying the special favor of God, and devoting themselves exclusively to the work, contributed to extend and deepen its sphere and to multiply its fruits. No such characters appeared in this country as Richard Weaver, Reginald Radcliffe, Brownlow North, and E. P. Hammond, whereas in Britain the spirit of Revival culminated in them.

. . . Some in America may congratulate us as so far better off than the British people, but we differ from them. Had a class of men, pre-eminently endowed for the work, been in like manner raised up among us; had some American Radcliffe or Weaver been divinely commissioned to speak to the poor and outcast of our cities at that time, the result must have been far in advance of what we actually behold. The Infinite Spirit in His sovereign appointment did not see fit to bestow upon us this crowning gift—a personal embodiment and representative of the work—a Leader whom all might recognize and who might have marshalled the Christian hosts to far greater victories even than those they did achieve.

While his comments were justified, that one observer wrote his conclusions much too soon. When those words were written, the armies of the Union and the Confederacy were locked in a titanic struggle. An American leader, not until afterwards generally recognized, was already busy in a steady ministry to soldiers and civilians in camps and cities: and the Infinite Spirit was soon to give Dwight L. Moody an opportunity of moving mightily two great countries.

The emergence of leaders in Great Britain was a distinct feature of the British Awakening of the 1860s. In Ulster, the movement was more like that of the American Revival of 1858, a spontaneous, leaderless turning to God. In Wales, excepting the work of David Morgan, it was the same. In Scotland a number of prepared evangelists participated in the general Awakening there, and then moved south for a greater work to be done in England. And in England, as in Southern Ireland, the emerging evangelists—both workers and converts of the first period of Revival—accomplished the main evangelistic mission of the Awakening.

Nearly all outstanding evangelists in England assisted in the intense Revivals in Ulster, Scotland, and Wales. The Palmers had seen the Spirit at work in Canada and America, and the Booths doubtless had witnessed the startling Revival across the Tyne from Gateshead. Most of them, therefore, served their apprenticeship in a spontaneous type of Revival, and carried the fire to less combustible areas where the fuel had to be first gathered and dried of the damp of indifference.

The evangelists of the British Awakening were of various denominational loyalties within the evangelical school of thought. The records of the Revival reveal no clashes between them, and they seemed to work like members of a very agreeable family. There was a division of labor according to the evangelist's background. The converted chimney-sweep did not lead drawing-room meetings for the elite of society, nor the converted aristocrat form Hallelujah Bands of cock-fighters, bear-wrestlers, prize-fighters, and jail-birds, but they helped one another, and introduced one another to suitable opportunities in evangelism.

Foremost among the British leaders of the 1859 Revival was Henry Grattan Guinness, a preacher of great power for half a century. He was born in 1835, in Kingstown, near Dublin. In his first twenty years, he indulged his adventurous desires in globe-trotting, then he came under deep conviction of sin and was converted.[21]

Grattan Guinness was the most popular evangelist in Ulster during the 1859 Revival, on one occasion addressing 20,000 people from the top of a cab. Fifty years afterward, revival memories were still vivid with him:

> . . . the predominating feature was the conversion of people of all ranks and positions, in ways sudden, startling, amazing . . . Before that time, I had seen tens or scores brought to Christ under Gospel preaching; but this new movement of 1859 was something quite different . . . Ministers were occupied until midnight, or even till two or three o'clock in the morning, conversing with crowds of inquirers who were crying: 'What shall I do to be saved?'

It was at the house of Grattan Guinness that Tom Barnardo met Hudson Taylor. After the crest of the Revival wave had passed, Grattan Guinness began to take an ever-deepening interest in foreign missions. His greatest contribution to the Christian Churches was surely in winning multiplied thousands of converts in the days of revival, and in training 1330 men and women for missionary service under thirty denominations in forty missionary societies. Dr. Barnardo, on holiday in Venice, said: 'I can never tell what Guinness has done for me; it is through him that I am what I am.'

Among the outstanding men of God becoming harvesters in the Years of Grace were several gentlemen-evangelists, Brownlow North, Grant of Arndilly, Reginald Radcliffe and Gordon Forlong, all of whom were much-used evangelists when the Revival began, but whose ministry developed phenomenally in Revival opportunities. W. Hay M. H. Aitken was another gentleman-evangelist, but he became an ordained Churchman.[22]

Similar to the group of gentlemen-evangelists was a group of working-class evangelists——Richard Weaver, Duncan Matheson, John Hambledon, James Turner, and William Carter, each of whom was busy in evangelism before the 1859 Revival but developed amazingly during the movement, preaching to vast crowds in the great industrial cities of Great Britain.

Among the pastoral evangelists of the Awakening were William Pennefather, William Haslam, Samuel Garratt, John Venn, C. H. Spurgeon, Henry Varley, Baptist Noel, Newman Hall, Denham Smith, Andrew Bonar, Horatio Bonar and David Morgan—and many others in both State Church and Nonconformity.

Several of the Church of England's most spiritual and successful Bishops were 'impressed' in the Revival of 1859. Perhaps most outstanding were F. J. Chavasse of Oxford and Handley C. G. Moule of Cambridge, whose spiritual unfolding in the Revival has been noted. The former became Bishop of Liverpool, following in the footsteps of the evangelical Bishop Ryle, himself active in the Revival in Suffolk. The latter became Bishop of Durham, in succession to the evangelical Bishop Baring, another active evangelist in the period of the Revival.[23]

The Methodist Conference of 1903 described Hugh Price Hughes as one of the most conspicuous and successful ministers ever ordained within its fellowship, and said that no Methodist minister in its British constituency was ever more widely lamented. Hugh Price Hughes (of partly Jewish stock) was converted in the Welsh Revival in 1860, at thirteen. He was an ardent evangelist, an advocate of temperance, an agitator for social purity, founder of the Central Hall movement in the downtown of cities.[24]

Alexander Whyte, of St. George's, Edinburgh, 'the prince of Scottish preachers,' was actually impressed by the Awakening of 1860, a student in Aberdeen at the time. There was 'no preacher . . . of greater personality, preaching power, and abiding influence' . . . the last of the Puritans. In 1909, he penned his reminiscences of the Revival, saying that the sovereignty of God was in it. After fifty years, Whyte knew that the glow had not died away.[25]

Dr. Hugh Black (of Edinburgh) described John McNeill, Scottish preacher of Ulster parentage, as the greatest living preacher of his day, rather than Joseph Parker, Alexander MacLaren, or Alexander Whyte. John McNeill was converted in the after-glow of the Scottish Revival, and gave his own testimony of the impression made on his young mind when the tide of Revival was still running high in Scotland.[26]

Dr. F. B. Meyer was baptized on confession of faith in New Park Road Chapel, near Denmark Hill, on 2nd June 1864.[27] Meyer had been brought up in a Christian home in London, and had grown in grace in his childhood; but it was during the Revival in the metropolis that he heard the call to the ministry and entered upon a truly fragrant life of service. From his first sponsoring of Moody to his founding of the National Young Life Campaign with the Brothers Wood in the present century, he was an ardent evangelist.

Other converts were Professor James Orr, Sir Robert Anderson, Principal John Anderson, Shuldham Henry and Robert Annan. There were so many others.

In Europe, a host of revived workers extended the great Awakening. Professor Theodor Christlieb, one of Germany's greatest evangelistic forces, served a Lutheran Church in London during the Revival. Another power, Theodore Monod in France, had been converted in the United States in 1858. Lord Radcliffe, whose ministry in the Russian Empire was the start of a nation-wide movement, was a product of 1859 Revival evangelism in Britain.

In India, there were national evangelists of great power, such as John Christian Arulappan of Tamilnad, Yerraguntla Periah of Andhra, and Justus Joseph of Kerala, converts or leaders of the Awakening. In South Africa, Andrew Murray arose to fame, as did the Fingo chief, Charles Pamla.

Three of the products of the American Awakening of 1858 were destined to have a worldwide influence for good— D. L. Moody, William Taylor, and A. B. Simpson. William Booth exercised a worldwide ministry also. Hudson Taylor and Grattan Guinness influenced the sending countries as well as the mission field. Several of the evangelists of the British 1859 Revival exercised an American ministry, and Gordon Forlong operated in New Zealand and Australia.

The subject is inexhaustible. Throughout Evangelical Christendom, there is room for research in each country, and even then the half could not be told.

18

CHRISTIAN ACTION

The English-speaking denominations, which carried the greater part of the responsibility for evangelizing the non-Christian world, received a mighty impulse from the 1858-1859 Awakening.

This was true both in Great Britain and the United States. There were thirty million or so people inhabiting the United States of America in 1860. More than five million of this total were communicants of evangelical Protestant Churches, the aggressive Methodist and Baptist bodies claiming a total of three million members between them.

The Methodist Bishop, Warren C. Candler, has stated that fully a million people were converted in the 1858 American Awakening.[1] Others have estimated between three hundred thousand and a million. The author has calculated the total accessions in the two year period following the outbreak of revival as exceeding one million, a figure confirmed by 1855-1865 statistics.

At the same time, the population of the United Kingdom exceeded twenty-seven million, of whom a third attended the worship services of the State and Free Churches. The Awakening beginning in 1859 in Northern Ireland had affected all parts of Great Britain by 1865. There were a hundred thousand converts in Ulster, a hundred thousand additions in Wales, three hundred thousand auditors 'impressed' in Scotland, and more than half a million converts in England, 370,000 joining the Methodist, Baptist and Congregational connexions.[2] More than a million were converted in Britain.

Halfway through the nineteenth century, the Anglican Establishments of England, Wales and Ireland, with the Episcopalians in Scotland, the Colonies and the United States, comprised the largest of the Protestant denominations within the English-speaking world.

In America, most Anglican Churchmen shared in the Awakening, as did those in Ireland and in Wales; Scottish Episcopalians of a more traditional and less evangelical churchmanship were lukewarm toward it. In England, some

Bishops supported the movement, some were indifferent, and some opposed. Evangelical clergy cooperated with other Christians in the interdenominational prayer meetings and evangelism; in certain dioceses, the revival meetings enjoyed the episcopal blessing as well as a Divine benediction; in others, only the Divine benediction.[3]

The Tractarians were usually opposed to the Evangelical Awakening, the Evangelicals usually in support. Indifferent Anglicans, unreached or unmoved or unhappy about a revival which seemed utterly alien to their easy-going religious way of life, reacted thus not because of convictions but on account of the lack of them. The observation of an historian (fully a century afterward) that the Anglican churches 'dissociated' themselves from the movement is unsupported—for not one instance was reported of any Evangelical Churchman 'dissociating' himself.[4] Anglican friends remained enthusiastic.

Among the Free Churches in the English-speaking world, the Baptists cooperated wholeheartedly in the 1858-59 Awakenings in America, Ireland, Scotland, Wales and England. Spurgeon built his Tabernacle on the crest of the Revival, and new Baptist churches arose everywhere to garner the increase, which numbered 300,000 baptisms.[5]

Likewise, the Congregationalists in America and Britain officially approved of the Awakening and gained greatly by it.[6] Less than 150,000 were added to the denomination which possessed a numerical strength inferior to the Baptists.

In keeping with the numbers of their world constituency, the Methodists were the greatest gainers in the Awakening in America and Britain, 400,000 members being added in the respective periods of revival.[7] In home mission ministry, the most outstanding convert was Hugh Price Hughes, and in foreign missionary work James Thoburn, the enterprising Bishop in India and the Orient. English Wesleyans limited their benefits by restrictive legislation on evangelists such as William Booth. The greatest extension of the Awakening by any one individual was by the Methodist, William Taylor.

In both Establishment and Free Church situations, the Presbyterian support of the Awakening seemed unanimous. It is difficult to calculate Presbyterian gains for, in both Ulster and Scotland, membership in the church was considered a family affair, hence many converts were already known as members. It is possible that 400,000 converts continued in Presbyterian fellowship in America, Scotland, Ireland, England and Wales.[8]

In keeping with their churchmanship of various brands, the Lutherans of European stock in America showed mixed reactions to the Awakening. Reports suggested that the 1858 Revival had brought great blessing to congregations which were normally suspicious of informal meetings of revival and evangelism, and even those associations which disdained fellowship with all others enjoyed the floodtide of enthusiasm. The Lutherans in Scandinavia, much like the Anglicans in Britain, reacted to the Revival Movements according to their theology and churchmanship. In Germany, the Awakening was felt for a generation through the ministry of individual clergy and laymen moved in the 1858-59 Revival.

The Quakers were deeply moved by the Awakening both in Great Britain and the United States. The unprogrammed nature of the meetings made a great appeal to Friends, but there was not much evidence of Quaker 'silences' in the 1858 Revival meetings. The evangelistic Gurneyite Friends, who multiplied west of the Alleghenies, welcomed the Awakening, and in turn were transformed by successive waves of revival following the Civil War. Friends' churches in the West became more like their Evangelical Protestant contemporaries, adopting the pastorate, regular evangelism, and instrumental music, abandoning peculiarities of speech and dress.

Likewise, the Christian Brethren (popularly known as the Plymouth Brethren) gained converts out of all proportion to their numbers. Laymen, who found the widest opportunity for witnessing during the Awakening, were reluctant to sit back in clergy-dominated congregations.

The 1858 Awakening began among Dutch Reformed folk in New York, but its extension to South Africa produced the greatest spiritual uplift in the Dutch Reformed Church there.

Most significant in the 1858-59 Awakenings was the rise of the laity to play a fuller part in the affairs of the churches:

> The working forces of the churches were immeasurably increased. The Revival of 1858 inaugurated in some sense the era of lay work in American Christianity. Wesley's system of class leaders, exhorters and local preachers had done much at an early date in the same direction but now the layman's day fully dawned on all churches. No new doctrine was brought forward but a new agency was brought to bear in spreading the old truth through the efforts of men who, if they could not interpret the scriptures with precision or train souls to perfection, could at least help inquiring sinners to find the Lord by relating how they themselves had found Him.[9]

So declared Bishop Candler.   And Beardsley added:[10]

> This divine visitation, providential in its character,
> was emphatically a lay revival. There was no evangelist
> of national reputation, no minister however influential
> to whom credit could be given for this mighty work
> of grace——even as the indirect instrument of its
> accomplishment.
>
> The revival was carried on independently of the
> ministry and almost without their aid. The ministry
> were not ignored, nor was there in any sense an op-
> position to them. They carried on their regular services,
> but to greatly increased congregations which were the
> immediate fruits of the revival, and by their preaching
> and prayers they gave encouragement to the work and
> cooperated with it. Laity were especially active. The
> movement commenced with the efforts of a layman,
> enlisted the sympathies and energies of other laymen
> throughout the country and was carried on chiefly through
> their instrumentality.

In the first place, most of the organizers of the daily
union prayer meetings were businessmen. The Fulton Street
Meeting was commenced by a lay-worker, the John Street
meeting begun and sustained by young businessmen.   The
Burton's Theatre meetings were launched by the downtown
merchants. The Jayne's Hall service in Philadelphia was
maintained by businessmen.   And so on, all over the country.

Another significant lay development was the way in which
meetings were provided by Christian men for their fellows
in industry and the professions. For example, the policemen
of the City of New York requested a meeting and filled a
church with men in uniform and their families.[11] The Y.M.C.A.
packed out the Academy of Music with firemen and friends.
In Philadelphia, 1779 firemen from 38 companies attended
a meeting in National Hall.

Paralleling the larger assemblies, the Revival initiated
a host of smaller meetings held in the stores and counting-
houses of all sorts of commerical companies. The workers
in a certain concern, or the manager of a store, or an out-
sider would propose a daily meeting on the premises.   The
idea spread throughout the length and breadth of the country.
These were overwhelmingly lay efforts. Beardsley noted:[12]

> The revival, moreover, served as a great training
> school for laymen, and brought to light the abilities of
> such men as D. L. Moody, who has left a lasting impress
> upon the history of American Christianity.

Much of this applied to the movement in Britain and was expanded into a host of lay enterprises in the 1860s and 1870s. When Moody crossed to Britain, his first idea in every great city was to establish permanent union prayer meetings, daily at noon. Likewise, Moody made a point of trying to contact various classes and groups of people in all of his great campaigns. Also the Y.M.C.A., which backed the 1858 Awakening wholeheartedly, became Moody's chosen organization, for undoubtedly the work of that body in the 1858 Revival commended itself to Moody's practical mind. Again, Moody's greatest success was in his ability to set laymen to work in Christian activity. The widespread Bible Institute movement provided testimony of this.

Long before Moody began his work in Great Britain, the 1859 Revival had produced a host of new agencies both social and evangelistic, and these were generally initiated and sustained by laymen of all denominations. Ordained ministers often inaugurated new enterprises, but none of them seemed to complain when laymen went ahead of them. It was all that the clergy could do to keep up with the spontaneous outpouring of lay energy.

As a natural corollary of the movement of the laity, the trend toward a practical interdenominational unity developed rapidly. Generally, lay movements are interdenominational, and usually revivals of religion also are interdenominational. Furthermore, in the Awakening of 1858-59, the various denominations were so busy trying to care for an influx of new members that there was scarcely room for sectarian jealousy. With hardly an exception, the Churches were all working together as one man. Arminians and Calvinists ignored their differences; Baptists and Pædobaptists were blessed together; and cooperation was almost 'too good to be true.' By common consent, doctrinal controversies were left alone, and the idea worked well.

These factors, the rise of the laity and their promotion of interdenominational fellowship, had greater effect in the Moody and Sankey Crusades and in the great interdenominational fellowships and agencies supported by Moody. The 1858-59 Awakening was noted for its home missionary work. The campaigns of a score of years later brought about an emphasis upon foreign missions. It is the writer's opinion that this regeneration of foreign missionary interest in the United States would have come earlier had it not been for the slavery issue and the Civil War of 1861-65.

Yet there were many calls for a revival of missionary interest. In October 1858, a Baptist missionary magazine issued in Boston asked: [13]

> Many of the churches of America have been recently blessed as never before. The question now arises: what ought to be the effects of this great revival on the missionary cause?

Before an answer could come, fratricidal war between the States drained the nation's energy and provided the churches with a Crusade. The oppressed at home were liberated first. In the absence of Civil War in Britain, there was immediate flowering of the Awakening in the revival of many existing organizations and the creation of new ones. The Revival brought a flood of blessing down the old channels and broke through all obstacles to form new rivers of missionary enterprise in newer and older organizations.

The British and Foreign Bible Society had celebrated its jubilee in 1854. Five years later, the Awakening brought a host of helpers to the band of workers in the noble enterprise. Little credit is given by historians to the cause of the sudden expansion of the 1860s, although it is noted.

The circulation of Scriptures among revived and converted multitudes in Ireland soared, and the Hibernian Bible Society became a supporter instead of a subsidiary[14] of the parent society. In 1861, the National Bible Society of Scotland was founded. The 1860s were years of expansion for the Bible Society's Welsh auxiliaries. Advances were made in every direction in England, and by 1863 'there was scarcely a city or town in England which had not its Biblewoman supported by local contributions.'[15] At the same time, the circulation of the Scriptures at home and abroad exceeded two million, a 50% gain over the Jubilee figures. During the War between the States, the presses of the American Bible Society were working at full pressure to keep up with the demand for Bibles, and these were supplied to both armies, while the financial response of civilians increased in proportion.

The Evangelization Society was founded by the supporters of the mid-century Awakening,[16] and engaged in extensive evangelism throughout the length and breadth of Britain. The City Missions entered into expanded evangelism in theatres, open-air meetings, slum visitation and the like. The Open Air Mission, founded 1853, gained its strength in the 1860s through the ministry of its teams of evangelists under the direction of Gawin Kirkham. Clergy of the Establishment as well as ministers and laymen of other churches preached in the open-air during the Awakening, with crowds of twenty thousand reported in some places.

In 1860, William Pennefather, son of an Irish nobleman, became the leader of a revival movement in Barnet.[17] He opened a training home after the Fliedner model to prepare Church of England deaconesses whose ministry was soon greatly in demand in the Evangelical parishes. In Mildmay, a North London suburb, Pennefather built a conference hall as a base for home and foreign missions. It was at Mildmay that the interdenominational conference on missions was held in 1878, preparing the way for the Edinburgh Conference.

Hugh Price Hughes, the best-known convert of the Revival in Wales, founded the Sisterhood of the Methodist Church, and with Collier and other pastor-evangelists he helped build the Central Hall movement which revitalized Methodism in the hearts of British cities.[18] Home Missions of the other denominations were likewise revived.

The most significant and fascinating home missionary development of the 1858-59 Awakening was the birth of the Salvation Army, which extended the evangelistic and social ministry of the more general movement.

The achievements of the husband-and-wife evangelistic team, William and Catherine Booth, during the years of the Revival were notable. Booth's experience in Cornwall taught him a connection between holiness of Christian living and power in successful evangelism, for he preached one to achieve the other. His experience in the Black Country Awakening taught him that the masses could be most successfully reached by their own kind bearing witness. His frustration at the hands of unsympathetic denominational directors must have determined him to shape an organization of his own. He was an interdenominationalist, yet his Wesleyan convictions were strong; so his creation, the Salvation Army, became interdenominational in the support commanded from all manner of Christians, yet denominational enough to be reckoned a convinced Arminian fellowship, more Wesleyan than contemporary Methodists in doctrine and practice.

Prophetically, in the New Year of 1861, a conference was called in Sussex Hall, Leadenhall Street, in the City of London to consider the appalling need of the slums of the East End.[19] The Reverend Baptist Noël there predicted that some far-reaching work was about to begin, and so the East London Special Services Committee began operations.

Six months later, William Booth visited London friends to seek employment in a home mission capacity, and was put into contact with leaders of the East London committee. They invited him to become their evangelist, but four years of success in revival ministry elsewhere elapsed before Booth accepted their invitation.   Into this opportunity for service, William Booth poured his passion for soul winning and his experience of ministry in the Awakening. The committee became the Christian Revival Association; then the East London Christian Mission; then, as its efforts were extended, the Christian Mission—which Booth finally named the Salvation Army.[20]

The Salvation Army thus arose as a lasting extension of the 1858-59 Revival in its double ministry of evangelism and social uplift. Many activities developed by Booth had already been initiated by other workers in the Awakening—its indoor and outdoor evangelism, its mission to fallen women, to criminals, its welfare work, and its missionary enterprise.

While the Army bore the indelible stamp of the personalities of William and Catherine Booth, it was cast by them in the mold of the 1858-59 Revival; and its pioneers entered country after country, becoming a world-wide movement still committed to evangelism and social welfare.

The mid-nineteenth century Awakening was primarily an urban rather than a rural phenomenon. The English-speaking world was fast becoming one of ever-enlarging cities, with huge concentrations of population that forever had left the influence of the rural churches behind.

It seemed that some new method was needed to reach the city populations. While the United States was preoccupied with the Civil War, the Revival in Britain produced a number of very effective evangelists who achieved their greatest success, not in rural Wales or Ulster or Scotland, but in the industrial cities, particularly in Glasgow and Cardiff, and the big towns and cities of England.

Soon these British evangelists were crossing the Atlantic to preach in the post-bellum United States. Men like Henry Moorhouse of Manchester made a profound impression upon D. L. Moody in Chicago. Moody, who had engaged first in evangelism in the 1858 Revival, was later to repay his debt.

With the Revival of 1858 came the successful introduction of the Y.M.C.A. to American cities, and the flowering of the movement in the United States. The influx of converted young men into Christian churches found an excellent outlet in the evangelistic activites of the early Christian associations of young men. The Y.M.C.A. took the initiative in the evangelizing of the masses.

R. C. Morgan, chronicler of the 1859 Awakening, noted as early as 6th August of that year:[21]

> It does not necessarily follow that because the Young Men's Christian Association has been so blessed in the American Revival, the same must be the case in this country. There might be an attempt at imitation followed by humiliating failure. But we think it will not be so. Our connexion with the Association is, indeed, but of recent date, but we have seen enough to lead us to expect God's blessing upon it in a very marked manner when His time is come.

From the beginning of the Revival in Britain, the Y.M.C.A. not only shared in the ingathering, but often sponsored the meetings which brought Christians together for united prayer and united evangelism. A conference of provincial and city Y.M.C.A. delegates met in London at the start of the Revival, and reiterated an early principle of the Y.M.C.A., binding it on all branches—a decided and authenticated conversion to God as the requirement for membership. From that time forward, the Y.M.C.A. increased with the Awakening.

The lasting effect of the 1858-59 Revivals on the Y.M.C.A. is scarcely mentioned in standard histories on the subject. The year 1864, indeed, is officially recognized as 'the turning point of the Y.M.C.A.,[22] the beginning of certain success.' The 1864 Edinburgh Conference of the Y.M.C.A. laid the foundations of the movement with its liberal provision for all-round requirements of young men, spiritual and social, physical and individual, initiated in evangelism.

Likewise, the Awakening of 1858-59 infused new vitality into the Sunday School movement. A Chicago businessman, Benjamin Franklin Jacobs, began his Sunday School career during the 1858 Revival, at a time when the Sunday Schools of the country were crowded with children. Jacobs engineered the International Sunday School Convention within seventeen years. Henry Clay Trumbull, likewise active in the Revival, became the leading Sunday School editor in 1875. In Ulster, the Awakening crowded the Sunday Schools, and the upsurge was felt in all three Kingdoms. The statistics of British Churches showed some denominational gains in numbers of pupils in Sunday School as high as 33% to 50% in seven years. Other agencies for child evangelism were springing up.

19

THE MISSIONARY EXTENSION

The friends of missions in the United States immediately asked themselves what effect the extraordinary Awakening of 1858 would have upon the overseas missionary enterprise, and Henry Venn, the able director of the Church Missionary Society expressed the same concern in London in 1859:[1]

> Yet I am so confident that we must either rise on the wave or be overwhelmed by it, that I shall propose on Monday to send a deputation to Ireland to the revival region to visit the great towns, and to obtain the prayers, sympathy, and hearts and hands, if possible, of some of the awakened servants of God. I am anxious thus to connect the Revival with missionary zeal for the sake of the Revivalists themselves as well as for our cause.

In 1860, while war clouds were gathering in the United States and before Abraham Lincoln was elected President, the British friends of the Awakening convened at Liverpool a Conference on Missions. Andrew Somerville, the Foreign Missions Secretary of the United Presbyterian Church in Scotland, told how the Revival was already making itself felt on foreign mission fields; and he declared that every recent letter he had received from foreign missionaries thanked God for the increase of intercession at home and expressed hope of an increase of effectiveness abroad:[2]

> They had heard of those blessed outpourings in America, in Sweden, in Ireland, in Scotland, in various parts of the metropolis and other places . . . they had come together knowing that God would bless them from day to day . . . Let all differences be forgotten: let them not remember that they were Churchmen or Dissenters, Baptists or Wesleyans, Presbyterians or Episcopalians.

Lord Shaftesbury, chairman of a great public assembly meeting in Liverpool's Philharmonic Hall, struck the same happy note, claiming that 'this union of all evangelical and orthodox denominations is a great sign of the times,' greeting delegates and representatives as an 'Ecumenical Council.'

How prophetic were his remarks can be seen in the development of the Ecumenical Movement.[3] Preceded by both trial conferences arranged by Dr. Alexander Duff in New York and London in 1854, the historic 1860 Liverpool Conference passed its responsibility to the Mildmay Conference of 1878, followed by the London Conference of 1888, crowned by the Ecumenical Missionary Conference in New York in 1900. Thus the Revival of 1859 helped to lay the foundations of the modern international and interdenominational missionary structure. The initiative for cooperation was Evangelical; and the objectives were evangelistic.

The 1858-59 Awakening produced new missionary modes. The missionary zeal created by the Awakenings at the beginning of the nineteenth century became denominational in organization, although the denominations often worked together for a more successful prosecution of their objectives.

In the next generation, there was a reaction against the evangelical ecumenism of the revival fellowship, leading to a resurgence of denominational exclusivism, weakening the cooperation of denominational societies, not so much by a lack of cooperation by missionaries on the missionfield as by a rise of tension in the home constituencies.

A movement of the Spirit of God reversed the divergent trend; the great worldwide movement of the mid-nineteenth century brought a tremendous expansion of the operations of the existing societies, but it also brought into being a new type of foreign mission enterprise, the interdenominational and nondenominational 'faith' mission. In the Bible Societies and in specialized organizations, true interdenominationalism already existed, but was confined to organizations with very limited objectives, never the founding of churches. An altogether new venture in evangelical ecumenism began.

Every revival of religion in the homelands is felt within a decade on the foreign missionfields. The records of missionary enterprise and pages of missionary biography after the year 1860 prove this conclusively.

Thanks to the Revival in America and Britain, the work of established societies revived,[4] and new societies were formed in the 1860s. New recruits of outstanding ability were provided for both. A missionary of the highest capability, Timothy Richard, soon came out to China. He had been converted in the Welsh Revival of 1859. Joining the Baptist Missionary Society, he became its best-known missionary in that vast Empire, famed for his educational ministry.[5]

In 1866, missionary forces in China were increased by twenty-five per cent through the landing of the Lammermuir party of the newly-formed China Inland Mission under the direction of Dr. J. Hudson Taylor, justly described as one of the greatest missionaries of all time.

The founding of the China Inland Mission was epoch-making in a world sense as well as in its relation to China. The story of the call of James Hudson Taylor is well-known but his relation to the 1859 Revival, and its relationship to the new Mission, has only recently been stressed by any historian.   This first organization of its type in missions was begotten in the 1859 Revival, both its founder's vision and its earliest realization in candidate-missionaries.[6]

While serving with the Chinese Evangelization Society, Hudson Taylor had already come under the influence of the revivalist, W. C. Burns. A letter sent in 1860 by George Pearse— 'You will be glad to know that the revival has reached London and hundreds are being converted,'— thrilled him. Much in need of physical, mental and spiritual recuperation, Hudson Taylor then returned to London.

Hudson Taylor devoted all his spare time, especially his Sundays, to revival ministry in a fruitful training ground, the East End of London.[7] In particular, he helped in the Twig Folly Mission in Bethnal Green which carried on daily prayer meetings and preaching services. A noted infidel was converted there and many converts of the Revival were there baptized as believers.

The Revival then in progress (said Marshall Broomhall) was a revelation in the homeland of God's power to bless, while a million a month dying in China without God made its appalling contrast in the mind of the burdened missionary.

While visiting George Pearse in Brighton in the afterglow of the wonderful Brighton Revival, Hudson Taylor faced his life's greatest crisis. On Sunday, 25th June 1865, unable to bear the sight of a thousand Christians rejoicing in their own security while multitudes perished for lack of knowledge, he walked along the beach and made a great decision.

The prayer life of British Christians had risen to record heights. George Müller's example in launching out by faith was being followed elsewhere. The need of China was appreciated by Hudson Taylor as by few others. So he applied the prayer and faith and action as exemplified by the 1859 Awakening to China's need, and the China Inland Mission became its dynamic extension to China's millions.

This newest venture was not denominationally indifferent. The China Inland Mission as envisioned by Hudson Taylor was interdenominational rather than undenominational. Its missionaries were sent to interior provinces of China where others of the same denomination served—Szechwan, for example, was an Anglican diocese. In due course, the China Inland Mission became the largest of all the missionary bodies, Protestant or Roman.

The example of the China Inland Mission had a profound effect on worldwide missionary enterprise. Interdenominational Faith Missions and other interdenominational societies spread until they supplemented the work of the older denominational societies all over the world. Not all societies copied the China Inland Mission's constitution wholly, but few there were owing nothing to its principles and practice. It maintained its spirituality in a remarkable way.

The 1860s were years of expansion for all the missions in China.[8] Under Griffith John, the London Missionary Society reached out into the midlands and north of China. James Gilmour, a convert of the 1859 Revival, ventured north into Mongolia, suffering privation and hardship. In the 1860s, the American Board opened stations in the north. In the same decade, the American Baptists entered the Swatow area. Southern Baptists maintained themselves in Shantung, in spite of the raging Civil War. The American Episcopal Church moved up river. The Church Missionary Society expanded its mid-China work. American Presbyterians spread from Canton southward. Around Amoy, the English Presbyterians and the Reformed Church of the United States organized a presbytery, and the former opened a work in Formosa among the Chinese. The Methodists of the United States spread from Foochow, opened a work up river on the Yangtze, and entered the north. And Josiah Cox brought the British Methodist enterprise up river also. On all this, Kenneth Scott Latourette made the comment:[9]

> Whatever the denomination, the large majority of the supporting constituencies and the missionaries were from those elements which had been affected by the Evangelical Awakening and kindred revivals . . .

In 1865, R. J. Thomas, a London missionary serving in China, went to Korea as an agent of the National Bible Society of Scotland. He lost his life in a fracas on the beach on landing.[10] Twenty years elapsed before any Protestant missionaries were permitted to reside in the country.

In the 1860s came a development of Protestant missions in Japan, drawn chiefly from American denominations. The American Episcopal Church, the American Presbyterians and the Reformed Church of America were first in the field. The Japanese were still prejudiced against Christian teaching, but there was a desire to learn English and this provided evangelistic contacts.

Until 1872, only ten Japanese had been baptized by Protestant ministers. Neesima, an unusual man, smuggled himself out of Japan and was able to obtain a good education in Christian schools in United States, returning as a missionary to found the Doshisha University.[11] In 1872, the American Baptists sent in two missionaries, one of them a marine (Jonathan Goble) who had been with Commodore Perry in the opening up of Japan by treaty.[12] The Canadian Methodists followed in 1873. Then came the Bible Societies. By 1882, there were five thousand adult church members in Japanese Protestant churches and a beginning had been made.

As in China, the majority of these Christians were under the tutelage of evangelical teachers. Evangelicalism was the dynamic of the societies raised up in the denominations, for neo-Protestantism was still in its incubation stage. Apart from zealous Roman Catholic missionaries, the missionary thrust in the Orient was overwhelmingly evangelical.

At the opposite end of Asia, the missionary drive was encountering Muslim resistance. Foothold were secured in ancient Christian enclaves. In the 1860s, American Board teachers opened colleges in Beirut (later named American University) and Istanbul (Robert College). In the 1870s, the American Presbyterians and the Church Missionary Society opened work in Iran.[13] In the 1880s, a small beginning was made at Aden in coastal Arabia under Ion Keith-Falconer.

In Indonesia, the greatest growth of Christian churches occurred within the 'Great East' cluster of islands, in folk movements on Celebes, Ceram, Amboina, and other communities where the native Christians began an aggressive missionary work in nearby islands and extended the limits of the Faith.[14] In Muslim Java, there were fewer converts.

In 1861, the Rhenish Missionary Society began work in Sumatra, where American missionaries had earlier been killed and eaten. Under the keen leadership of Ludwig Ingwer Nommensen,[15] the mission to Bataks was eminently successful, a Christian community of 160,000 gathered in fifty years of evangelism and revival.

In Inverary in the Scottish highlands, during the Revival of 1859, a high-spirited, unconverted lad tried to disrupt a meeting addressed by two Irishmen from the Ulster Revival but instead came under an intense conviction of sin, being brought in from the streets in the middle of the night. James Chalmers was trained for active service in the Glasgow City Mission, and proceeded to the South Seas.[16] He arrived in Rarotonga in 1867, and spent ten years there.

In 1871, the London Missionary Society began its work in New Guinea, a huge island difficult to penetrate. The missionaries and nationals from other Pacific islands made initial landings, and in 1877 Chalmers joined them, soon becoming one of the greatest pioneers of the Pacific area. In 1901, he was martyred.

In the 1880s, the northeast portion of New Guinea territory came under German control, and the German missionaries pioneered there. In 1890, the L. M. S. divided the southeast portion with Anglicans and Methodists of Australia. The western part of New Guinea, under Dutch rule, had been opened at mid-century by the Gossner Mission.[17]

The impact of the 1858-59 Awakenings was felt in all the Polynesian kingdoms, Hawaii, Tonga and Tahiti. As a result, in the 1860s, the evangelical Polynesians carried the Gospel to the remaining groups of islands in Polynesia, till then unevangelized. In 1863, the American Board turned over its work in Hawaii to the Hawaiian Evangelical Association, which inaugurated missionary work in Micronesia.[18]

Meantime persecution raged in Madagascar. Ranavalona the queen was determined to stamp out Christianity.[19] In 1837, martyrdom was thrust upon believers, nine being speared to death in 1840, others poisoned in 1842, fourteen cast over cliffs and others burned to death in 1849. In 1857, a score were stoned to death. Thousands were flogged, fined or sold as slaves. But Christians grew in numbers, meeting in secret to read the Scriptures which fortunately had been translated into Malagasy before the persecutions actually started.

A faithful body of believers awaited their liberation. The revived British churches found openings in Madagascar when the death of the persecuting Ranavalona I relieved a secretly growing church of its worst sufferings. William Ellis brought a contingent of the London Missionary Society and a vigorous evangelistic and educational enterprise to the aid of the Christians in the 1860s.[20]

The Church Missionary Society entered the island of
Madagascar in 1864, at the same time as the Society for the
Propagation of the Gospel.[21] The C. M. S. withdrew when the
S. P. G. brought out a bishop consecrated by the Scottish
Episcopal Church but opposed by the non-Anglican groups.
The High Churchmen were unsympathetic to the revival
movement which impressed Malagasy Christians.

In 1866, the Norwegian Missionary Society, a fellowship
born of revival in Norway,[22] sent out a team of missionaries
to cooperate with the L. M. S., which alone had more than
260 churches, twenty thousand members, and a hundred and
thirty thousand adherents. By 1880, there were more than a
thousand churches, seventy thousand members and two hundred and twenty five thousand adherents. Dispensaries and
clinics were opened and Malagasy given medical training.
Schools were maintained in nearly every church building
and a teacher's training college was set up. As yet, there
were no indigenous revival movements.

As in Asia and Oceania, the Evangelical Revival of 1858-
1859 had an immediate effect on missionary work in Africa.
This was most noticeable in the South, which had been the
object of the most thorough missionary penetration.

In Britain, the Anglo-Catholic section of the Church of
England remained antipathetic to the Revival of the 1860s.
There was little sympathy within the predominantly Anglo-
Catholic Church of the Province of South Africa either, but
Anglican missions to the Bantu arose from a plan made by
Bishop Gray to appoint bishops and employ Anglo-Catholic
orders to staff mission stations.[23] The controversial Bishop
Colenso also left a successful Zulu Mission that continued
to be more evangelical than sacramentarian.[24]

The Presbyterians sent out choice recruits. Christina
Forsyth, a convert of the Revival in Scotland, pioneered in
Fingoland.[25] To Africa in 1861 came James Stewart, first a
companion of Livingstone on the Zambesi, then explorer of
the highlands of Nyasaland—where Presbyterians in later
years built their great mission— then back to the Lovedale
Institution to become its outstanding principal.

The Awakenings of the years before and after 1860 had
a profound effect on the Bantu majority in South Africa as
Dutch Reformed and Methodist South Africans and missionaries from America and Europe extended missionary operations and native converts of the Revival kept on preaching
powerfully until the twentieth century.

The work among Bantu tribes was deep and lasting. The missionaries and native pastors who had experienced a baptism of the Holy Spirit went everywhere preaching both repentance and faith, pardon and purity, to illiterate and semi-literate tribesmen. Great days of harvest followed.[26]

Mission stations were transformed from half-Christian-ized 'cities of refuge' under missionary management into Christian communities. Education received a great impetus as native Christians sought learning for their children. An 'era of education,' so designated in Whiteside's account of Methodism in South Africa,[27] followed the great awakening. Converts of the '60s became forerunners of a native ministry. A third of all Xhosa hymns came from the 1860s Revival.

The spiritual sons of William Taylor continued in minis-try into the twentieth century, and the indigenous bands of local preachers arising from the Awakening became the Wesleyan Native Home Mission.[28] Methodism became the greatest force in evangelizing the Bantu in South Africa, more than a third of all Bantu Christians being recognized as the fruit of Wesleyan missions therein.

Charles Pamla continued his preaching as a Methodist evangelist throughout all South Africa.[29] When he died, the Methodists regarded him as father of 25,000 converts, and the community agreed to bury him in Kokstad Cemetery, an unusual tribute in racially conscious European towns.

In the Awakenings of the 1860s, the revival had occurred, more or less, among people of European and mixed blood and the Africans in European hinterlands. But the power began to affect native communities outside the colonies. A decade later, shortly after the death of Moshesh, the king of the Basuto, a spiritual awakening began at the main station of the Paris Evangelical Missionary Society, spreading to almost all of Lesotho.[30]

The leaders of the Paris Evangelical Mission in Africa recognized that the work of French and Swiss Protestant Missions as a whole owed its being to the Haldanes and the evangelical forces they set in motion at the beginning of the century. Coillard, an apostle to Southern Africa, himself was converted in a revival in the Jura in 1851. Such men of God expected to see similar awakenings in Africa.

Using South Africa as a base, missionaries in turn moved north into central and eastern Africa. The Paris Missionary Society directed Francois Coillard to Barotseland, north of the Zambesi,[31] and in 1887 he developed a mission there,

Lozi people having been found to use a Sotho-type language. Older Protestant societies entered Rhodesia in force with the British South Africa Company, and South African Dutch Reformed missionaries built an outstanding mission station at Morgenster, a many-sided institution.

Before and after the Revival, Livingstone was turning the light of exploration and evangelization upon the Continent of Africa. His was the example and his also was the challenge given in the right places so often by tongue and pen.

The challenge of Livingstone and the dynamic of the Revival of 1860 were responsible for the pioneering of the Mission to Nyasaland by the Free Church of Scotland which sent to Capetown its main advocate, James Stewart, in 1861. After a discouraging survey in 1862, little was done until Livingstone's death, when Stewart and his friends revived the project, a party pushing up the Zambesi and reaching Lake Nyasa.[32] The Church of Scotland also entered Malawi, and the Dutch Reformed Church of South Africa followed.

Frederick Stanley Arnot was a lad who heard Livingstone speak in times of revival and decided to follow in his footsteps. He became a pioneer, accomplishing a great work as a Brethren missionary, making nine long pioneering journeys in thirty years of service before his death in 1914.[33] He led out to Africa yet another pioneering missionary, the valiant and intrepid Dan Crawford 'of the long grass.'[34]

The ubiquitous William Taylor, American revivalist and evangelist, was appointed Bishop for Africa by the American Methodist Episcopal Church, and landed at Loanda in 1885. From Angola the Methodist work spread across the continent through the Congo to Mozambique, girdling Africa.[35]

In 1877, the British Baptists were challenged to invade the Congo. Unlike their American colleagues, who concentrated upon the lower Congo, the British Baptists pressed inland. The cause in the Congo was greatly aided by the arrival of George Grenfell, whose 'earliest impressions of a serious kind' dated back to the 1860s, just 'when the great wave of awakening which followed the Revival of 1859 was passing over the country.' Grenfell became the greatest of Baptist pioneers in Africa and an able mission director.[36]

The revivalist, H. Grattan Guinness, launched a work in the Congo in the 1870s, known as the Livingstone Inland Mission,[37] a title which suggested two of Guinness's heroes (Hudson Taylor and David Livingstone) at a time when there was talk of naming the Congo the Livingstone River.

The Guinness party established stations in the vicinity of Matadi.[38] One enthusiastic worker there was Adam McCall, an experienced hunter who had roamed South Africa, and another was Henry Richards who soon witnessed a movement of revival among his Bantu converts at Banza Manteke, the first 'Pentecost on the Congo.' Two thousand were baptized during the awakening. In other stations, similar awakenings occurred in turn. It was an auspicious beginning.[39]

Grattan Guinness transferred the promising field to the American Baptists, under whom the revival movement continued.[40] It was reported: 'We are in the midst of a great spiritual revival upon the field which equals the Banza Manteke Pentecost in intensity and surpasses it in extent.'

In 1862 the explorer Speke declared that the kingdoms of Uganda were by far the most inviting in Africa for missionary enterprise.[41] Stanley was of the same opinion and his challenge stirred the Church Missionary Society to enter Uganda, a task by no means easy.

Alexander Mackay, a convert of the Revival of the 1860s in Britain, arrived with a party of pioneers in Zanzibar in 1876, but only two of them established themselves in Uganda, two dying of fever and two being murdered. The entrance of a militant Roman Catholic mission added to their troubles, which increased when the friendly king Mtesa died and was succeeded by his vicious son, Mwanga. Mwanga was responsible for the murder of James Hannington, Anglican bishop, in 1885. Converts of the Christian missions refused to submit to Mwanga's practice of sodomy. So the Kabaka roasted three martyrs slowly to death, and burned alive thirty-two young men in one funeral pyre. Perhaps two hundred martyrs died by fire, and another bishop perished through fever.[42]

The West African pioneer, Mary Slessor of Calabar, was converted in Dundee during the Revival of the 1860s, joined the United Presbyterian mission in Nigeria, and became an extraordinary pioneer among the tribes.[43] In 1867, Samuel Adjai Crowther, a rescued slave educated in England, was consecrated as Anglican Bishop of the Niger territories, working without European help, then a handicap.[44]

Grattan Guinness, George Pearse, and other leaders in the British 1859 Revival joined in founding the North Africa Mission, which sought a foothold in Algeria, Morocco and Tunis in the 1880s.[45] It was difficult indeed to win converts from Islam in the Maghreb or Libya or Egypt.

In the 1860s, Protestant missionary work in the Sudan began, and during the same decade a Swedish Mission, sent out by the Rosenius revival movement, entered Ethiopia.[46]

There is no doubt that the nineteenth century Revivals opened up many countries of Africa to the Gospel, providing at first societies and men, then half a century later adding liberally to them. What were the effects of this expansion of Evangelical Christianity throughout Africa in the latter decades of the nineteenth century?

The missionaries reduced the languages of the natives to writing, prepared translations of the Scriptures, taught the people to read and write, set up schools for the young, established hospitals for the sick, introduced arts and crafts, and built up Christian communities.

The missionaries hastened the disintegration of native cultures. Polygamy was discouraged by most, marriage-purchase by many; initiation rites at puberty were discountenanced as being breeders of immorality. Missionaries struggled against murder and ritual killing and opposed witch doctors, undermining ancestor worship and animism, everywhere. Their attitudes were often intransigent.

The missionaries fought the exploitation of the natives by Europeans, and adamantly opposed slavery and the slave traffic, evangelicals being leaders in the opposition. They also encouraged their native charges to become self-reliant, in this way preparing them for self-government to come.

In tropical and sub-tropical America, Negro slaves and freemen alike were already detribalized, learning to read and write, delivered from polygamy and marriage purchase. Emancipation accelerated the processes of Christianization and civilization and prepared the Negroes of America for separate-but-equal, then equal status before the law.

The Revival of 1858-59 onwards provided the enterprise and also the volunteers for the invasion of the vast southern continent and the countries of the Caribbean. High Church parties still advocated respecting Rome's prior claim.

In 1862, an Anglican Evangelical, W. H. Stirling, became superintendent of the South American Missionary Society, and seven years later was made the Bishop of the Falkland Islands nearby. Charles Darwin was greatly impressed with the success of the mission's work among savages in Tierra del Fuego whom he had declared to be hopelessly degraded, and he became a financial contributor to the work until his death. The Society maintained its evangelical stance.[47]

Immigration opened the doors of the southern republics of South America. The British colonists in Argentina were cared for by chaplains.[48] Americans from the defeated Confederacy emigrated to Brazil and were followed by Baptist, Methodist and Presbyterian ministers.[49] German settlers in south Brazil were followed by Lutheran clergy. There were other Protestant immigrants.

In Chile in the 1860s, a liberal government came to power and interpreted the constitution to sanction Protestant evangelism.[50] So Spanish-speaking churches were organized in Valparaiso and Santiago. Italian Waldensians emigrated to Uruguay and Argentina and maintained churches. The South American Missionary Society in the 1860s sent a chaplain to Callao, port of Lima, in Peru.

William Taylor, following a missionary urge, focussed the attention of the Methodist Episcopal Church on Latin America. Taylor developed a plan for self-supporting missions and, touring several republics, helped to plant churches.[51]

The Scottish physician, Robert Reid Kalley, developed an interest in Brazil, where churches of Congregational organization were springing up after 1858.[52] The first missionary of Presbyterian affiliation arrived in Brazil in 1859, a presbytery being organized as early as 1865. In 1867, the Methodists sent a pastor to Brazil, followed by Portuguese-speaking missionaries. In 1879, the Southern Baptists supplied a pastor, followed by missionaries to the Brazilians also. Foundations were being laid for a great work of God.

The first Protestant communion was shared in Mexico in 1859. Then in 1860, the American Bible Society sent an agent to Mexico. He was followed by James Hickey, an Irish convert who gathered a congregation in Monterey. Melinda Rankin, founder of a school for Mexicans on the Texas side of the border, moved to Monterey in 1865.[53] Presbyterian, Baptist and Methodist missionaries met with the fiercest opposition from Roman priests. Converts were won from among the mestizo masses rather than the upper class and educated Spanish elite or lower class Indian peasants.

From such small beginnings, made after the 1858-59 Revival, came the vast missionary enterprise in Brazil and Hispanic America. The evangelical zeal of the pioneers, in the decades following, gave birth to evangelical convictions and evangelical activities among their national converts. For a full century to come, the temper of Latin American Evangelicals remained evangelistic.

20
THE HOLINESS MOVEMENT

The Keswick Convention for the Deepening of the Spiritual Life, an evangelical movement with a truly worldwide influence, budded at gatherings in London, Oxford and Brighton in 1873, '74 and '75, and blossomed into early maturity at a Lake District resort in 1875; but the seed was sown in the great Revival of 1858-59 in the English-speaking world. Its origins may be traced to the American Middle West.

William Edwin Boardman had published at the height of the Awakening of 1858 a treatise upon the 'Higher Christian Life.' He was a zealous young Presbyterian businessman when he started his search in the 1840s for a holier life. His book was a huge success on both sides of the Atlantic (circulation, 200,000), being published in Britain in 1860.[1] It produced its greatest effect in the Old Country.

The year 1860 dated the conversion of a young English clergyman, Evan Hopkins, and it was not long before a copy of Boardman's treatise found its way into the eager hands of Hopkins, then engaged in an engrossing revival ministry. It was on 1st May 1873 that Hopkins with fifteen other people met in Mayfair to discuss the subject of the deepening of the Christian life. He entered a fuller experience so real that his wife was the first to follow him into it.[2]

In July 1874, a conference was conducted at Broadlands estate in Hampshire, the seat of Lord Mount Temple, the leaders being Mr. and Mrs. R. Pearsall Smith. Before he could participate in a conference announced for 1875, Smith suffered a nervous breakdown, brought about by charges more serious than the indiscretion which provoked them.[3] It is of interest that Pearsall Smith's daughter married Lord Bertrand Russell, whose anti-Christian bias increased.

Meetings for promoting Scriptural holiness were begun at Oxford in August 1874, with the help of Canon Cristopher. The Convention at Oxford was followed by a larger one at Brighton, begun on 29th May 1875.[4] Henry Varley, of 1859 Revival fame, spoke several times. D. L. Moody, in London, sent the good will and prayers of eight thousand people.

The Vicar of St. John's, Keswick, Harford Battersby, had been active in the 1860 Awakening in Carlisle.[5] He attended the Oxford Convention, committing himself. He invited his friends to the Lakeside town, and thus began the conventions for deepening of the Christian life that gained for 'Keswick' a unique place of leadership in the evangelical world. A majority of its leaders were either evangelists or converts of the 1859 Revival, as were a number of new speakers.

Canon Harford Battersby continued to preside until his death; Evan Hopkins emerged as the leader; William Haslam ministered; Theodore Monod participated. After an address by Evan Hopkins, Handley C. G. Moule was moved to stand publicly as a seeker after blessing, and as Principal of Ridley Hall, Cambridge or as Bishop of Durham, he warmly addressed the Keswick Convention thirteen times.[6]

Andrew Murray entered a deeper experience at Keswick in 1882, and became a mouthpiece of its message all over the world. In 1887, a new speaker was F. B. Meyer, converted during the Revival in the 1860s in London. Another was Charles Inwood, the Irish Methodist evangelist, whose ministry extended its message far and wide.

The Keswick Convention became a missionary force after Reginald Radcliffe in 1886 borrowed its tent for a missionary meeting. Hudson Taylor and Eugene Stock used the Keswick platform to enlist young people for the mission fields. The Keswick line of teaching was supported within the United States by such evangelical leaders as D. L. Moody, Reuben Torrey, Adoniram J. Gordon, A. B. Simpson and J. Wilbur Chapman, but it never became the unifying force in United States that it had become in Great Britain.

Keswick borrowed its evangelical ecumenism, with its slogan 'All One in Christ Jesus,' from the Revival of 1858-59 and the movements which followed it. Unlike certain other products of the Revival, the Keswick Convention maintained its evangelical and evangelistic character.

It is strange to notice that both the Keswick movement in Britain and the Holiness movement in the United States owed much to the circulation of W. E. Boardman's writings. How diverse were the two movements: Keswick became an evangelical and ecumenical force; the Holiness movement in the United States led to division after division, as splinter denominations lacking a sense of revival unity were formed. After a hundred years, most divisions between the Holiness denominations were still definite, though less pronounced.

Timothy Smith has offered four reasons why the Holiness movement in America separated from the old main-line denominations—the persistent opposition of ecclesiastical officials to holiness associations; the recurrence of outbreaks of fanaticism in these Holiness associations; the attacks upon Holiness doctrine in the 1890s; and the increased activity of urban holiness preachers in many states.[7] One other reason was the intransigent American temperament developed by the existence of a western frontier that incited independence.

The pursuit of holy living took very different directions in Britain and America. Keswick doctrines represented a synthesis of Calvinistic and Arminian ideas, or rather a statement of the doctrine of holiness acceptable to more moderate Calvinists.[8] Throughout its history, the Keswick movement enlisted the support of Calvinists and Arminians —Anglicans, Baptists, Methodists and Presbyterians of either party without the dispute being ever heard of, except in rare instances in the case of hyper-Calvinists or hyper-Wesleyans and then only in the most cordial fraternity. But in the United States, the vehemence with which the doctrine was propounded and the bitterness with which it was opposed led to a severance of relations rather than a diffusion of influence. In American holiness agitation, schism produced several major and many minor denominations— each one stressing sanctification in its own Wesleyan terminology.

Methodists in America as in Britain had begun to lose their interest in their founder's doctrine of entire sanctification. A majority of them was beginning to treat it as a creedal statement, even though lip service was paid to the experience. Not that the major bodies of Methodists were left without witnesses to the doctrine of holiness.[9]

When William Taylor, later the astonishing Methodist missionary bishop, returned from his tour of duty in California, he renewed an earlier association with the Palmers and then preached in the Eastern and Midwestern States, between 1858 and 1860, before taking off for his meteoric missions to the other five continents.[10] Phœbe Palmer was a 'Priscilla who taught many an Apollos the way of God more perfectly'—Wesley style. Taylor's commitment to holiness theory and practice explained much of his effectiveness in extraordinary revival movements overseas.

The agitation of the Holiness movement also affected the Mennonites, being of Arminian theology. Boardman's views made an impression in Baptist circles also and produced an

evangelist, A. B. Earle,[11] outstanding until the rise of D. L.
Moody. The gruff Baptist evangelist, Jacob Knapp, when he
encountered Earle's 'sanctified Baptists' in Boston, stated
that holiness troubled him but little.[12]

The effect of the American holiness agitation was to make
a powerful plea for holiness of life a sectarian appeal rather
than an ecumenical one as in Britain. Where the subject was
tenderly expounded in British countries, drawing together a
cross-section of denominational membership, in the United
States it was on occasion hotly debated.

The Holiness movement in Germany proved to be ecumenical rather than sectarian. It produced the Gemeinschaftsbewegung (German Alliance for the Cultivation of Fellowship
and Evangelism), often called the Gnadauer Band.[13] Theodor
Christlieb, revived in the 1860 Awakening in London, had a
part in transplanting the 'Keswick' impulse to Germany.

The movement spread through the German States, until
in 1898 the Gemeinschaftsbewegung was formed, remaining
in association with the denominational organizations, maintaining seven hundred seminary trained preachers and five
thousand lay ministers and circles.

The Keswick Convention movement itself spread to the
countries of the British Empire and to other communities.
It became a world movement, in which Christians of all
denominational loyalties sought a closer walk with God, and
in which many a missionary heard his call to service. The
movement was not without its critics, and periodically there
were those who disputed its theology or terminology. While
remaining unaffiliated, its adherents shared in many drives
for evangelism at home and abroad.

Keswick theology, mediated through a tract written by a
Tamil evangelist, stirred up George Pilkington in Uganda
and through him provoked an extraordinary awakening that
added tens of thousands to the Anglican mission churches.

A Keswick speaker, Charles Inwood, brought the same
message to Malawi, and witnessed another extraordinary
revival of the Presbyterian churches and ingathering of the
heathen, less than twenty years later, in 1910.

The adherents of the Keswick Convention developed their
own kind of ecumenism, based upon a recognition of the
oneness of all truly regenerate believers. They were less
concerned with organizational mergers of denominations,
and less disturbed by obvious denominational distinctions,
though not committed against the drive for organic union.

In the United States, the holiness movement enjoyed no such central focus as Keswick. The Wesleyan Methodists had come into existence fifteen years before the Revival of 1858; the Free Methodists seceded from the major body of Methodism in 1860, after an agitation begun long before; after the Civil War, a National Camp Meeting Association for the Promotion of Holiness was formed, and successive splinter denominations were organized, each stressing the Wesleyan theology of perfection. And this process continued until the end of the century. It cannot be said that the 1858 Revival played a responsible part in the development of the holiness movement in the United States, other than contributing a considerable interest in holiness of living to the denominations generally.

21

THE EVANGELISTIC EXTENSION

The impact of the 1858-59 Awakening was felt in the field of evangelism for more than forty years—the span of D. L. Moody's ministry—and continued on until the outbreak of World War I, before which disaster another worldwide awakening had become interdenominationally effective.

As the figure of Charles Grandison Finney dominated American evangelism in the middle third of the nineteenth century, so the figure of Dwight Lyman Moody dominated the final third, not only in the United States but Britain. Finney was a well-educated scholar; Moody an uneducated countryman who never learned to spell or punctuate his pungent speech. This they had in common, that they were full of zeal to win men and women to Jesus Christ.

In Northfield, a pretty village in rural Massachusetts, family circumstances scarcely suggested a career as a world evangelist for Moody.[1] His father had died when Dwight was four years old, leaving his mother and eight other children (including twins born posthumously) without provision. Nor did family religion suggest it. All the Moody children were christened in the local Unitarian Church. As an eighteen-year old lad in Boston, Moody was professedly converted. It proved to be a simple rather than a profound experience, for when he was examined for admission to church membership, he had so little to say that his candidacy was deferred until he had learned a little more.[2] A little over a year later, Moody moved to the frontier town of Chicago. It was here that his great career began.

The Awakening of 1857-58 in Chicago made a profound impression on the life of the zealous young man from New England.[3] The churches of every denomination were packed to overflowing, yet the rapid growth of the town provided all the raw material for evangelism needed.

In Chicago, Moody became interested in winning young folk to Christ through the Sunday School and through the Young Men's Christian Association. So successful was he that he became an expert in 'drumming up' scholars for

Sunday School.[4] In 1858, he started a Sunday School of his own in a vacant saloon, and before long it was the largest Sunday School in Chicago. All the while, he continued active in his business as a salesman.

Moody's Sunday School developed into a church. In 1860, Moody decided to give up his business income (then bringing him $5000 a year) and to 'live by faith' (which brought him $150 the first year).[5] In 1864, the congregation occupied its own building on Illinois Street, and next year Moody was elected president of the Y.M.C.A. in Chicago. He remained a layman.

His first trip to Britain Moody made in the year 1867, seeking out leaders of the evangelical movement there, such as C. H. Spurgeon, George Müller, George Williams, Lord Shaftesbury, R. C. Morgan, Henry Varley, Harry Moorhouse, and those who seemed to Moody to have something to share with him in the work of the Lord.[6]

Events in Chicago encouraged Moody to revisit Britain. In 1868, the great Farwell Hall of the Y.M.C.A. was burned, scarcely three months after its dedication. It had cost the sum of $200,000, its loss a crushing blow. The members worked hard to raise the funds to rebuild the hall, which was reopened in little more than a year. None worked harder than Moody, but the effort took him away from his work at times and made him restless.

Moody had been married in 1862 to a young English-born girl, Emma Revell. In 1870, he met a helpmeet of a different kind, Ira D. Sankey, who became his soloist in his world ministry. In 1871, a great fire destroyed the city of Chicago, reducing to ashes fifty churches and missions. In 1871, while visiting New York, Moody experienced a mighty enduement of the Holy Spirit, an answer to two old ladies' prayers.[8] He was being prepared for a greater ministry.

In 1872, Moody paid a second visit to Britain. After a night of prayer in Dublin, Henry Varley said to him: 'Moody, the world has yet to see what God will do with a man fully consecrated to Him.'[9] That comment startled Moody. His visit brought a local awakening in a North London church and a number of invitations to return to Britain for a wider ministry followed. An Anglican clergyman, William Penne-father, sent him an invitation by letter to America.[10] Moody tried to settle again in Chicago, but he felt restless until he decided to return to Britain and win 10,000 souls to Christ there.

Moody persuaded Sankey to go along. Their plans made, in June 1873, the Moody and Sankey families arrived in Liverpool to learn that Pennefather had died. Moody crossed to York and commenced meetings on short notice. The response was slow but definite. There was still no movement in the next campaign, in Sunderland. But in Newcastle-on-Tyne, Moody and Sankey's evangelism enjoyed success.[11]

From there, the evangelists proceeded north to Scotland. A turning point in Moody's ministry came in their Edinburgh Campaign.[12] Despite the local Calvinistic conservatism, the evangelist won the enthusiastic approval of the people, both inside and outside the churches. The ministers studied the movement carefully, then began to back it without reserve. Moody introduced the noonday prayer meeting of the 1858-59 Revival again. His evening meetings were crowded, taxing the largest auditoriums.

After three weeks in Dundee, Moody began a mission in Glasgow that made a lasting impact on the city. Not only were thousands converted, but the United Evangelistic Committee transformed itself into the Glasgow Evangelistic Association and maintained a dozen subsidiary organizations of evangelism and relief work.[13]

Thus encouraged, the evangelists crossed over to Ireland. The Belfast Mission of the Moody and Sankey team commenced in the autumn of 1874. A daily noonday prayer meeting was begun in a Donegall Square church. The evening meetings attracted an enormous attendance of young men. The Anglican, Presbyterian and other ministers reinforced them. Dublin's Roman Catholic majority noted Moody's own avoidance of affront to their faith, and proved friendly, if not enthusiastic. Again, there were several thousands of professed conversions.[14] The Irish had seen the greatest expression of evangelism since the '59 Revival.

The Manchester, Sheffield, Birmingham and Liverpool Missions followed, each with success.[15] They were moving towards a climax in London. Twenty thousand people nightly heard them in the Agricultural Hall in Islington. While William Taylor of California continued there, D. L. Moody preached in a tabernacle in Bow to the poor and in the Opera House in the Haymarket to the rich each evening. The London meetings lasted twenty weeks and attracted 2,500,000.

As in Scotland, Moody's work in England gave birth to many Christian enterprises besides giving a breath of revival to existent organizations. It made such an impact that

Friedrich Engels, the collaborator with Karl Marx in his Communist propaganda, explained the whole business as a plot of the British bourgeoisie to import Yankee revivalism to keep the proletariat contented.[16]

In August 1875, Moody returned to the United States and commenced a campaign in Brooklyn in October, followed by a greater one in Philadelphia in late November. Vast crowds attended, for news of successes in Britain had excited the American church people. In February 1876, Moody held a campaign in New York City, with attendance in the tens of thousands, many responding to the challenge.[17]

Moody returned to Chicago to campaign in the winter of 1876, and received a hero's welcome from a city which claimed him as a son. Early in 1877, he commenced ministry in Boston, another city of his youth, but there he encountered opposition from both Roman and Unitarian sides. A year later, he was still campaigning in New England. Sankey parted from him to conduct a singing ministry in England, but failing there returned to work with Moody as before. In 1880-81, together they ministered in cities across the country as far as the Pacific Coast.[18]

In Newcastle-on-Tyne, Moody began his second British campaign in October 1881, again moving north to Edinburgh for six weeks, then to Glasgow, in which metropolis he held forth for five months. He then conducted short series of meetings in Welsh cities and towns and in provincial cities in England.[19] In 1883, Moody conducted an eight months' mission in London.[20] Two large temporary structures were built, first one in North London, the other in South London. As soon as a three weeks' mission had been completed in one, it was moved and rebuilt in another location on the same side while the other building was being used across the Thames.

After 1884, Moody conducted his evangelistic campaigns in smaller American cities,[21] besides giving much of his time to educational promotion at Chicago and Northfield, and to Bible conferences. It was rare for him to visit non-English-speaking countries, though in 1894 Moody preached in Mexico City, triggering a year of blessing there.[22]

Moody conducted a great campaign in 1893 at the World's Columbian Exposition in Chicago. Approximately two million visitors attended this evangelistic series at the World's Fair, sponsored by Moody with the help of his Bible Institute. Points of preaching were chosen on the north-side, west-side and south-side of Chicago, and, on Sunday mornings, Moody rented a huge circus tent near the lake front.[23] To reach those speaking French, German, Polish and other languages of Europe, Moody invited Monod of Paris, Stoecker of Berlin, Pinder of Poland, and other European notables to conduct special meetings, and he also shared ministry with Thomas Spurgeon of New Zealand, Henry Varley of Australia, John McNeill of Scotland—famous English-speaking evangelists.

In Kansas City, Missouri was held Moody's last series, commencing November 1899. His committee was composed of Anglican, Baptist, Congregational, Disciples, Methodist and Presbyterian ministers.[24] There were the usual great crowds, but Moody showed signs of exhaustion. He told his friends: 'This is the first time in forty years of preaching that I have had to give up my meetings.' He rushed home and lingered little, leaving his loved ones 22nd December 1899.

Moody's ministry was a puzzle to unbelieving scholars. The distinguished historian, William Warren Sweet, insisted that 'the attempts of sociologists and psychologists to explain him seem trite and foolish.'[25]

It seems appropriate to point out that Dwight Lyman Moody was an evangelist, and that his organized campaigns of evangelism were not necessarily 'revivals' in the historic sense of the word, and that his calling cannot therefore be described as a revivalist, if such a word is also used to describe the ministry of men such as Evan Roberts.

Among classes that despised his homely ways, Moody stirred up supercilious enemies, yet he also inspired both loyalty and esteem in the best products of the universities. A man is known by his associates and his friends. Moody's co-workers were extremely able men. He made use of the musical talents of Philip P. Bliss and George C. Stebbins, besides those of Ira D. Sankey. Associated with him in preaching were men like D. W. Whittle, Reuben A. Torrey, A. C. Dixon, and J. Wilbur Chapman, Americans; and from Britain, Henry Varley, John McNeill, Henry Drummond, G. Campbell Morgan, and F. B. Meyer.

There were contemporary evangelists in sharp contrast. An Australian, John Alexander Dowie, born in Edinburgh in 1847 but pastor of a Congregational Church in Melbourne, withdrew from his denomination to build up an independent congregation in Melbourne. He appeared at the World's Fair in Chicago in 1893, and decided to stay in the Illinois metropolis. By 1895, Dowie had won a great following which met weekly in the Chicago Auditorium.[26]

In 1901, Dowie founded a Christian community on the shores of Lake Michigan forty miles north of Chicago, calling it Zion. The sale of tobacco, liquor, and drugs was prohibited and the use of pork banned. Every industry in town was under the control of the founder, John Alexander Dowie. His doctrines were generally evangelical, but he claimed to be Elijah the restorer, and he looked the part with his long white beard and benevolent appearance.

In 1903, Dowie proposed to take his gospel to the nation and the world and began by renting the vast Madison Square Garden in New York City in October. Vast crowds attended, but the doubters heckled him in the press. Something snapped in his brain one night, and out of his mouth there flowed 'a seething torrent of defiling invective.' The campaign was a huge failure, leaving Zion $300,000 in debt. Dowie died in delirium two years later, repudiated by his own denomination, next directed by Glenn Voliva who said the earth was flat.

While Moody dominated the American scene in evangelism and conducted a great campaign in Toronto in 1884, Canada produced its own effective evangelists in the Crossley-Hunter team in Canadian cities between 1887 and 1889. Crossley and Hunter followed the Moody pattern. A series in Ottawa was reported as 'the most extraordinary revival' ever known in Canada.[27]

Many other evangelists arising in the United States copied Moody. The 'Moody of the South'—Samuel Porter Jones of Alabama—had been converted in 1872. It was not till 1884 that Jones attempted evangelism on a city-wide scale, his campaigns in Memphis and Nashville launching him to fame. His preaching was blunt to a point of coarseness and vulgarity, but his evangelism was much in demand in the South.[28]

In 1887, B. Fay Mills became an evangelist, specializing in district combination of churches. Within seven years, he veered away to a kind of social gospel preaching, his elementary gospel message being more and more muted until he was backed chiefly by Unitarians. In 1899, Mills abandoned such evangelism—though in 1915 he resigned his Unitarian connections and returned reconciled to Presbyterianism.[29]

In Moody's opinion, the greatest evangelist of the late 1890s in the United States was J. Wilbur Chapman, whose ministry reached its greatest usefulness in the next decades. Britain's greatest evangelists of the Moodyan period were the Anglican Hay Aitken and the Presbyterian John McNeill, both of whom were related to the 1859 Revival in Britain.

Towards the end of Moody's lifetime, a genial Anglican, George Grubb, became an outstanding evangelist throughout the British Empire, being particularly successful in South Africa and Australia,[30] at which time, Gipsy Rodney Smith (born in 1860) arose to fame as a Free Church missioner.

There was much interest in Moody in South Africa, though he never visited the country.[31] Andrew Murray, a leader in the extraordinary awakening there in 1860, was thrust forth by a general movement in the 1870s, and in 1879, 1884, 1886, 1887, 1888, 1890, 1891 and 1897, engaged in campaigns of evangelism while maintaining his leading position in the Dutch Reformed Synod. Spencer Walton, an Englishman but domiciled in South Africa, became an effective evangelist among Europeans and Africans alike.[32]

The movement under Moody in Great Britain was paralleled by a series of awakenings in the Scandinavian countries, influenced by Anglo-Saxon Christianity more and more. A great revival commenced in Norway in the 1880s, it being particularly powerful in the town of Skien, but also effective in the western and the southern parts of Norway.[33]

Carl Olof Rosenius had died in Sweden in 1868, but his great work continued in strength within the state church. In 1876-77, yet another revival of evangelical Christianity occurred in Sweden.[34] One of the leaders of this movement was August Skogsbergh, who was called 'the Swedish Moody.' Another was Paul Peter Waldenström,[35] who had succeeded Rosenius as editor of the revival magazine founded by Scott.

Waldenström adopted an Anselmic view of the atonement of Christ, as a result of which those who followed him received much criticism from the leaders of the Church of Sweden.[36] They then formed in 1878 the Evangelical Mission Covenant (or Svenska Missionsförbund), retaining formal membership in the Church of Sweden but in fact operating as a free church somewhat as did the Wesleyan movement before separating from the Church of England. Those of the Rosenius revival movement in Sweden who did not follow Waldenström's lead continued their support of the National Evangelical Foundation (Evangeliska Fosterlands Stiftelsen), begun in 1856.[37] It was equally evangelistic. In United States, the Evangelical Mission Covenant denomination was itself formed of two revivalistic Lutheran synods in 1885.[38] It was entirely a free church, of evangelistic low-church traditions, as also was the Augustana Synod which served the Lutherans from Sweden without the approval of Swedish ecclesiastics.

A Swedish-born emigrant, Fredrik Franson, thoroughly converted in Nebraska, came to Chicago in 1875 to study the methods of Dwight L. Moody.[39] He became a member of the Moody Church and went forth as an evangelist with its blessing. In 1881, Franson crossed to Sweden, where he began to exercise a fruitful ministry in the chapels of the evangelistic sections of the Church. He extended his ministry to Norway with striking success. In both countries, the clergy of the State Churches offered opposition to his ministry, and this was repeated in Denmark in a greater degree. Yet in Copenhagen, in the New Year of 1884, Franson became the prophet of a great revival in the city. In 1885, Franson was arrested on false charges, imprisoned until some influential Norwegians at court interceded with Danish royalty, and was then finally banished from Denmark.

Theodor Christlieb, who had ministered in a Lutheran Church in London as pastor during the mid-nineteenth century Awakening, returned to serve later as professor of theology at Bonn, supporting fully the evangelistic cause in all the German States.[40]

Elijah Schrenk, a German missionary from Africa, attending Moody's meetings in London, wrote home: 'I want to become an evangelist.' Shortly thereafter a German-American Y.M.C.A. secretary named Frederick von Schlümbach held evangelistic campaigns in Berlin and Hamburg, resulting in a revival and in the foundation of the first German Young Men's Christian Association.

These and many other movements were soon brought together by Professor Christlieb, who founded the German Committee for Evangelism and a seminary to train evangelists. He began at Gnadau (in 1888) a series of conventions for both pastors and evangelists. Thus the forces of the Revival in Germany developed an evangelistic drive and the movement went on for thirty years. It took permanent form. From this resulted the German Association for Evangelism and Christian Fellowship which sent evangelists throughout the German lands, most remarkable of whom were Samuel Keller and Elijah Schrenk, who were inspired by Moody. German historians claim that the movement began a 'thirty years' revival' in Germany between 1880 and 1910 especially effective in the Established Church, and that several hundred thousand people were converted. The origins of this great German Awakening were mainly Anglo-American though the movement soon became thoroughly Germanic in personnel.

Protestantism in Poland, which had declined from its strength in early Reformation days, was mainly identified with Germans.[41] The same was true of Germanic landlords and their tenants in the Baltic States of Estonia and Latvia, where a peasant interest in Moravianism existed in spite of Russian imperial and German local tyranny.[42] In Hapsburg royal dominions, where a reactionary Romanism obtained, there were minorities of Protestants suffering disabilities.

In Hungary, the rationalism of the Napoleonic period gave way to an evangelical awakening, in which the British and Foreign Bible Society took part by promoting the sale of the Karoli Bible in Magyar. With the revival came a strong Scottish influence through a mission in Budapest. In 1849, full religious rights were first granted Protestants, then rescinded, and then renewed again in 1867.[43]

In Moody's days, Sunday Schools, Y.M.C.A. and Y.W.C.A., the Evangelical Alliance, the Student Christian Movement, and the Christian Endeavour movement entered Hungary. It is strange that although the Protestants of Hungary were equal to those of Denmark, Norway or Finland and were more than half of those of the Netherlands or Sweden, there was less revival and less missionary activity. In fact, Hungarian missionary activity did not even match that of the tiny French Protestant minority.

Lord Radstock, a product of the 1859 Revival in Britain, who had served against the Russians in the Crimean War, returned to Russia to witness to the upper classes in St. Petersburg in 1874 and again in 1877-78.[44] Among the converts within the aristocracy were Colonel Pashkov and Princess Natalia Lieven. Lord Radstock was followed by Friederich Wilhelm Baedeker, German-born British subject, who journeyed throughout the Russian Empire encouraging the evangelical believers, including Baptists, Mennonites, Stundists, Brethren and other Protestant groups.[45] That the two British evangelists made an impression on the Russian intelligentsia is seen by the fact that Dostoievsky wrote about Radstock in his works, while Tolstoi referred to Baedeker.

The Awakening of 1858-59 affected others parts as well. Among the humble peasants of the Ukraine, a revival had begun about 1860. Oncken, a Baptist leader from Germany, visited them in 1869. In 1884, a twenty years' persecution began, hurting both nobles and peasants. The Evangelicals continued to thrive. An engineer, I. S. Prokhanov, converted in 1886, founded the All-Russian Evangelical Union.[46]

22

VOLUNTEERS FOR SERVICE

A direct outcome of the 1858-59 Awakening was the formation of Christian Associations in the state universities of the United States and of daily prayer meetings (later to be known as Christian Unions) in the universities of Great Britain. Thanks to the energy and influence of a student leader named Luther Wishard, the Christian Associations affiliated themselves with the burgeoning Y. M. C. A. in the United States and Canada, an alignment that brought great good when the latter movement was evangelical in doctrine and evangelistic in practice, but which contributed to the dissolution of the student movement in the twentieth century.

In 1877, fifty or so of the two hundred student societies scattered across North America were affiliated with the Y.M.C.A., necessitating the formation of an Intercollegiate Young Men's Christian Association.[1] That same year, the student society at Cambridge formed the Cambridge Inter-Collegiate Christian Union. Oxford followed suit.[2]

Across the Atlantic, D. L. Moody had made an impression upon a brilliant young Scot, Henry Drummond. Drummond had shown real ability in at least two fields, science and theology, and commanded the respect of faculty and students in the University of Edinburgh.[3] Drummond lined himself up with Moody, and engaged in evangelistic personal work in university circles during Moody's campaigns and afterwards.[4] Drummond and student helpers participated with great effect in Moody's meetings elsewhere. Often Moody would summon Drummond by telegram to share in the conclusion of a campaign and continue the work. This cordial association between the unlettered Moody and the literate Drummond was to have effect upon the student world not only in Britain and America, but around the world.

In the Christian unions at the universities, the leaders were studying D. L. Moody carefully, wondering whether he would be able to reach the cultured and sophisticated undergraduates of Cambridge and Oxford. Edinburgh and Glasgow were not residential universities, their students residing in lodgings nearby in their respective cities. Nor were the Scots inclined to snobbery. Would Moody be able to touch Oxford and Cambridge? Little did they know that he would be able to reach universities around the world thereby.

From the resultant university contacts grew a movement among students which reached a quarter of a million in its membership, and from its missionary arm in North America alone, more than sixteen thousand went to the missionfield.

One of the many upper-class Englishmen moved by D. L. Moody was Edward Studd, a wealthy, retired tea-planter, who had made his fortune in India. Studd had three sons at Cambridge: Kynaston, George and Charles. Kynaston was a member of the university cricket team; George was captain of cricket; and Charles, better known as C. T., was an all-England cricketer of national fame.[5]

Three hundred Cambridge men had petitioned Moody to come to Cambridge during his earlier British tour, but now Kynaston Studd had rounded up support among his colleagues to invite the American to conduct a mission at the University. Handley Moule signed the invitation reluctantly, and so did other Cambridge men. The Cambridge Prayer Union through its committee invited its friends to join in asking Almighty God 'that it would please Him to grant to our university a measure of the religious revival which has lately been vouchafed to other parts of His church.'[6]

Moody was already famed in Britain when, in 1882, he consented to conduct a preaching mission in Cambridge for university students.[7] The aristocratic undergraduates were utterly outraged that 'an illiterate American' presumed to lecture to them. They determined to show their objections and rebuff the trespassing evangelist. Word soon spread of the pranks that were to be played. Even Moody's friends were concerned, Handley Moule (the future Bishop) penning in his diary: 'Lord, be Thou really with me in this coming anxious, responsible time.'[8]

'There never was a place,' said Moody, 'that I approached with greater anxiety than Cambridge. Never having had the privilege of a university education, I was nervous about meeting university men.' He was not concerned without good reason, as events quickly proved.[9]

It was arranged that Moody and Sankey should speak and sing in meetings for the townspeople first, and these went off without an incident. The Corn Exchange, ill-suited to purposes evangelistic, was well-filled each time.

Seventeen hundred university men, attired in cap and gown, noisily crowded into the hall for the university meeting. Seventy undergraduates, displaying rare courage, joined in singing hymns, but the majority responded with vulgar songs. The Rev. John Barton, vicar of Holy Trinity parish, opened with prayer, to which some 'ill-mannered youths' responded with 'Hear, hear!' Sankey's first solo produced derisive shouts of 'Encore!' Cambridge proctors ejected several of the more rowdy disrupters.[10]

The proceedings went on in an uproar. Moody decided to preach upon 'Daniel in the Den of Lions,' a very appropriate topic. The Hebrew name Daniel has three syllables, and in English it may be pronounced with two, but Moody managed in one, which brought the house down in cheering and jeering, clapping and stamping. It was a trying time for Moody, but he kept his temper and his poise.[11]

Next day a ringleader, Gerald Lander of Trinity College, called at Moody's lodgings to apologize, saying that he had supposed that Mr. Moody was unfit to speak to gentlemen, but concluded that he, unlike his critics, was a gentleman.

Although seventeen hundred students had been counted in the first meeting in the Corn Exchange, only a hundred attended the second in a seated gymnasium, but they included Gerald Lander. On Wednesday, before a larger crowd, Moody gave an evangelistic appeal and after repeating it saw more than fifty men make their way to the inquiry room. One was Gerald Lander—afterwards Bishop of Hong Kong.[12]

Next night, a hundred or more waited behind for counsel. All through the week, clear-cut conversions were professed by intellectuals and athletes, many of them proving to be both deep and lasting. The final meeting in the Corn Exchange brought eighteen hundred hearers, and concluded a mission which proved to be the beginning of a worldwide, interdenominational student movement. Moule, kneeling beside Moody on the platform, heard him say: 'My God, this is enough to live for.'[13]

The next day, without the benefit of a Sunday start, Moody opened his mission in the Corn Exchange in Oxford, which was filled to overflowing. Bolder, he quenched attempts at rowdyism several nights running and gained a hearing for his messages. Audiences moved from Clarendon Assembly Rooms to the Town Hall, where Moody gathered inquirers in an aftermeeting, and a number made personal decisions for Christ.[14]

Moody's Oxford and Cambridge campaigns, like his earlier visits to Edinburgh and Princeton, had continuing effects in the lives of key personalities.

C. T. Studd had played for England against Australia, but was away in Australia playing against Australia's cricket elevens during Moody's Cambridge campaign. His brothers communicated the Moody challenge to him so he responded. Together with Stanley Smith, another outstanding athlete, he visited Edinburgh and stirred another generation of students, encouraging numbers remaining behind for counsel. Kynaston Studd and his brother Charles assisted Moody in his great London meetings. It is recorded that, on one occasion, D. L. Moody called upon a clergyman to offer prayer in the huge gathering, but the man of the cloth was so overwhelmed by the privilege of addressing Deity on behalf of so many thousands of people that he prayed on and on and on—-until Mr. Moody cheerfully invited the assembly to join in singing a hymn while 'our brother is finishing his prayer.' This utter frankness intrigued a young atheist, a medical student, who had wandered into the meeting. He returned and heard the Studd brothers speak, and thereupon committed his life— and the story is well known in the work of Sir Wilfred Grenfell of Labrador.[15]

Sir Montague Beauchamp, William Cassels, D. E. Hoste, Arthur and Cecil Polhill-Turner, Stanley Smith and C. T. Studd, all Moody's helpers and some his converts, offered themselves to work in China under the China Inland Mission, founded by Hudson Taylor in the wake of the 1859 Revival. They first became a remarkable witness team, named the Cambridge Seven, touring the British universities with their message, stirring up the students. No doubt, part of their extraordinary influence was due to their family circumstances as well as their reputations as athletes.[16]

Beauchamp was a nephew of Lord Radstock; Cassels was the son of an importer from Portugal; D. E. Hoste was the son of a brigadier-general; the Polhill-Turners were sons of a Member of Parliament; Stanley Smith was the son of a London West End surgeon; and C. T. Studd was the son of a wealthy man, a Master of the Hounds, a turf enthusiast. They were not all as famous as C. T. Studd as athletes; but they had each a reputation in sport.

The Cambridge Seven as a team or in pairs set about visiting Edinburgh and Glasgow, Liverpool and Manchester, Leicester and other English towns, delivering the message.

All this had an exciting effect upon the universities of Great Britain. Their visit had brought to white heat (to quote John Pollock, historian of the Cambridge movement) the religious revival among the students at Edinburgh kindled by Moody. There the theological colleges were overcrowded with Scots preparing for the ministry and missionfield. At Cambridge, five years of religious enthusiasm followed, with a marked increase in attendance at the Daily Prayer Meeting.[17]

D. E. Hoste, not a Cambridge graduate, was a dashing young officer of the British Army, whose brother William had been impressed by Moody at Cambridge. Hoste was converted through his brother's witness and Moody's ministry at Brighton, in 1882.[18] He succeeded Hudson Taylor as the general director of the China Inland Mission, which, until the 'liberation' of China by the Communist armies, was considered the largest Protestant missionary society in the world. Cassels became the first Anglican Bishop in West China. Each of the others served in China with distinction. (Later, Studd was to found a mission in the heart of Africa— this in turn became the Worldwide Evangelization Crusade, an international organization.)

Moody invited Kynaston Studd—in the present writer's youth, Sir Kynaston Studd, Lord Mayor of London and father of his good friend, Commander Ronald G. Studd—to spend an academic term on American campuses.[19] Another wave of awakening swept twenty colleges in those thirteen weeks. At Cornell, a law student named John R. Mott made a full commitment of his life, and emerged as the best-known student leader for half a century.[20]

Evangelical awakenings generally develop in four phases, reviving, evangelizing, missionary and social. The student movement of 1858 was primarily one of reviving the work of God among students, then evangelistic; Moody's ministry at Princeton and Cambridge, for example, was evangelistic with overtones of revival; now the rolling movement seemed about to develop into a missionary enterprise, one of the most remarkable in the history of the Christian faith. This movement was to last for thirty years.

A friend of Luther Wishard, Robert Mateer of Princeton, became leader of an Inter-Seminary Missionary Alliance which held its first convention in 1880 with two hundred and fifty students from thirty or more seminaries present;[21] these missionary-minded students, like their Y.M.C.A. friends, were strongly evangelical and evangelistic.

LutherWishard, as organizer and evangelist of the Inter-Collegiate Y.M.C.A., had tried hard to interest Moody in collegiate ministry, but had been rebuffed by the modest Moody, conscious of his academic deficiencies.[22] In 1884, after Moody's powerful impact on Cambridge became known, Wishard pleaded again with Moody, who consented to preach at a few colleges in 1885, including Dartmouth, Princeton and Yale. His college-slanted sermons, he knew, were few. He looked for help from his many faculty friends.

An outcome of Moody's growing interest in the student world was the convening of a college conference at Mount Hermon in Massachusetts in the summer of 1886, when some two hundred and fifty students from one hundred colleges attended, and Moody was as popular as any eminent lecturer. This first conference was entirely unprogrammed, and the students followed a course of lectures and activities which came about 'as the Spirit directed.'[23]

One of the college delegates was Robert P. Wilder, son of a retired missionary to India, who had already formed a student foreign missionary association at Princeton. The Wilder family, whose head had been one of the Williams College group of missionaries in the early 1800s, had been praying that a thousand students from American universities might be enlisted for foreign missionary enterprise. To every student who would listen, Robert Wilder presented the call of missions.[24]

Wilder succeeded in persuading Moody to set aside time for missionary talks, and this combination of prayer and presentation had its effect. One hundred delegates signed a declaration signifying their willingness to serve overseas.[25]

Consciously following the example of the Cambridge Seven, a team of committed students was formed to carry the call of missions to the college campuses: R. P. Wilder of Princeton; John R. Mott of Cornell; W. P. Taylor of Yale; and L. M. Riley of DePauw. Only Wilder was able to go, but he enlisted the help of a Princeton classmate.[26]

Robert Wilder and John Forman toured the universities and succeeded in enlisting about two thousand volunteers for missionary service.[27] McCosh of Princeton asked: 'Has any such offering of living men and women been presented in our age?' Seelye of Amherst replied that the movement was of larger proportions than anything of the kind in modern times. At first, Moody was cautious about the overflowing enthusiasm of the youngsters, but he continued to help them.

The volunteers increased their own numbers to about three thousand in the academic year, 1887-88.

Before Robert Wilder commenced his second missionary journey, it was decided to create a new organization, to be called the Student Volunteer Movement for Foreign Missions. Mott was made chairman of the new movement, a position that he held until 1920. John Forman crossed the Atlantic to communicate the enthusiasm for service to student hearers in the universities of Aberdeen, Edinburgh, London, Oxford, Cambridge and Belfast. Prof. Henry Drummond crossed the Atlantic and addressed the students. He received a welter of invitations to address scientific societies, but refused almost all of them. He returned to minister in American universities, Williams College being stirred, Dartmouth suspending all classes, Princeton pre-empting his time from morning till night, Yale giving him one of the busiest weeks of his life. Even Harvard heard him graciously. Drummond was attacked by conservatives for his attempt to bring both religion and science into harmony, and, although Moody had lined up with the conservatives, he stood by Drummond as a zealous evangelist and a great scholar. Drummond so extended his student ministry around the world.[28]

Luther Wishard returned the British visitors' calls by touring the universities of Cambridge, Oxford, Edinburgh and Glasgow in the spring of 1888. The summer he spent in Germany, France, Switzerland and Sweden.[29] Wishard extended his journey around the world, reporting conversions and calls to service everywhere.[30]

James B. Reynolds, another student volunteer, crossed the Atlantic to Oslo University. He also visited Stockholm, Lund and Copenhagen in 1889. In 1891, Robert Wilder visited universities in Britain, enlisting three hundred volunteers for missionary service.[31]

In 1890, Henry Drummond sailed for Australia and spent a profitable time challenging students in the universities of the southern continent. His days were numbered, however, for he fell ill in 1894 and died in 1897.[32] John R. Mott had organized the Student Volunteers in the universities of New Zealand and Australia before Drummond died.[33]

In 1893, a conference was called at Keswick, attended by a hundred delegates from twenty universities, and from it was created the Inter-University Christian Union. Donald Fraser, later a successful missionary in Central Africa, became its first secretary.[34]

These various developments resulted in the formation of the World's Student Christian Federation. The chief engineer was none other than John R. Mott.[35] The federation was fully consummated at the castle of Vadstena in Sweden, Dr. Karl Fries becoming Chairman and John R. Mott Secretary. (Both Mott and Fries—the writer met them in the 1930s—were ardent evangelists.)

The Student Volunteers sought to enlist every Christian in the objective of evangelizing the world. Their watchword was 'the evangelization of the world in this generation.' In their main objective, they were hugely successful, for in half a century, more than twenty thousand students reached the foreign mission fields of the Church, an astounding and heartening achievement. The greatest of church historians, Kenneth Scott Latourette declared his measured opinion that it was through the Student Volunteers in the various countries that a large proportion of the outstanding leaders in the spread of Protestant Christianity were recruited.[36]

Moody himself made provision for training of students who felt called to home and foreign missionary service. In 1883, some of his personal friends in Chicago were praying that he might (in proper time) found an institute for preparation of workers for worldwide missions.[37]

Once Moody was committed to the project, he announced his plans to his friends. Young Cyrus McCormick, a wealthy manufacturer, leaped up and offered fifty thousand dollars, which Moody calmly suggested he should make one hundred thousand dollars. C. T. Studd, on his twenty-fifth birthday, inherited a share of his father's fortune, and he decided to give it away to Christian causes. He sent five thousand pounds to Moody for the Bible Institute, expressing a hope that he would use part of it to evangelize Indian people.

In 1889, the Bible Institute was opened, with Reuben A. Torrey as its first superintendent.[38] Dr. Torrey was a staunch evangelical, and was a man of intellect, widely trained and as widely read, a product of Yale, Leipzig and Erlangen, devotionally reading the Greek New Testament.

Another convert of the 1858 Awakening built a following. Albert B. Simpson was born in the Maritimes, on Prince Edward Island, at the end of 1843, and was converted near Chatham in Western Ontario shortly after the beginning of the 1858 Awakening which had first appeared in Hamilton, Ontario, the previous October. Simpson had been convicted under the pungent preaching of Grattan Guinness.[39]

In 1861, Simpson appeared before the London (Ontario) Presbytery and was approved for study at Knox College in Toronto. He had already begun to preach, and continued to do so during college training. He was graduated in 1865 and became the minister of Knox Church in Hamilton eight years after the worldwide Awakening had begun there.

Simpson's second pastorate was in Louisville, Kentucky, where he led the ministers of the city in sponsoring a campaign of evangelism with Major Whittle and P. P. Bliss. He resigned after six years, and in 1879 moved to New York. After two years, he launched a wider evangelistic ministry, opening in 1884 a Gospel Tabernacle, completed 1889.[40]

In 1886, A. B. Simpson organized a summer convention at Old Orchard, Maine, out of which came the Christian and Missionary Alliance——at first interdenominational. Simpson laid emphasis upon sanctification and healing, but his primary motivation was the preaching of the Gospel to all nations before the coming again of Jesus Christ. When he died in 1919, the Alliance was worldwide.[41]

In the winter of 1880-81, there was a time of revival in Williston Congregational Church, in Portland, Maine. Its pastor, Francis E. Clark, wishing to conserve the blessing, organized a 'Young People's Society of Christian Endeavor' to call youth to greater dedication and service. The idea caught on, becoming an organization for encouraging young folk to participate in churchly activities.[42]

In 1886, one thousand delegates attended the first convention of Christian Endeavor, held at Saratoga Springs, two thousand the second one. In 1888, five thousand Endeavorers attended the convention in Chicago, and next year six thousand five hundred in Philadelphia, including overseas delegates. In 1890, eight thousand attended the St. Louis convention, followed by fourteen thousand in Minneapolis. In 1892, ten years after the foundation of the first society, thirty-five thousand Christian Endeavorers met in New York.

Denominational authorities adapted the idea, there being the Baptist Young People's Unions of Christian Endeavor, and Epworth Leagues also. During 1888, Francis Clark visited England, and three years later there were a hundred societies there, in six years a thousand.

In 1895, there were thirty-eight thousand C. E. Societies in the world, with 2,225,000 members. The movement was evangelical, evangelistic and church-related, suited to the climate of the day, which was evangelical and ecumenical.

23
MISSIONARY REINFORCEMENT

Moody's evangelism stemmed from the mid-nineteenth century Awakening, and in its turn was responsible for the movement among students. World missions owed much to reinforcements from the Student Volunteers, for more than five thousand volunteered in North America alone in thirty years, 1078 going to India, and 1615 to China.[1]

The Student Volunteers reinforced existing missionary enterprises throughout most of India. The older missions were supplemented by newer organizations from Britain and other parts of the British Empire, and from the United States, and from the Continent of Europe. A dozen societies in the second quarter became two dozen in the third quarter and fifty in the fourth quarter of the nineteenth century.[2]

The Young Men's Christian Association began its work in India in the 1880s,[3] and had founded thirty-five Indian Y.M.C.A.s in a single decade. It was less than a generation since the Y.M.C.A. had felt the impact of the mid-century Awakening, so it was natural to expect its ministry in India to be evangelistic as well as social in emphasis.

In 1862, the Salvation Army invaded India, spear-headed by Frederick St. George de Latour Tucker (son of an Indian civil servant, grandson of an East India Company director) who was converted through the ministry of D. L. Moody and became interested in the work of the Army. Later, Tucker married a daughter of General Booth. Under the Booth-Tuckers, the Salvation Army adapted itself to Indian conditions very thoroughly. Its uniform was modified to suit Indian custom, and its officers even went barefoot for a while, later adopting Indian sandals as footwear. There were many arrests suffered for outdoor preaching, but in due course public and legal toleration followed.[4]

The Student Volunteers were followed by the Christian Endeavour movement which reached India also in the 1880s, through the medium of American missionary organizations already in operation. Within a generation, there were 849 Societies, averaging forty members each.[5]

The Student Volunteers made a contribution to China too. At the time of the 1858-59 Revival, China had been scarcely opened to the Gospel. The China Inland Mission was organized to carry the Word to inland China, and to begin this work the first party had sailed for Shanghai in 1866.[6] In 1875, Hudson Taylor prayed for eighteen missionary reinforcements to raise the mission strength to about fifty; in 1881, he prayed for seventy; and in 1886, he prayed for one hundred more.

Where did Hudson Taylor find his men? As in the Cambridge Seven, he reached for the best and often found them in the universities. W. W. Cassels became a missionary bishop in West China.[7] (Gerald Lander, Moody's critic converted at Cambridge, became a missionary bishop in South China.) Within thirty years, the China Inland Mission counted more than six hundred missionaries in two hundred and sixty stations, with nearly five hundred national workers and more than five thousand communicants, though the mission did not set out to build churches.[8]

In the 1880s, the older missionary societies also moved into new territories—Anglican, Baptist, Congregationalist, Lutheran, Methodist and Presbyterian. Likewise, in 1888 the Christian and Missionary Alliance began its operations that were to extend all over China.[9]

As in India and elsewhere, the Young Men's Christian Association organized in China in the middle 1880s. The Y.M.C.A.s were evangelistic, hence enjoyed a rapid growth, stressing Chinese leadership which was immediately forthcoming.[10] H. H. Kung, later Prime Minister of China, in his early days served as a Y.M.C.A. officer—one among many professing Christians (such as Sun Yat-sen or Chiang Kai-shek) in the government of the Republic of China, one full generation afterwards. Christians were being prepared in China for a generation of leadership.

The practical ecumenism of the 1858-59 Revival was felt; the fact that almost all the missionaries in China were of revival-evangelistic background made it very easy to convene them in missionary conference to establish cooperation and comity.[11] In 1890, the second such conference sent out an appeal to the Protestant homelands to equip and send to China a thousand missionaries within five years. The numbers of Chinese communicants were about 50,000; they doubled in ten years, to increase five-fold within twenty-five years—following another worldwide awakening.

At this time, an awakening began in Japan. The work of evangelization had been proceeding slowly in Japan in the 1860s. In 1872, a Week of Prayer sponsored by the World's Evangelical Alliance was held in Yokohama, and there was an encouraging local revival.[12] In 1883, James Ballagh recalled the encouragement of the prayer times of the decade previous, and such was the effect on hearers that an intense revival ensued in all Japanese evangelical circles. Within a short time, the missionaries reported: 'A spirit of religious revival bringing times of refreshing from the presence of the Lord is spreading in Japan.'[13]

The awakening spread to the Aoyama Gakuin in Tokyo, whose staff and students were deeply moved. In 1884, the Week of Prayer at Doshisha University could not be stopped but ran on until March, two hundred students being baptized. The revival spread to Sendai in 1886. 'There were intense emotional upheavals, much confession and restitution, and many testimonies to the joy of new life in Christ.'[14]

Otis Cary has titled the sixth chapter of his history of Christianity in Japan 'Rapid Growth 1883-1888,' when the Protestant enterprise in Japan experienced remarkable growth through 'the beginning of a series of remarkable revivals that exerted a powerful influence upon Christians and through them upon the unbelievers.'[15] Churches became crowded with eager listeners. The word 'rebaiburu' gained a place in the Japanese Christian vocabulary. There were 'tears, sobbings and broken confessions of sin' among these supposed Oriental stoics. The Japanese showed themselves susceptible to the same religious feelings as Westerners.

Concurrently with revival, a dozen societies entered the country.[16] Japanese denominational organizations were then taking shape, such as Nippon Sei Ko Kwai, the Anglican Church of Japan. In 1890, foreign missionary personnel numbered more than five hundred, with about three hundred organized churches and thirty thousand members.

In seven years, adult membership increased from four to thirty thousand, evangelists from a hundred to four hundred, and self-support gained ground among virile Japanese congregations,[17] 'the springtime of Japan and the Church.'

Both Otis Cary (1909) and Iglehart (1959) in turn designated the decade following the period of rapid growth, a period of 'Retarded Growth,' and both attributed the decline to the theological speculations that chilled the faith of the pastors.[18] In the 1890s, a wave of liberalism in theology caused some pastors to leave the ministry, and within ten years, theological students declined in numbers from three hundred to less than one hundred. The optimistic predictions of the full conversion of the Empire to Christianity were not being fulfilled. The Christian faith was less influential in Japan than in China, yet Christianity had ceased to be an alien way of life in the sunrise kingdom.

The pattern was different in nearby Korea. It was in the 1880s that the Evangelicals made an entrance to Korea. American Presbyterians and Methodists bore the brunt of the invasion, though other nationalities and communions participated.[19] Not only was the background of the missionaries largely evangelical but the methods advocated by them were evangelistic, encouraging the Koreans to evangelize the country themselves. In Korea, the ground was being prepared for an evangelical revival on a national scale.

The same forces were at work in the Indonesian islands. Thanks to the influence of the revivals in the Netherlands, the policies of exploitation of the Netherlands Indies began to give way to policies of uplift.[20] The revivals not only affected colonial administration but gave birth to new missionary societies, generally of a more orthodox or a more evangelistic motivation. At the same time, in Indonesia the missionary societies drew closer in cooperation and comity. The next century was to witness indigenous awakenings.

American Methodists and Presbyterians had entered the Philippines even before annexation (in 1898) by the United States.[21] They were followed by American Baptists and other denominations, and the Christian and Missionary Alliance.

At the same time, the long-smoldering anger of many Filipinos against their Spanish regular priesthood led to the schism of the Independent Catholic Church of the Philippines, with Aglipay as its Archbishop. At first this church developed a Unitarian tendency, but afterwards swung into fellowship with the American Episcopal Church, regarded as a catholic-evangelical body. There were also other long hidden pro-evangelical movements coming to the surface.

In that other Malaysian-related island world, the austere French imperial domination of Madagascar brought travail to the missions operating there. Towards the end of the nineteenth century, a rebellion against French domination became an anti-Christian movement. Churches, schools and hospitals were destroyed, and many missions were left in ruins.[22] It was a severe setback to all Christian work.

Deliverance from the decline was manifest unexpectedly. A great awakening began through a movement known as the Disciples of the Lord which arose from the conversion of an old Betsileo solider, Rainisoalambo, who had dabbled in pagan sorcery.[23]

The Disciples of the Lord multiplied so fast that in the space of a few years they were found in every part of the great island of Madagascar. The revival, which was truly an indigenous work, emphasized the necessity of a personal experience of grace and the obligation of holy living. Belief in evil spirits played a large part in the awakening, and exorcisms were practised. Yet the movement increased a desire for self-improvement, added an impetus to social reform, and gave encouragement to national evangelism.

There were also stirrings on the western Asian mainland. The American Board missionaries reported an evangelical revival in Asia Minor in the year 1889 among the Armenians. The chief evangelist of the movement was the Rev. Haratune Jenanian of Tarsus.[24] There were three large Evangelical churches in Aintab, a town of 35,000. Response began in the smallest and spread to all three. Half the hearers were Gregorians. So great was the movement that missionaries and helpers around joined in the work. The attendances ranged from a thousand to two thousand, taxing all available space. Among the converts were gamblers and drunkards. In the accounting of several weeks, more than a thousand had professed conversion to God, 500 joining the church in services on two Sundays.

The work of the American Board in Turkey was marked by a number of seasons of revival.[25] In the 1830s, the mission was begun in Istanbul in the face of great opposition. The first church was formed in the late 1840s. Forty years later there were more than a hundred and twenty-five churches with weekly attendances trebling that figure, served by nearly ninety ordained pastors and by nearly nine hundred trained lay helpers.

As the years passed, the hostility of the old Gregorian Church towards Evangelicals passed, and not only were Evangelical pastors asked to preach in Gregorian churches but students were trained for the Gregorian priesthood by Evangelical teachers.

At this time, medical missions were planted in Palestine. The work begun in Syria under Mrs. Bowen-Thompson became an interdenominational British Syrian Mission,[26] later

Lebanon Evangelical Mission. In Baghdad in Iraq, Church Missionary Society work began in 1882, while Bishop Stewart of New Zealand reinforced the work in Iran.[27] The famed Islamic scholar and Christian missionary, Samuel Marinus Zwemer, arrived in Basra as a student volunteer in 1890, beginning a significant career.[28]

From 1875 to 1895, the United Presbyterian Mission of North America increased its Egyptian membership ninefold, drawing many Copts. In 1892, the North Africa Mission sent a scout to Egypt, but it was the Egypt General Mission, a revival product with its bases in Belfast in the North of Ireland, that developed a considerable work there.[29]

The Church Missionary Society moved into the Sudan in the 1890s, as did the Presbyterian Mission in Egypt, but their greatest gains were in the south among the pagans, Muslim resistance against Christianity being tenacious, as elsewhere in Islamic lands.[30]

In the late 1880s, the North Africa Mission extended its foothold in the cities of Morocco, Algeria and Tunisia, and in 1888, its work was seconded in Morocco by the Southern Morocco Mission and in Algeria by the Algiers Mission Band, both societies uniting with it three generations later. In the 1890s, North Africa Mission workers entered Libya.[31]

In 1893, the Sudan Interior Mission entered Nigeria and spread its chain of mission stations across the full width of the continent to Ethiopia.[32] Based on Canada, it became one of the largest interdenominational societies in the world.

In 1887, a student under Grattan Guinness, Samuel A. Bill, penetrated the Qua Iboe area of Nigeria, backed by a strong board in Northern Ireland.[33] The staunchly evangelical work grew to a Christian community of great proportions as the tribes became predominantly Christian.

In other parts of West Africa, the churches continued to grow. Much the same was true of East Africa, in spite of the initial hardships, and again, as elsewhere noted, the greatest advances came through indigenous awakenings.

Difficulties had multiplied in Uganda in 1885, yet the Anglicans gained a foothold. In 1888, the Baganda themselves overthrew Mwanga, but the Muslims counter-revolted and drove out the missionaries and dispersed the Christians. Civil war ensued, until those very men who had been so persecuted by Mwanga replaced him on his throne which in 1890 came under British control, a full protectorate being established in 1894.[34]

Alfred Tucker was appointed bishop in 1890, the year that Alexander Mackay succumbed, but the mission was still precarious until 1893 when a chain of circumstances changed the situation, from trial to triumph.

A Muganda reader, Musa, announced his intention of apostatizing to heathenism, and this so discouraged the missionaries that one, George Pilkington, sought mental and spiritual recovery on an island in Lake Victoria. Recovery came from a surprising quarter.[35]

Far away in South India, a Tamil Christian had found the secret of the victorious Christian life, becoming a great revivalist who won many thousands to Christ in Tamilnad and Kerala.[36] He penned a tract on the work of the Holy Spirit, a tract which found its way to Pilkington on a tiny island in a lake in East Africa. The message transformed Pilkington's life and ministry. He returned to his work a changed man and, like Tamil David, saw the message provoke a general revival, followed by thousands of conversions.

Roscoe, a colleague of Pilkington, described the outbreak of the revival at Mengo after the return of Pilkington from the island of Kome: 'We are in the midst of a great spiritual revival ... after the morning service, fully two hundred stayed behind to be spoken with.'[37]

The awakening spread throughout Uganda. In fifteen years the number of native lay teachers increased from 75 to 2032, communicants from 230 to 18,041, baptized Christians from 1140 to 62,716, and catechumens from 230 to 2563.[38]

George Pilkington lost his life in a Sudanese uprising in 1897, but the Baganda became ardent native evangelists, reaching many other East African tribes around them. An encouraging growth of the churches followed.

About the same time as the Uganda Revival, a spiritual awakening was reported from Jilore, north of Mombasa. The Anglican missionary reported an hour of preaching followed by a three hours 'endless song of praise.' In review in 1894, the Church Missionary Society noted that at the same station, Jilore, 'a season of revival a year and a half ago produced permanent effects in the spiritual earnestness of converts.'[39]

The Church Missionary Society in the 1880s had extended its work in Kenya, and (in 1891) the Church of Scotland missions among the Kikuyu developed into a considerable enterprise. They fell short of the success in Uganda which called forth commendations of significance.

A young statesman, Winston Churchill, added (1908) to the vindication of missions by leaders qualified to judge, contrasting the grotesque and pitiful welcome his party received from tribes in other parts of the African continent with the experience of entering Uganda—'another world' of 'clothed, cultivated, educated natives.'[40] In the account of his African journeys, he claimed that he had never seen better order or happier homes than in Uganda, 'where a few years ago pioneer missionaries were mercilessly put to death.'

Theodore Roosevelt, one of the world's great wayfarers, and an observer of keen insight in those days, completed a tour in East Africa in 1910. He commented:[41]

> . . . As soon as native African religions—practically none of which have hitherto evolved any substantial ethical basis—develop beyond the most primitive stage . . . they tend to grow into malign creeds . . .   Even a poorly taught and imperfectly understood Christianity, with its underlying foundations of justice and mercy, represents an immeasurable advance on such a creed. . . . Where, as in Uganda, the people are intelligent and the missionaries unite disinterestedness and zeal with commonsense, the result is astounding.

In 1886, the Evangelical Missionary Society for East Africa was formed in Berlin. Its main sponsor was Pastor Friedrich von Bodelschwingh of the Inner Mission at Bielefeld, a leader in the German Evangelical Awakening.[42] It soon moved across the newly acquired German territories, sharing opportunities with older German groups in East Africa.

Another interdenominational mission started operations. The Africa Inland Mission was begun in 1895 by Peter C. Scott, who revived Krapf's dream of planting a chain of mission stations across Africa, beginning in Kenya, Tanganyika, and the Congo.[43] Throughout the 1880s and 1890s, missions of various kinds, denominational and otherwise, spread throughout the Congo basin.

In 1885, A. B. Simpson and the Christian and Missionary Alliance sent their missionaries to the Congo and began a great work.[44] Guinness sent out another mission, Congo Balolo Mission, in the 1880s.

The Swedish Mission Covenant, a product of the Awakening in Sweden,[45] commenced its Congo operations in the 1880s. The Paris Evangelical Mission shared Equatorial Africa (Congo) with the American Presbyterians, who also entered

Cameroons, where a Baptist effort begun in 1848, extended by George Grenfell, was transferred to the Basel Mission when the Germans raised their flag in 1887.[46] A mass movement of Bantu folk toward Christianity soon followed, which built in twenty-five years a church of 15,000.

In South Africa, Charles Pamla ministered in Lesotho until the outbreak of the Basuto War of 1880, which almost cost him his life as an open advocate of peace. He returned to Butterworth in the Transkei and ministered the Word with much success. At East London, Pamla's fiery preaching resulted in the conversion of Xhosas, Cape Coloured and Europeans. So many servants of the Europeans were detained at the penitent form that angry Europeans complained to the magistrate, who forbade a native drummer to beat the drum calling the people to the meetings. When the African police went to arrest whoever was beating the drum, they found a European converted through Pamla's preaching.[47]

Wherever he ministered, in Queenstown or East London, in Pondoland or Tembuland, it was said that the mantle of William Taylor had fallen on Charles Pamla. Among the Baca on the banks of the Umzimkulu River, Pamla lived in danger of his life because of his challenge to the forces of darkness; yet whole kraals of heathen professed conversion. In 1890, when superintendent at Tembeni, Pamla raised the membership from about 300 to more than 5000.

W. Spencer Walton, an English protege of the Afrikaner, Andrew Murray, made a great contribution to African evangelism. He had visited South Africa prior to his conversion, and in 1888 he accepted an invitation to campaign in Cape Town. The Y.M.C.A. Hall became too small, so meetings were adjourned to the Metropolitan Church, thence to the great Exhibition Buildings, where hundreds of people were converted to God and the city was stirred.[48]

The awakening continued in revival meetings up country. Spencer Walton returned to England, but in 1889 he helped organize (with Andrew Murray's backing) the Cape General Mission. The object of the Mission was to evangelize the European population of South Africa, but the sponsors were so committed to Keswick doctrine and dynamic that they soon set up the South African Keswick Convention in Wellington.

Walton and his associates were led to invade one of the neediest of Bantu areas in South Africa, Swaziland. It was not long before the Mission became the interdenominational South Africa General Mission (Africa Evangelical Fellowship)

Each new invasion of Latin America by the forces of Evangelicalism followed an awakening in sending countries. This was true in the case of the Student Volunteer movement between 1890 and 1920.

The Christian and Missionary Alliance began its missionary enterprise in Latin America in the 1890s, stressing revival and evangelism.[49] At the same time, the Regions Beyond Missionary Union founded by the revivalist Grattan Guinness entered Peru. The Help for Brazil Mission and the South American Evangelical Mission working in other Latin countries joined forces to form the Evangelical Union of South America.

In 1890, through C. I. Scofield, an associate of D. L. Moody, the Central American Mission was formed as an interdenominational society to take the Gospel to the republics of Central America.[50] After the close of the Spanish-American War, Protestant missions entered the islands of Cuba and Puerto Rico, gathering adherents very rapidly.[51] The character of these missions thus engaged was, as usual, evangelical and evangelistic, and so remained.

Meanwhile, the Moravians at the mid-century had begun a mission on the Mosquito Coast, on the Caribbean side of Nicaragua. Originally an English buccaneering settlement, its population was Negro and Mulatto as well as Indian. In the year 1881, an extraordinary awakening started with confession of sins and restitution of wrongs which resulted in so many conversions that the church membership increased from a thousand or more to three thousand or more in one decade.[52] There were awakenings in many other fields as dedicated missionaries and revived people responded.

In most cases, a generation of pioneering and teaching passed before the infant churches were themselves to experience the phenomena of true revival. When these awakenings came in their courses, unparalleled advances were made in a vast territory which less evangelical societies were willing to leave to the Roman-established Churches long moribund. If ever an invasion of a territory were justified, the invasion of Latin America by Protestant missions was obviously a necessity.

It can be seen that the decades following the rise of the Student Volunteer movement were years of advance wherever an Evangelical cause existed. Volunteers on the field, as at home, were committed to the dynamic that won them in the first place.

24
SOCIAL INFLUENCE, I

It is not easy to gauge the social influence of a spiritual awakening. Lasting benefits have been secured by individuals (influenced therein) either working alone, organizing action groups, mobilizing public opinion or lobbying for legislation.

If it is legitimate to trace the influence of an awakening through a revived or converted disciple to his life work in Christian ministry at home or abroad, then it is legitimate to do the same in the life of an enlightened Christian moved in the same revival to devote himself to service (in the social or political sense) for the good of humanity. The same Lord is interested in the material as well as the spiritual welfare of His creatures, regenerate or unregenerate.

The great social reforms were seldom spontaneous. So Wilberforce did not wait for the accord of the Convocations of Canterbury and York, nor did Howard enlist the Wesleyan Conference. Rather they went straight to the seat of power and the heart of the matter, and spoke as enlightened saints possessing the privileges and responsibilities of citizens.

There have been conscientious Christians on either side of every great social issue that has agitated either Church or society or both. Social action cannot wait on unanimity among the companies of believers, influenced as they are by upbringing, prejudice, vested interests, popular ideas. If unanimity is impossible, the Church must minister to those who differ as well as to those who agree.

The forum of the Church is not the fulcrum of reform. It is in parliament or palace that the decisions are made. But it often takes preaching or propaganda or public protest, as well as prayer, to persuade possessors of power. Violence is forbidden the servant of God, though there is no denial of the use of force against evildoers by legitimate authority.

Social progress is the interest of every citizen, and not of Christians only. A Buddhist in Thailand cannot join with a missionary in proclaiming the Good News of Jesus Christ, but they can work together for the good of the country. Social witness, therefore, must be mainly a matter of persuasion.

Following the mid-century Awakening, Britain maintained the lead assumed fifty years earlier in undertaking social reform and relief. There were many reasons for this.

It is an American historical opinion that the 1858 Revival had little effect on the social welfare of the American people. Rather its effects were suspended while the nation's energies were being consumed by the War between the States,[1] a war with far-reaching social after-effects.

During that war, Christians engaged in social action; the United States Christian Commission brought spiritual good, intellectual improvement, and social and spiritual welfare to Federal troops; there were Christian organizations also that cared for the welfare of Confederate soldiers.[2]

Negroes were given as much protection as war permitted. Suddenly, in the course of hostilities, slavery was swept away. What Christians were striving for by peaceful agitation became mandatory almost overnight by military decree. Emancipation, however, did not occur in a moral vacuum.[3]

In post-war years, the American Evangelicals found British social enterprises ready to adopt. The 1858-59 Evangelical Awakening, while it was primarily evangelistic, had developed a humane spirit as liberal as its theology was conservative. Commenting on a single outcome of the great Revival, G. M. Trevelyan affirmed that it had 'brought the enthusiasm of "conversion" after Wesley's original fashion to the army of the homeless and unfed, to the drunkard, the criminal and the harlot,' treating 'social work and care for the material conditions of the poor and outcast as being an essential part of the Christian mission to the souls of men and women.' This tribute belongs to the 1858-59 Awakening as a whole, not only to a very worthy part.[4]

One of the first effects of the Awakening of 1858-59 was the creation of new and intense sympathy with the poor and suffering. 'God has not ordained,' protested Lord Shaftesbury, 'that in a Christian country there should be an overwhelming mass of foul, helpless poverty.'[5]

A revival school of Christian philanthropists soon arose, seeking to go straight to the heart of the slums with its practical Samaritanism, yet always ready to cooperate in all wise legislative improvements. So, as this Awakening intensified the fervency of faith, denominational schemes, organizations and committees were multiplied; numberless philanthropic institutions, asylums, homes, refuges, and schools were founded.[6]

As before, Shaftesbury was spokesman for evangelical social reform.[7] He originated more Royal Commissions of social investigation than any parliamentarian in all British history, extending benefits to all classes of working people.

During 1864 and 1867, Industrial Extension Acts were passed, practically universalizing provisions of workmen's protection. In 1865, Lord Shaftesbury tackled the problem of agricultural gangs and so relieved the children of the countryside from a bondage as brutal as that endured by their townsfellows in earlier decades. In 1872, Shaftesbury worked for the abolition of use of children in brickyards. His most striking victory was passing legislation forbidding the use of little boys to clean house and factory chimneys.

The Seventh Earl of Shaftesbury was not without faults, of course. As an aristocrat of class-conscious times, he upheld the superiority of his order, detested trade unions, and was occasionally a narrow-minded diehard. He bitterly opposed the Salvation Army and refused to reconsider an opinion hard to excuse.[8]

There is an immediate connection between an evangelical awakening and educational hunger.[9] In Great Britain in 1815, elementary schools were entirely private.[10] Two decades later, Lord Ashley (later Shaftesbury) petitioned the Queen to provide education for the working classes. As insisted by Evangelicals, the State contributed a measure of support to elementary schools. In 1870, their recommendations were fulfilled in an Education Act, setting up public day schools. A million or more were in attendance in England in 1870; two million or more in 1885. This had a profound effect upon the countries of the overseas Empire.

During the 1859 Awakening in Dublin, some members of a brilliant family named Barnardo professed to accept Christ as Saviour in the Metropolitan Hall series. Two of these Barnardo brothers tried to persuade their younger brother, Tom, but he scoffed. Nevertheless he attended the meetings and witnessed the striking demonstrations of spiritual conviction. These he explained away as emotional hysteria and psychological phenomena, yet in spite of his subtle arguments he was set to thinking. An address by John Hambledon in the same place some weeks later caused him such conviction that long after midnight he sought, in great distress and with many tears, his brothers' help.[11] Young Barnardo heard a call to missionary service and soon volunteered— but tragic discoveries in the dismal East End of London

led him into his life-work, the founding of Dr. Barnardo's
Homes, the world's largest private orphanage system. Other
great orphanages were founded throughout the country.[12]

Young and Ashton, in their study of British social work
in the nineteenth century, specified Evangelicalism as the
'greatest single urge' of humanitarianism, saying that the
sentiment of human benevolence and its practical expression
derived directly from religious influence. 'It came from the
quickened knowledge, born of religious revivalism, that all
men were the children of God and loved by Him.'[13]

The same forces were at work in American experience.
A Christian man, John Augustus, a cobbler in Boston, offered
in 1841 to bail out a drunkard. The Massachusetts Court
agreed to it and, in the next two decades, this Christian man
bailed out two thousand people who might have otherwise
become criminals.[14] By the time of the Awakening, the vital
experiment had succeeded. The example was followed.

The Probation of First Offenders became law first in the
State of Massachusetts in 1878, and a similar law passed
in Britain in 1887, though preceded there by the Youthful
Offenders Act of 1854, and the Discharged Prisoners Act of
1862, likewise through Christian prompting.[15] Sarah Martin
and Mary Carpenter, who achieved so much for the care of
prisoners in Britain, were both dedicated Christian women
who had before them Fliedner's example from Germany.

The Awakening of 1858-59 had an immediate effect upon
the ancient practice of prostitution. It was a far cry from
medieval days when the Bishops had licensed a row of houses
of ill-fame near London Bridge; and a long time since the
Puritans of Cromwell's day had made fornication a felony,
punishable by death on the second occasion.

The industrial revolution aggravated the problem. Slum
squalor and drunkenness made many women reckless. By
the mid-nineteenth century, venereal disease was rampant
in London, and in the 1860s became the target of regulative
legislation, approved and disapproved on moral grounds.[16]

One of the first startling stories from the Ulster Revival
of 1859 was that of a prayer meeting being held by the newly
converted inmates of a brothel. A policeman reported seeing a group of fourteen prostitutes making their way to a
home of rehabilitation, the result of a visit to a prayer
meeting in Belfast. Dr. Hugh Hanna, in the same city, noted
that prostitutes were prompted to seek salvation after noting
the falling off in business.[17]

In the earlier months of the 1860 Revival in the city of London, attempts were made to reclaim the prostitutes who frequented the West End. A series of evangelistic meetings was held for prostitutes only, arranged at midnight or later. At the outset, many fallen girls burst into tears when addressed by the saintly Baptist Noël who talked very tenderly to them. The sponsors took a score of penitents to houses of rehabilitation. A thousand women were rescued in a year of the operation of the mission.[18]

The work was carried on by a rare champion. In bereavement, Josephine Butler sought to share the greater pain of other unfortunates, and thus found her life work in social welfare in London. In visits to prisons, where she shared in the menial tasks of the women, Josephine Butler was confronted with the evil of state patronage and regulation of vice. She dedicated herself in righteous indignation to the abolition of the evil. Concentrating upon the inequality of suspected women before the law, Josephine Butler worked for repeal of the obnoxious legislation that made government the official supervisor of iniquity.[19]

By the year 1877, more than eight hundred committees (provincial and metropolitan) had gathered eight thousand petitions with more than two million signatures submitted to Parliament. A Select Committee of Parliament (1879 onward) reported adversely, so Mrs. Butler rallied Christian forces in prayer 'so that the prayers of the people of God would be as the incense of Aaron, when he ran between the living and the dead.' The Acts were suspended in 1883, and repealed in 1886.[20] 'No other woman in history,' said Dame Millicent Fawcett, the social reformer, 'had such a far-reaching influence or effected so widespread a change in public opinion.'

Other great victories in social reform were won, for example, by Ellice Hopkins, and by Bramwell Booth with his associate, the journalist W. T. Stead. In a nationwide crusade against the white-slave traffic, Stead demonstrated (in a morally innocent but technically guilty way) that young girls could be inveigled into involuntary servitude of the most vicious kind.[21] His crusade was followed by national and international action carried on by the League of Nations.

For ninety years, the charge was reiterated by enemies of the 1859 Revival that the excitement brought about a sad increase of sexual promiscuity. Even Charles Dickens was guilty of declaring that 'the most immoral scenes take place on Sunday nights.'[22] There was much evidence to the contrary.

Most of the instances quoted by observers of the Revival concerned the reform of professional prostitutes rather than promiscuity and its outcome, illegitimacy. There were no compulsory registrations of births in Ireland in those days, but the Scottish figures indicated a decrease in rural cases, and a considerable reduction of the annual increase in urban areas; the all-Scotland figures showed a tiny fractional rise in illegitimacy year by year, except in 1860, when the 1859 Awakening had its full effect.[23]

A charge of increased promiscuity is easy to make in the absence of statistics to contradict selected examples of sin. Since the first publication of the present author's studies on the subject, this charge has not been repeated. Without a doubt, the excitement of the times provided more temptation for young people, due to sympathetic reaction.

In the year 1859, the young Swiss businessman Henri Dunant followed the French Emperor Napoleon III to North Italy, hoping to arrange business contracts. Unwittingly he found himself a spectator at the bloody battle of Solferino, fought between the armies of the French and Austrians.

Henri Dunant was of a prominent evangelical family and already active in the Young Men's Christian Association of Geneva.[24] Among those who had made a profound impression upon his thinking were Elizabeth Fry, famed as a prison reformer, and Florence Nightingale, famed as a military nurse.[25] Dunant was expert in both business and evangelism and maintained his family interests.

Dunant was horrified by the suffering of the wounded and dying on the battlefield. He helped as best he could in the days that followed, noting the sincere if unskilled efforts of local people to alleviate their suffering. He wrote 'A Memory of Solferino' and published it in 1862, sending it to statemen and leaders throughout Europe. As a result, a Geneva Convention was held in 1864 and from its findings and decisions came the Red Cross Movement.[26]

Not everyone expected to help proved willing. Some of the military leaders resented the intrusion of civilians on the battlefield. To Henri Dunant's sorrow, even Florence Nightingale witheld her support,[27] saying that the succor of the wounded in war was the business of government. But there was enough help forthcoming to speed the Red Cross on its mission of mercy and it spread throughout the world, by no means an evangelical agency but an evangelical idea whose time had come.

Timothy L. Smith, in his able study of 'revivalism' and social reform, made a pertinent observation concerning conditions in the United States at that time:[28]

> The rapid growth of concern with purely social issues such as poverty, working men's rights, the liquor traffic, slum housing, and racial bitterness is the chief feature distinguishing American religion after 1865 from that of the first half of the nineteenth century.

The United States was being rapidly industrialized, and the Christian Gospel was beginning to influence the situation. Evangelical sentiment was expressed by Mrs. Barnardo thus: 'The State should deal with it, but does not: the Church of Christ must!'[29] Responsibility of the State was recognized.

In the same sequence of logic, once the State has undertaken its responsibilities in the way of education, medicine and the like, there is no longer the same urgency or even reason for missioners to shoulder the burden. Their very limited funds could be put to better use elsewhere.

In the homelands of Evangelical Christianity, the step-by-step improvement of social conditions, the leavening of the lump by the Christian conscience, was accompanied by a development of a social impetus by Society itself, so that it was no longer necessary for Christians to initiate ideas for new social improvements—they simply joined efforts with other enlightened citizens. Their ministry of pioneering was channeled more and more into needier fields abroad. There, where the social conscience was often feeble, they were free to combine their urgent evangelism with urgent social betterment, their hosts accepting the former so long as it was accompanied by the latter.

This Christian service was so very different from the practice of the Communists, who were often committed to the worsening of conditions so that bloody revolution would follow the frustration of social progress.

The founding father of Communism, the anti-Christian Karl Marx, was of purest Jewish stock, but his father had become a Protestant, and had him baptized in infancy. Marx was not ignorant of Christianity of the evangelical conscience. He was raised during the Lower Rhineland revival, and his sister-in-law was active in it, when tremendous social improvements were being accomplished by Evangelicals, such as Theodor Fliedner. Marx was educated during a time of social betterment, rather than oppression, and it was not until 1848 that reaction set in.

Arnold Toynbee has described Communism as a Christian heresy, and certainly it sprang out of the Christian social conscience rather than out of Islam or Buddhism, even though it reacted bitterly against many basic Christian beliefs and practices.

Marx was in London during the great Revival of 1860 onward.[30] Marx founded his International in 1864 and stayed in its company or at the desks of the British Museum. He was a contemporary of Lord Shaftesbury and of his reforming friends, and he was still a resident of London when D. L. Moody came to preach.[31] He derided the Moody campaigns, if his friend Engels be accepted as a reliable authority. Marx became so obsessed with his dogma that he learned to hate Christians for doing good and so delaying the day of violence. He was impatient with the evolutionary methods of all Christian social reformers.

As Marx had rebelled against Christianity and its ethics and methods, he did not understand the Acts of the Apostles who turned their world 'upside down' by persuasion rather than by resort to violence. Christian meekness Marx considered cowardice; Christian humility he considered self-contempt; Christian steadfastness he put down as abasement; and Christian obedience he put down as subjection; while Christian kindness he called obsequiousness. For the rule of God in society he substituted a war of the classes; for love, he substituted hatred. He denied God's existence, and promoted atheism.

It was interesting that Marx published in 1859 (the Year of Grace) a trial volume of what was afterwards re-written and entitled 'Das Kapital,' published eight years later. In it was found the rationale of revolution.

Communism was little more than a nuisance movement until well into the twentieth century. After the Russian Revolution, it took on itself the fervency and trappings of a cult, calling for whole-hearted dedication of life and purpose. Its atheistic character remained unmodified despite expediences of propaganda and policy.

Christian socialists found the Marxist spirit very different to their own temper and motives. They disagreed with Marx about God, about the nature of man, about the Christian morality and the purpose of life—about so many things that it was obvious that they agreed in only a few points, the need of reform of society and its regulation. They believed that man could not live by bread alone.

25
SOCIAL INFLUENCE, II

One of the most overlooked factors in the development of backward countries has been the contribution of missions and missionaries. No other voluntary agency in all the world has achieved so much good and so little harm. Hence missionaries have stayed on where civil power evacuated.

The social influence of the 1858-59 Awakening carried over to the mission fields of the world. The influence of the missionaries was circumscribed by their relationship to the holders of power: in other words, in India and in southern Africa, the missionaries could appeal to the British as the colonizing or protecting power, either directly or by stirring up the evangelical conscience at home; whereas, in a country such as China or Japan, the missionaries had no power at the imperial courts, other than good example and persuasion. The same was true of Argentina and Brazil, where a different form of Christian faith held sway.

Generally speaking, the colonial powers were indisposed to interfere with their subjects' way of life, providing the government and commerce were not disrupted thereby. They welcomed the aid of the missionaries, but supported them only up to a point, and, in certain countries, they opposed them and ardently defended the native religion and culture.

The missionaries were scarcely ever able to achieve results in such fields as the rights of working men, for the simple reason that the working force was nowhere as near full development as in the industrialized countries. There were other factors also, the gap between employers and employed in standards of living, which was considerable in countries of homogeneous race as well as in those where the race factor further complicated matters.

There was little that the missionaries could do regarding sexual morality. They discouraged polygamy among their own converts, but were unable to alter public opinion about the matter. They discountenanced primitive puberty rites as breeders of immorality, but their rules were not binding outside their followings. They disapproved of promiscuity, but what did that matter to the tribes people who tolerated it? Their influence was not fully effective until cultural disintegration occurred, and the detribalized people sought a more suitable way of life in modern times.

It was necessary, therefore, for the missionaries to concentrate upon education and medical services, for in every country there was manifested a minimum of objection to such benefits to all classes, including the lowest. And in these two fields, they were second to none.

The 1860 Revival's effect on South Africa has been noted. Not only did the Awakening move the Afrikaners to engage in missionary activities on their northern frontiers, schools being founded along with churches, but the Taylor Awakening profoundly moved the Xhosa and Zulu communities, leading to 'an era of education' among them, to quote an historian.[1]

Using Southern Africa as a base, missionary societies penetrated Central Africa. As late as the year 1875, there were in Malawi 'no schools, no teachers, no pupils, and nobody who could read.'[2] The Church of Scotland, influenced by its educational tradition and its recent renewal in the Awakening, initiated a successful educational system based at Blantyre, with 57 schools and 3643 scholars; and the United Free Church of Scotland, based at Livingstonia, maintained an even more remarkable system of schools, 15,765 pupils attending 207 institutions—all built up in thirty years.

In Central Africa, industrial missions were maintained by several societies so specializing. At the turn of the twentieth century, the Zambesi Industrial Mission cultivated thousands of acres, largely in coffee and cotton, and useful trades were taught in forty schools based on ten stations, useful at a time when there were thousands of refugees from the terror of the Ngoni and other raiders.[3]

It was the same in other parts of the African continent. By the end of the nineteenth century, the Church Missionary Society alone was maintaining in East Africa a grand total of 262 schools, with 26,847 pupils. The educational policy of the society was concerned with the elementary schooling of its entire body of converts and inquirers. Sir Harry Johnston estimated that 200,000 of these had been taught to read in a single generation.[4]

It was many years before the rest of Africa was opened up for education. But it is significant that the earlier the missionary penetration, the higher the proportion of the population in school today. Even so, education was a mission by-product, and not the major emphasis of missions. Most missionaries engaged in it automatically. And the same was true of medical work. The missionaries built hospitals all over Africa, and provided the only worthy medical service.

It was after the 1858-59 Revivals in America and Britain that medical missionaries were activated in all India. The Scottish Presbyterians began a medical work in Rajasthan in 1860, employing medical evangelists who dispensed medicine and the Gospel.[5] Other Scots established hospitals at principal mission stations in the same period. Other missions adopted the plan. Before the '58 Revival, there were only seven medical evangelists in the entire Indian sub-continent, but their numbers quadrupled by 1882 and increased to 140 in 1895, with 168 Indian doctors assisting them.[6]

In the decade of the Revival, Clara Swain as a fully qualified doctor began her work among Indian women at Bareilly, where she opened a women's hospital in 1874.[7] Other lady doctors followed, British sponsors founding Zenana Medical missions to meet the needs of secluded women.

Christian Institutes for training doctors and nurses followed the foundation of hospitals. In 1881, a training hostel was begun at Agra, and in the years following, Dr. Edith Brown founded a School of Medicine for Christian women in Ludhiana, Dr. William Wanless one for men at Miraj, and Dr. Ida Scudder another for women at Vellore, serving north and central and south India, attracting capable students.[8]

Their standards were necessarily low, but, as a result of upgrading, the Medical Colleges at Vellore and Ludhiana and Miraj became fully-fledged Christian Medical Colleges for men and women from all parts of India.

The evangelical impact on nursing was felt in India too, and it is sufficient to say that 90% of all nurses throughout India (surveyed in World War II) were Anglo-Indian or Indian Christians, and that four-fifths of all Christian nurses were trained at mission hospitals.[9]

The missionaries tackled the 'white scourge.' The leading tuberculosis sanatorium in all of Asia is that of the Union Mission in southern Andhra. Sixty hospitals, homes and clinics for lepers were founded or subsidised by the Mission to Lepers which began in 1874 when three ladies in Dublin collected money for relief of leprosy. Cochrane and Brand, evangelical missionaries, became world famous specialists in Hansen's disease, and other missionary doctors made significant contributions to medicine and health in India.[10]

From the days of William Carey, evangelical missionaries sought to improve Indian agriculture. Carey had published valuable horticultural catalogues, and urged the missionary societies to send out men qualified to teach agriculture and to preach. The contribution of missionaries to agriculture in India is beyond computation. A case in point is Allahabad Agricultural Institute, founded by Sam Higginbotham, well-known agricultural missionary and evangelist.[11]

Mission schools, though by no means the last word in technology and education, introduced not only better animal husbandry and agricultural methods, but inculcated much-needed ideas of personal and social hygiene, prophylaxis against disease, and improvement of diet, resulting in a vast enlargement of living standards which in turn challenged traditional Indian superstitions.

The 1858-59 Awakenings were felt in India in the 1860s. Not only did they bring out a contingent of dedicated missionaries, but they stirred the Indian Christian communities too. Kerala, at the southwest corner of India, shared in a like movement beginning in 1861 and climaxing in 1873. People in Travancore, as the native state was known, were 33% nominal Christian. Compared with other rulers, the Rajahs were enlightened men. Among the non-Christians, women were held in higher respect than in other parts of India.

Entrance of the Church Missionary Society to Travancore had had a startling effect on the ancient community of Syrian Christians in Kerala. English schools were begun in 1834, and thirty years later a vernacular education committee, using Malayalam, was established by the state.

Kerala early had the benefit and blessing of two Christian colleges, Kottayam College which was begun by the C.M.S. and Alwaye College, a wholly Indian Christian institution. A University was established in Trivandrum.[12]

By 1891, there were 2,418 institutions of all classes and grades with 104,616 pupils. By 1901, there were a hundred and fifty thousand pupils, 25% in state schools. In 1931, there were 2700 students in Kerala colleges, more than fifty thousand in English schools, and more than half-a-million in primary schools. Travancore led the rest of India in literacy in 1931, with 23.9%. Kerala maintains its lead.[13]

Missionary education in China developed the same way as in India, with obvious differences, the absence of a conscientious colonial power, the lack of a caste system, the use of a hallowed system of classical education.

The Protestant missions became involved in education, beginning with primary schools, then secondary schools and a few colleges. The moot question, whether English should be taught as a language or medium of instruction was debated. The missionaries' schools and high schools and colleges were not designed to prepare for the traditional civil service. They were in the modern mold, arts and sciences.[14]

During the 1859 Awakening in Wales, David Morgan conducted a meeting in a Carmarthen village, reporting pessimistically: 'It was a very hard service.'[15] One of the converts, a lad named Timothy Richard, went to China as missionary. Richard engaged in famine relief in Shansi. In the capital, Taiyuan, he sought to interest the Chinese scholars in Western science. He later proposed to his London committee the founding of a college in each of the eighteen provincial capitals. He resigned from the society and set about influencing the literati of China in other ways. The great reformer, Kang Yu-Wei, said: 'I owe my conversion to reform chiefly to the writings of two missionaries, the Rev. Timothy Richard and the Rev. Dr. Young J. Allen.'[16]

After the Boxer Uprising, Timothy Richard proposed that the Chinese authorities use half a million taels of indemnity toward establishment of a University in Shansi. Curriculum, faculty, and funds were placed in his charge for ten years.[17]

By 1911, there were 543 Protestant secondary schools in China, with 33,000 pupils, one-third girls; 33 colleges and universities, with 2000 students, one-fifth women—out of a total of 115 colleges and 40,114 students—including Canton Christian College (Lingnan University); St. John's University, Shanghai; the University of Nanking; the Shantung Christian University; and Peking (Yenching) University).[18]

The medical missionaries, numbering in 1895 nearly a hundred men and fifty women, laid the foundation of a medical service which produced a number of medical schools, including the famed Peking Union Medical College, leading medical college in all China until the Communist dictatorship took over the country and all its social services.[19]

Likewise, in Korea, missionary penetration in the 1880s was followed by evangelism and by education, from primary to secondary schools and to colleges. Mrs. Mary Scranton, a Methodist, founded Ehwa, to give women education through to the college level. The six major missions coordinated their educational projects. The Union Christian College, in Pyungyang, was begun in the following year.[20]

One of the first pioneer missionaries to Japan, J. C. Hepburn, a Presbyterian, arrived in 1859. He prepared an English-Japanese dictionary as well as a major part of an early translation of the Scriptures. He and Mrs. Hepburn eagerly provided a Western education for all and sundry, beginning the first Western-type school for girls. Among their pupils were men who rose to high station in national affairs. Hepburn, a trained medical man, practised medicine and founded a medical school in Tokyo.[21]

Samuel R. Brown, a Reformed Church missionary with experience of pioneering education in China, spent twenty years in Yokohama and round about, pioneering in Western education.[22] Another mission pioneer, also Dutch Reformed, was Herman F. Verbeck, who operated a school at Nagasaki, then an official school for interpreters and finally a school in the capital which became the Imperial University.[23]

In Japan, there existed a national system of education, and to this advantage was added an avid desire for Western civilization. It was not necessary for missionaries to convince young Japanese of the benefits of Western education.

Neesima, a remarkable Japanese, journeyed at some risk to United States and studied at academy, college and seminary in Massachusetts, where he declared his faith.[24] There also he conceived the idea of founding a Christian school to become a university in Japan. A wholly Japanese company took title to property in Kyoto, the old capital, and Doshisha University was begun.[25] It was at Doshisha that an extraordinary evangelical awakening began in 1883, leading to times of expansion of the Christian Church in Japan.

Within thirty years of the opening of Japan, Protestant missionaries had established 250 churches—more than a third self-supporting—with 25,000 members, and they operated a hundred schools with ten thousand pupils.[26]

Although evangelization was their main object, the pioneer missionaries in Brazil devoted much attention to education. Their schools were later recognized as the forerunners of the Brazilian system of education that evolved in due course in the twentieth century.

Fernando de Azevedo, in his outstanding work on Brazilian culture,[27] attributed a large share of the inspiration for the educational reforms of Leoncio de Carvalho in the late 1870s and of Caetano de Campos and Cesario Mota in the early 1890s to the work of Evangelical institutions. Of these early Presbyterian, Methodist and other schools, he said that they helped to change didactic processes, influenced by the imported ideas of North American pedagogical technique, and for a long time they were to be among the few innovating forces in education—those living forces which keep the temperature of spiritual institutions from a kind of moral cooling off due to uniformity and routine.

In 1869, a Presbyterian missionary, Nash Morton, laid the foundation of Colegio Internacional in Campinas, near Sao Paulo. In 1870, Escola Americana was founded in Sao Paulo, becoming later the Mackenzie Institute, comprising educational projects from kindergarten to university.[28] In 1891, Mackenzie College was chartered by the Regents of the State of New York, graduating its first class in 1900.[29] It conferred degrees in literature and science. A Brazilian leader wrote to the president of Mackenzie University and expressed a widely-held opinion:[30]

> A great change has come over us here in Sao Paulo. We firmly believed that scientific thought and religious thought were incompatible or equally hostile. We have however, found that religious thought is perfectly compatible with efficient scientific thought. You people at Mackenzie do not parade your religion, but you have made it felt and stand for it on any suitable occasion, and you are doing the best scientific training that is being done in Brazil today.

Between 1858 and 1908, more than three million immigrants from Europe entered the Argentine. The majority were Roman Catholics, a minority Protestants from Britain, Germany and Italy (Waldensians). Unlike Brazil, the Evangelical missionaries did not establish a school system in the Argentine. Evangelical influence was otherwise exercised through the training of teachers.

Argentine politics had driven to exile in Chile Domingo F. Sarmiento, an educator, journalist and author. He returned to become one of Argentina's greatest presidents, serving first as ambassador to the United States in 1865. Elected in 1868 to highest office, he completely reorganized the Argentine educational system.[31]

Sarmiento knew that Thomson's Lancasterian schools had perished through the lack of trained teachers and the hostility of conservative churchmen. He decided to set up a stronger system of normal schools, and he personally enlisted a number of dedicated teachers from the United States to begin operations.[32]

The imported teachers were not officially evangelical missionaries but, of the sixty-five outstanding pioneers, sixty were Evangelical by conviction and five were equally dedicated Roman Catholics.[33] They came from a population which had enjoyed an evangelical revival within the decade. Sarmiento thus harnessed missionary idealism for a secular project. Among the teachers who came to head, reorganize or establish eighteen normal schools were a United States Army chaplain, Thomas Wentworth Higginson; Mary Elizabeth Gorman, daughter of a Baptist minister; and others. The Bishop of Cordoba excommunicated the parents of all those who patronized the new schools; the Bishop of Salta followed suit. Sarmiento dismissed one, suspended the other. By 1870, 20% of the Argentine population was literate; in 1895, 50%. Jose B. Zubiaur declared: 'This is the work of the normal schools, of which not one existed in 1869.' [34]

In 1885, a Chilean government chartered the Evangelical missionaries to 'promote primary and secondary instruction according to modern methods and practice.' From then on, their schools and colleges influenced the life of Chile.[35]

So also in Mexico. In 1865, Melinda Rankin founded her school in Monterrey.[36] In 1867, a Liberal Government set up a free, obligatory and lay school system, but this seemed to be limited to urban communities. As missionaries multiplied, so did their schools in rural areas, the first ray of hope for the mestizos in many a neglected district. The missionaries acted as schoolmasters as well as evangelists. The schools produced many a leader in national life.

SUMMARY

THE 1858-59 AWAKENING

The Evangelical Awakening which began in the United States before the end of 1857 and in the United Kingdom in early 1859 spread all over the world and remained effective for at least forty years.

The preliminary prayer meetings were commenced in New York City before the sudden bank panic of October in 1857, and the extraordinary conviction of sin in evangelism was first manifested in Canada, which was not immediately affected by the bank panic. (That bank panics do not cause religious revivals may be seen in the results of the crash of the stock market in 1929 and on earlier occasions.)

How did this great Awakening manifest itself? In the autumn of 1857 came the first signs of an awakening—great success in revival and evangelism in Canada, and an extraordinary movement of men to prayer in New York City which spread from city to city throughout the United States and over the world. Churches, halls, and theatres were filled at noon for prayer, and the overflow filled churches of all denominations at night in a truly remarkable turning of a whole nation toward God.

The Awakening of 1858 was received with enthusiasm by the secular press, which testified gladly of the changes for good in every place. With few exceptions, chiefly among doctrinaire anti-Evangelicals, the Awakening was supported by all the Protestant denominations, including the formalist Anglicans and Lutherans as well as informal Baptists and Methodists. The movement was singularly free of sectarian spirit. Its primary emphasis on prayer did not overshadow its augmented preaching of the Word. The meetings were commended for their quietness and restraint, and won the respect of citizens everywhere, enlisting some of the most mature minds of the community for Christ.

In addition to uncounted multitudes of nominal church members transformed by the power of God, more than a million converts were added to the membership of major denominations during the height of the movement. Beyond

all else, it was a layman's movement, in which the laymen
of all denominations gladly undertook both normal and extraordinary responsibilities in the service of God and humanity.

Despite the outbreak of the most devastating and bloody
war in all the world between the Napoleonic wars and World
War I, the awakening continued effective in the armies of
both North and South and in the civil population at home,
and the coming of peace brought about a renewal of zeal.

The social influence of the Awakening was felt in wartime services, but much impetus was held in suspense until
the cessation of hostilities, after which the social conscience
asserted itself, reinforced by the social achievements of the
same Awakening across the Atlantic.

The same movement also affected the United Kingdom,
beginning in 1859 in Ulster, the most northerly province in
Ireland. Approximately ten per cent of the population there
professed conversion, the same in Wales and Scotland, and
a great awakening continued in England for years, another
million being added to the Churches. Repercussions were
felt in many other European countries, and in South Africa
and Australia and elsewhere among European settlers.

The phenomena of Revival were reported in parts of
India, South Africa, and the East and West Indies among non-
European peoples. Any mission field that possessed an in-
doctrinated body of believers enjoyed the same reviving. In
many countries, the reviving was followed by extraordinary
evangelism and by folk movements of tribes and castes.

Out of the 1859 Awakening in Britain arose a phalanx of
famous evangelists—aristocrats and working men. Spurgeon
built his Tabernacle on the crest of this movement. The
intervention of the War between the States (in which there
was extraordinary evangelism and revival in every theatre
of operations) delayed the emergence of great American
evangelists from the 1858 Awakening. Yet the greatest of
world evangelists emerged in America in due course.

There was not so much unanimity of approval in Great
Britain as in the United States. While the established Church
of Scotland and other Presbyterian bodies overwhelmingly
endorsed the Revival, there was lukewarmness or opposition
in the broad-church and high-church sections of the Church
of England. The British Free Churches fully supported the
Awakening. Many of its supporters questioned the value of
the physical prostrations which marked the outset of the
movement, but these died away under sober direction.

The 1858-59 Awakenings extended the working forces of evangelical Christendom. Not only were a million converted in both the United States and the United Kingdom, but existing evangelistic and philanthropic organizations were revived and new vehicles of enterprise created—Bible Societies flourished as never before, Home Missions and the Salvation Army were founded to extend thus the evangelistic-social ministry of the Awakening in worldwide projects. The impact on the youthful Y.M.C.A. organization was noteworthy.

The mid-century Awakenings revived all the existing missionary societies and enabled them to enter other fields. The practical evangelical ecumenism of the Revival was embodied in the China Inland Mission founded by Hudson Taylor in the aftermath of the British Awakening, the first of the interdenominational 'faith missions.' As in the first half of the century, practically every missionary invasion was launched by men revived or converted in the Awakenings of the Churches in the sending countries.

For example, the first permanent missions in Brazil followed the 1858-59 Awakenings. In Indonesia and India, folk movements to Christianity followed. China was penetrated by the converts of the Revival from many countries. The missionary occupation of Africa was rapid, and the liberated Negro in the Anglo-American territories was hopefully evangelized.

In the 1870s, D. L. Moody rose to fame as a world evangelist. Beginning modestly in York in 1873, Moody progressed through Sunderland, Newcastle, Edinburgh, Dundee, Glasgow, Belfast, Dublin, Manchester, Sheffield, Birmingham and Liverpool, using the methods of the 1858 Revival in prayer and preaching. About 2,500,000 people aggregate heard him in twenty weeks in London.

In 1875, Moody returned to his native land a national figure, campaigning equally successfully in Brooklyn, Philadelphia, New York, Chicago, Boston and other cities. From then onwards, he ministered in cities on both sides of the Atlantic. A flock of successful evangelists was associated with him. Perhaps his greatest campaign was conducted at the World's Exposition in Chicago in 1893. Moody died in action in 1899.

In the Moody period, another awakening began in Sweden, extending the work of the National Evangelical Foundation (EFS) and an offshoot, the Evangelical Mission Covenant (SMF). Revivals continued in Norway, Denmark and Finland.

As a result of the impact of Anglo-American Revivalists —including D. L. Moody—a Thirty Years' Revival began in Germany, from 1880 until 1910. Outstanding leaders were Theodor Christlieb (who founded the German Committee for Evangelism and Gemeinschaftsbewegung), Elijah Schrenk and Samuel Keller.

In the same period, there was revival among the Ukrainian peasantry and evangelism among the Russian upper classes, the latter done by British gentlemen, Radstock and Baedeker. I. S. Prokhanov, converted in 1886, founded the All-Russian Evangelical Union which in the next century united in denominational organization with the Baptists.

It is curious to notice that Charles Darwin's most significant publication (1859) occurred at the time of the Awakening in Great Britain and the United States, heralding a clash between sceptics who interpreted many new scientific conclusions as anti-theistic and traditional theologians who too readily agreed with such a faulty interpretation.

Yet far from antagonizing the academic world, the Awakening resulted in the most extraordinary invasion of the universities and colleges by the Christian message and the most successful recruitment of university-trained personnel in the history of higher education and evangelism.

In the 1858 Awakening in the United States, revivals among students resulted in the formation of the College Y.M.C.A.s, and in the following year, prayer meetings at Oxford and Cambridge gave rise to Christian Unions which later united to form the Inter-Varsity Fellowship. In the local student fellowship at Princeton in 1875 were several outstanding young men—Robert Mateer, who became leader of the Inter-Seminary Missionary Alliance; T. W. Wilson, who became president of Princeton University and later (as T. Woodrow Wilson) President of the United States, and Luther Wishard, who as organizer and evangelist of the Inter-Collegiate Y.M.C.A., pleaded with a reluctant Moody to minister to a sincerely interested student constituency.

In 1882, Moody was persuaded to campaign in Cambridge University, where at first he stirred up scornful opposition. Out of the awakening, the Cambridge Seven (C.T. Studd and other first-rank varsity men) stirred the student world and proceeded to China as missionaries.

Thus encouraged, Moody acceded to Wishard's promptings to arrange a conference for students at Mount Hermon, in his home state. A youthful delegate, Robert Wilder, presented the claims of the mission fields and a hundred of the 250 present responded—within an academic year, two thousand from American universities and colleges. Thus was born the Student Volunteer Movement, with their watchword—to 'evangelize the world in this generation.' Under the direction of men like John R. Mott, Volunteers multiplied on every continent, as recruits or as emissaries.

Out of the 1859 Awakening arose the Keswick Movement for the Deepening of the Spiritual Life (1875). In the eastern hemisphere, it became a unifying force in Evangelicalism, a missionary recruitment rally of the highest quality. Out of the same agitation in America, the organization of the Holiness Movement resulted in splintering, giving birth to vigorous denominations in the Wesleyan tradition.

Christian Endeavor, a movement for training young people in church-related activity, began in a local revival in Maine in 1881, under Francis E. Clark. Within fifteen years, there were more than two million members in forty thousand local societies: they were ecumenical and evangelical. A number of the denominations promoted comparable young people's organizations on the same plan.

Toward the end of the century, an Anglican, George Grubb, excelled as evangelist in the British Empire countries, as did Gipsy Smith, Hay Aitken, John McNeill and Andrew Murray.

Singular advances were made in Africa. Charles Pamla continued preaching as the leading Bantu evangelist; Spencer Walton began a new missionary enterprise; an extraordinary awakening began in Uganda, Christianizing the country.

The 1880s witnessed advances in the evangelization of China, as well as a remarkable seven years' revival in Japan, but the years of rapid growth in the island empire were followed by a decline caused by an onslaught of rationalist theology among national pastors.

The awakenings in sending countries caused an extension of missionary enterprise on every continent. Albert B. Simpson, a convert of the 1858 Revival in Canada, founded the Christian and Missionary Alliance in 1886, at first as an interdenominational organization but later becoming more a denomination as missionary minded as the Moravians.

In the social impact of mid-century Revivals, greater effects were realized in the industrialized United Kingdom. Lord Shaftesbury continued his extraordinary parliamentary projects for the betterment of humanity. Great orphanages were begun. A Society was formed for the Prevention of

Cruelty to Children (1889), while Josephine Butler rallied evangelical opinion to abolish the licensing of prostitution in Great Britain (1886). Aroused evangelical interests motivated much of the agitation for the betterment of conditions for working people, many leaders in the Labour Party itself being avowed evangelical Christians. In the United States, there also was a growing concern with purely social issues such as rights of the working man, poverty, the liquor trade, slum housing and racial bitterness. Overseas, social action excelled in missionary education and medical services.

To achieve this reform, the crusaders of the Evangelical Awakenings did not stoop to engage in class warfare. Rather, under the guidance of the Spirit, they enlisted the privileged to serve the poor. The Seventh Earl of Shaftesbury single-handed accomplished as much in his lifetime as had been achieved by any parliamentarian, yet remained an aristocrat.

Out of this evangelical concern grew a liberal social gospel whose advocates became indifferent by degrees to the dynamic of the Christian gospel, the transforming of individual lives by the power of Jesus Christ.

Some effects of the 1858-59 Awakening were not immediately apparent—the relationship of the conversion of hundreds of thousands who soon developed an insatiable desire for education to the transformation of the public school systems; or the evangelical conversion of Keir Hardie under Moody's ministry and the introduction of that evangelical spirit into the Labour Movement in contrast to the atheism of Continental socialism. This evangelical leadership among British workers continued for three generations.

Unlike the Reformation, Puritanism and the Evangelical Revival, the Awakening of 1858-1859 onwards produced no cleavage among the Christian denominations, rather sewing together the rent patches of Evangelical Christianity with the thread of spiritual, if not organic, unity. The Anglo-Scottish Reformation rent the major part of British Christianity from the body of Roman Christianity. Puritanism led to the expulsion of the Baptists and Congregationalists from the Anglican Established Church, and the Evangelical Revival resulted in the separation of a considerable part of the religious population from the Church of England. But the Evangelical Awakening of the mid-nineteenth century produced no further divisions and rather indicated that the tide in inter-church relationship had begun to flow in the opposite direction.

There was nothing new in the theology of the 1858 Revival. All of its teachings were derived from the New Testament, and many of its strong points were doctrines recovered in the Reformation, and re-emphasized in the Evangelical Revivals of the eighteenth and early nineteenth centuries. The Revivalists as a whole shared the doctrinal views of the Evangelical Alliance, founded 1846.

The unity promoted by the Awakening of 1858-59 was of the spiritual rather than the organic kind. Its cooperation was typified by the inter-denominationalism of evangelistic campaigns, of conventions for the deepening of the spiritual life, and of missionary comity rather than union of differing bodies in a greater organization. And yet it could be said that the later ecumenical movement had its beginnings in the evangelical unity of the Revival rather than in ecclesiastical negotiations undertaken by denominational hierarchies, the ecumenism of the Spirit being one of the grass-roots.

The 1858-59 Awakening was an evangelical revival in the purest sense of the word. It was supported by evangelical Christians of all schools, and it strengthened evangelical Christians of all denominations.

The Revival affected impartially the two great divisions of Evangelicalism—the Calvinist and the Arminian. The Revival was soon at its greatest intensity among the traditionally Calvinistic denominations: and yet it affected as powerfully the Methodist groups and produced the Salvation Army, a convinced Arminian fellowship. It likewise moved the Lutheran constituency, in majority or minority.

In the 1858-59 Awakening, the two systems of interpretation were not reconciled. Rather they were blended. There was little friction between Calvinist and Arminian anywhere. One of the few instances uncovered by this research will suffice to show how mild the friction was: the editor of a London Methodist periodical complained that, in a united prayer meeting in Bath, the Baptists, Congregationalists and Churchmen seemed to avoid instinctively such controversial questions as baptism and church government, yet they kept on praying the most Calvinistic of prayers! The observers might have added that, although the revivalists prayed like Calvinists, they worked like Arminians for the salvation of souls. Though the Calvinist-Arminian controversy had been extremely bitter following the Evangelical Revival of the eighteenth century, there was the happiest harmony during the mid-nineteenth Awakening.

No serious charges were made by evangelical theologians on doctrinal grounds against the teaching of the Revivalists. The most hostile criticism considered was really very mild. Objections from the liberal and traditionalist sections of Christendom were expected and experienced: but, among Evangelicals, while some cloistered thinkers shook their heads about the phenomena and excitement of the Revival, few were able to raise a doctrinal issue of any sort.

Most of the offhand denigration of the movement noticed by the present researcher came from later—not earlier—twentieth century historians writing from the vantage point of a philosophy of 'revivalism' transposed across the hundred years. Suffice to say, one discovered no depreciation of the 1858-59 Revival (other than the temporary objections of a tiny minority at the time) throughout the rest of the century. Many Christians who lived in the latter half of the century regarded the movement as the greatest since Pentecost! In 1899, Moody declared: 'I would like before I go hence to see the whole Church of God quickened as it was in '57 . . .' from which may be deduced that nothing he had seen in forty years of effective evangelism matched the Awakening in which he first served God. The Great Revival of 1859 that 'shook the whole world' was still potent, the Evangelical Alliance claimed, while Principal Alexander Whyte of Edinburgh and Scottish scholars in 1909 declared that the 1859 Revival in Scotland was the most fruitful in the annals of Christianity since the Reformation. Documents confirm the view against superficial judgments made generations later.

Certain facts need to be highlighted, the most important of which is that consideration of the movement cannot be limited to the passage of the few years of the Revival's beginning. Who would limit the eighteenth century Revival to a few years? A comprehensive view of the mid-nineteenth century awakening and the evangelical movements issuing therefrom for forty years indicate a distinct and definite period of expansion of the Christian Church—a nineteenth century evangelical awakening comparable to its noted predecessor of the eighteenth century. If the revival of the earlier century be reckoned effective from 1725 until 1775, the 1858-59 Awakening may be held as effective from that time until the death of Moody who extended its ministry, as Whitefield also extended the eighteenth century movement of evangelization. How then did the movement compare with the earlier awakening in magnitude?

Geographically, the Evangelical Awakening of 1858-59 onwards affected Christian communities in every part of Canada and the United States, in England, Scotland, Wales and Ulster, the colonies overseas and several mission fields nearby, as the reports collated in this narrative indicate. In this respect, the movement was every bit as effective as the earlier evangelical awakening that stirred, in the days of the Georges, the Three Kingdoms and the Thirteen Colonies.

Numerically, the 1858-59 Awakening added approximately two million converts to the various Churches, and the testimony available suggested that the quality of the conversions was excellent and abiding. The revivalistic preaching of the Wesleys, Whitefield, and their contemporaries had deeply moved a vast mass of human beings, as noted by Dr. G. M. Trevelyan. Without any doubt, the 1858-59 Evangelical Awakening moved a greater mass of human beings, for the population had already doubled in the intervening period. In its setting, the Wesleyan Revival was incomparably effective; but the fact remains that no historian would claim for the redoubtable Wesley and his companions two million won to the churches in five years. There were less than 80,000 members in the British Methodist societies in 1791 when Wesley completed his half-century of powerful preaching.

Denominationally, every evangelical church fellowship gained from the 1858-59 Awakening. The gains were proportionate to their evangelical-evangelistic strength, and were inversely proportionate to the strength of their anti-evangelical or anti-evangelistic traditions.

Evangelistically, the 1858-59 Awakening revived all the older agencies raised up by the great Revivals of the early nineteenth century. It also created new organizations of a permanent character, and increased the efforts of Christians to fulfill the Great Commission at home and abroad.

Individually, the Revival of the mid-nineteenth century presented the Church and people with a crop of sturdy husbandmen in every field of life, contributing to the general store the priceless fruits of sanctified personality, not only in the home countries but in all the mission fields.

Socially, the mid-nineteenth century Awakening gave birth to a whole litter of active religious and philanthropic societies, which accomplished so much in human uplift — the welfare of children, and the reclamation of prostitutes, of alcoholics, of criminals, of the wounded and distressed, besides the development of the social virtues.

The 1858-59 Awakening occurred in three distinct phases. The first phase began in a revival of Christian life that followed an outpouring of the Holy Spirit, first clearly manifested in a remarkable movement to prayer with its attendant conviction of sin. In a general sense leaderless, this revival became the means of winning many hundreds of thousands to the Christian way of life. Its peak passed, but the Christian communities were by then operating upon a higher level of spiritual effectiveness everywhere.

The second phase took its rise in a development of evangelism. Dwight L. Moody, whose Christian service actually began during the first phase of the Revival, became after 1873 a force in Great Britain as well as in America. Moody extended the scope and the methods of the same Awakening, for he introduced little that was new—united prayer meetings, cooperative evangelism, zeal for home and foreign missions, promotion of lay ministry, development of leadership, and dependence on the Scriptures—all these were already in evidence in the movement of 1858 that affected young Moody's life in Chicago. Moody was without question the greatest single product of the Revival, but he was not alone in his heyday of usefulness from 1873 to 1899. Those years were outstanding in the history of English-speaking evangelism.

The third phase arose from the first and the second, a mobilization of the talents of the best trained young men for a missionary advance without parallel in the history of the faith. Student Volunteers and other dedicated agents helped reinforce missions in Africa and India, and to man ventures recently started in East Asia and Latin America.

It required the passing of time to give proper perspective. Church historians have united in recognizing gratefully the Moody period of mass evangelism in Britain and America. Actually, the period should be advanced fifteen years to date from the year 1858 when Moody served his apprenticeship (so to speak) in Chicago, during the world-wide 1858-59 Evangelical Awakening in which he 'learned his trade.'

The relating of these three movements as a period of forty years of expansion, a nineteenth century awakening, was a thesis not hitherto set forth, so far as one can gather, until the publication of the author's Oxford dissertation, in the year 1948.

NOTES

Notes on Chapter 1: THE SOURCES OF THE REVIVAL

1 F. G. Beardsley, A HISTORY OF AMERICAN REVIVALS, 1912, pp. 213-214.
2 see W. W. Sweet, THE STORY OF RELIGION IN AMERICA, chapter XVIII, 'Slavery Controversy and Schisms.'
3 F. D. Nichol, THE MIDNIGHT CRY, pp. 337-348, is cited to disprove charges of other excesses made against the Adventist folk.
4 F. G. Beardsley, A HISTORY OF AMERICAN REVIVALS, p. 216.
5 H. U. Faulkner, AMERICAN ECONOMIC HISTORY, p. 235.
6 F. G. Beardsley, A HISTORY OF AMERICAN REVIVALS, p. 217.
7 T. W. Chambers, THE NOON PRAYER MEETING, p. 284.
8 cf. CHRISTIAN ADVOCATE, New York, 13 May 1858, and THE REVIVAL, London, 17 September 1859.
9 CHRISTIAN ADVOCATE, New York, 5 November 1857.
10 R. Wheatley, THE LIFE OF MRS. PHŒBE PALMER.
11 CHRISTIAN ADVOCATE, New York, 13 May 1858.
12 PRESBYTERIAN MAGAZINE, September 1858.
13 S. I. Prime, THE POWER OF PRAYER, pp. 63-64.
14 PRESBYTERIAN MAGAZINE, September 1858.
15 THE WATCHMAN, 17 December 1857; cf. also W. C. Conant's NARRATIVE OF REMARKABLE CONVERSIONS, p. 358.
16 T. W. Chambers, THE NOON PRAYER MEETING, pp. 33-34.
17 cf. W. C. Conant, NARRATIVE OF REMARKABLE CONVERSIONS, regarding Visitation Campaigns.
18 T. W. Chambers, THE NOON PRAYER MEETING, pp. 42ff.
19 M. H. Smith, MARVELS OF PRAYER, p. 8.
20 Dr. W. G. McLoughlin (in MODERN REVIVALISM, p. 163) stated: 'As everyone recognized at the time, it developed out of the financial panic of 1857.' Christian contemporaries repudiated this point of view (see Chambers, THE NOON PRAYER MEETING, p. 284), and few besides cynical journalists supported the idea (see NEW YORK HERALD comment: 'Satan is busy all the morning in Wall Street among the brokers, and all the afternoon and evening the churches are crowded with saints who gambled in the morning'—a wisecrack, not a report, DAILY COURIER, Louisville, 6 March).

Notes on Chapter 2: THE RISING TIDE

1 H. Newcomb, THE HARVEST AND THE REAPERS, p. 16.
2 T. W. Chambers, THE NOON PRAYER MEETING, p. 69.
3 CHRISTIAN ADVOCATE, New York, 28 January 1858.
4 DAILY TRIBUNE, New York, 10 February 1858.
5 Report in DAILY TRIBUNE, New York, 24 February 1858.
6 W. F. P. Noble, A CENTURY OF GOSPEL WORK, p. 419.
7 NATIONAL INTELLIGENCER, Washington, 2 & 11 March 1858.
8 see S. I. Prime, THE POWER OF PRAYER.
9 NATIONAL INTELLIGENCER, Washington, 23 March 1858.
10 Conant, NARRATIVE OF REMARKABLE CONVERSIONS, p. 362.
11 NEW YORK TIMES, 20 March 1858.
12 NEW YORK HERALD, 26 March 1858.
13 J. Shaw, TWELVE YEARS IN AMERICA, pp. 182-184.
14 PRESBYTERIAN MAGAZINE, June 1858.
15 NATIONAL INTELLIGENCER, Washington, 20 March 1858.

16 CHRISTIAN ADVOCATE, New York, 11 February 1858.
17 THE EXAMINER, New York, q. in DAILY COURIER, Louisville, 30 March 1858.
18 CHRISTIAN ADVOCATE, New York, 3 June 1858, q. REVIVAL MESSENGER.
19 R. E. Francis, PENTECOST: 1858; an unpublished thesis, 1948, University of Pennsylvania.
20 H. Humphrey, REVIVAL SKETCHES AND MANUAL, p. 281.
21 THE EVANGELIST, New York, 19 November 1857.
22 CHRISTIAN ADVOCATE, New York, 13 May 1858; W. C. Conant, NARRATIVE OF REMARKABLE CONVERSIONS, pp. 379–380 & 429; OBERLIN EVANGELIST, 25 March, 28 April, 5 May, & 12 May 1858; THE EVANGELIST, New York, 11 March, 15, 22 & 29 April, & 8 July 1858.
23 S. E. Morison, THREE CENTURIES OF HARVARD, 1636–1936, pp. 244–245; THE EVANGELIST, New York, 11 March 1858; cf. CHRISTIAN REGISTER, Boston, 3 April 1858 & the MONTHLY RELIGIOUS MAGAZINE, 1858, pp. 333–356; THE EVANGELIST, NEW YORK, 15 & 22 April 1858; F. D. Huntington, PERMANENT REALITIES OF RELIGION AND THE PRESENT RELIGIOUS INTEREST, Boston, 1858; and A. S. Huntington, MEMOIRS AND LETTERS OF F. D. HUNTINGTON, Boston, 1906; OBERLIN EVANGELIST, 28 April 1858; EVANGELICAL REPOSITORY, June 1858, pp. 31ff; CHRISTIAN ADVOCATE, New York 13 May 1858; THE EVANGELIST, New York, 22 April & 10 June 1858; CONGREGATIONAL YEAR BOOK, 1859, pp. 147ff; Reynolds, Fisher & Wright, TWO CENTURIES OF RELIGIOUS ACTIVITY AT YALE, passim.
24 THE EVANGELIST, New York, 22 April 1858.
25 THE EVANGELIST, New York, 22 April 1858; A. Godbold, THE CHURCH COLLEGE IN THE OLD SOUTH, pp. 113, 142; see H. M. Bullock, A HISTORY OF EMORY UNIVERSITY, p. 98 & E. M. Coulter, COLLEGE LIFE IN THE OLD SOUTH, pp. 162–165; & J. M. Carroll, A HISTORY OF TEXAS BAPTISTS, p. 237.
26 G. W. Chessman, DENISON: THE STORY OF AN OHIO COLLEGE, p. 139; THE EVANGELIST, New York, 15 July 1858.
27 W. W. Ferrier, ORIGIN AND DEVELOPMENT OF THE UNIVERSITY OF CALIFORNIA, p. 273.
28 F. Rudolph, THE AMERICAN COLLEGE AND UNIVERSITY, p. 83.
29 F. Rudolph, THE AMERICAN COLLEGE AND UNIVERSITY, p. 83.
30 see C. P. Shedd, TWO CENTURIES OF STUDENT CHRISTIAN MOVEMENTS, pp. 98ff; and C. H. Hopkins, HISTORY OF THE Y. M. C. A. IN NORTH AMERICA, p. 38; THE EVANGELIST, New York, 20 May 1858; C. P. Shedd, TWO CENTURIES OF STUDENT CHRISTIAN MOVEMENTS, pp. 95ff.

Notes on Chapter 3: THE EASTERN STATES

1 H. Newcomb, THE HARVEST AND THE REAPERS, p. 26.
2 C. G. Finney, MEMOIRS, pp. 442–443. Finney was preaching then in Park Street Church.
3 DAILY TRANSCRIPT, Boston, 5 March 1858.
4 NATIONAL INTELLIGENCER, Washington, 20 March 1858.
5 CONGREGATIONAL QUARTERLY, January 1859.
6 CHRISTIAN ADVOCATE, New York, 15 July 1858.
7 J. Shaw, TWELVE YEARS IN AMERICA, pp. 182–184.

8   cf. THE INDEPENDENT, 7 January 1858 onwards, and Conant, NARRATIVE OF REMARKABLE CONVERSIONS, pp. 377–429.
9   CHRISTIAN ADVOCATE, 13 May 1858 & Conant, NARRATIVE OF REMARKABLE CONVERSIONS, p. 378.
10 Conant, NARRATIVE OF REMARKABLE CONVERSIONS, p. 426.
11 cf. THE WATCHMAN, 24 December 1857 onwards; Conant, p. 379.
12 Conant, NARRATIVE OF REMARKABLE CONVERSIONS, p. 430.
13 cf. THE WATCHMAN, 24 December 1857 onwards; see also THE INDEPENDENT, 7 January 1858 onwards; and Conant, pp. 377ff.
14 PRESBYTERIAN MAGAZINE, June 1858.
15 W. C. Conant, NARRATIVE OF REMARKABLE CONVERSIONS, pp. 379–380.
16 cf. MISSIONARY NOTICES of the Wesleyan Methodist Missionary Society, 6 January 1858; and MISSIONARY REGISTER OF THE PRESBYTERIAN CHURCH OF NOVA SCOTIA, June 1858; see R. Wheatley, THE LIFE AND LETERS OF MRS. PHŒBE PALMER, pp. 316ff; and WESLEYAN METHODIST MAGAZINE, 1863, p. 470; also P. C. Headley, THE HARVEST WORK OF THE HOLY SPIRIT (Life of Edward Payson Hammond).
17 Conant, NARRATIVE OF REMARKABLE CONVERSIONS, p. 370.
18 cf. CHRISTIAN ADVOCATE, New York, 4 February 1858; and W. C. Conant, NARRATIVE, p. 370.
19 Conant, NARRATIVE OF REMARKABLE CONVERSIONS, p. 371.
20 CHRISTIAN ADVOCATE, 4 February 1858, and Conant, p. 370.
21 Conant, NARRATIVE OF REMARKABLE CONVERSIONS, p. 431.
22 cf. issues of THE WATCHMAN, and W. C. Conant, pp. 369–370.
23 Conant, NARRATIVE OF REMARKABLE CONVERSIONS, pp. 430ff.
24 cf. issues of CHRISTIAN ADVOCATE, 4 February 1858; and Conant, NARRATIVE of remarkable conversions, p. 432.
25 Conant, NARRATIVE OF REMARKABLE CONVERSIONS, p. 372.
26 NATIONAL INTELLIGENCER, Washington, 23 March 1858.
27 Conant, NARRATIVE OF REMARKABLE CONVERSIONS, p. 372.
28 cf. issues of CHRISTIAN ADVOCATE, THE WATCHMAN, and THE INDEPENDENT, with Conant, pp. 431–432.
29 CHRISTIAN ADVOCATE, 22 October & 24 December 1857; and 7 January & 18 February 1858.
30 Conant, NARRATIVE OF REMARKABLE CONVERSIONS, p. 368.
31 cf. issues of CHRISTIAN ADVOCATE, THE WATCHMAN, and THE INDEPENDENT, with Conant, pp. 369, 432–433.
32 W. F. P. Noble, A CENTURY OF GOSPEL WORK, p. 420.
33 EVANGELICAL CHRISTENDOM, 1858, pp. 177–178, and W. F. P. Noble, p. 420.
34 W. F. P. Noble, A CENTURY OF GOSPEL WORK, p. 421.
35 CHRISTIAN ADVOCATE, New York, 6 May 1858.
36 EVANGELICAL CHRISTENDOM, 1858, pp. 177–178.
37 W. F. P. Noble, A CENTURY OF GOSPEL WORK, p. 422.
38 W. C. Conant, NARRATIVE OF REMARKABLE CONVERSIONS, pp. 373–374.   39 CHRISTIAN ADVOCATE, 24 December 1857.
40 Conant, NARRATIVE OF REMARKABLE CONVERSIONS, p. 375.
41 NATIONAL INTELLIGENCER, Washington, 4 April 1858.

Notes on Chapter 4: WEST OF THE ALLEGHENIES

1   J. Shaw, TWELVE YEARS IN AMERICA, pp. 182–184.
2   PRESBYTERIAN MAGAZINE, June 1858.
3   WESTERN CHRISTIAN ADVOCATE, Cincinnati, 10 March 1858.

4   PRESBYTERIAN MAGAZINE, June 1858.
5   DAILY COURIER, Louisville, 6 & 11 March 1858.
6   Conant, NARRATIVE OF REMARKABLE CONVERSIONS, p. 374.
7   DAILY COURIER, Louisville, 6 & 29 March, 8 April 1858.
8   Conant, NARRATIVE OF REMARKABLE CONVERSIONS, p. 374.
9   DAILY COURIER, Louisville, 27 March 1858.
10 Conant, NARRATIVE OF REMARKABLE CONVERSIONS, p. 433.
11 DAILY COMMERCIAL, Cincinnati, 2 April 1858; Conant, p. 434.
12 NATIONAL INTELLIGENCER, Washington, 30 March 1858.
13 Conant, NARRATIVE OF REMARKABLE CONVERSIONS, p. 433.
14 CHRISTIAN TIMES, Chicago, 27 January 1858; Conant, p. 373.
15 W. C. Conant, NARRATIVE OF REMARKABLE CONVERSIONS,
    pp. 374 & 434.
16 T. W. Chambers, THE NOON PRAYER MEETING, p. 196.
17 Conant, NARRATIVE OF REMARKABLE CONVERSIONS, p. 374.
18 CHRISTIAN ADVOCATE, 18 March 1858.
19 Conant, NARRATIVE OF REMARKABLE CONVERSIONS, p. 434.
20 cf. CHRISTIAN TIMES, Chicago, 21 April 1858, & Conant, p. 434.
21 Conant, NARRATIVE OF REMARKABLE CONVERSIONS, p. 434.
22 DAILY PRESS, Chicago, 5 January 1858.
23 CHRISTIAN TIMES, Chicago, 3 & 10 February; & DAILY PRESS,
    13 March 1858.
24 see issues of 13, 19 & 25 March 1858, DAILY PRESS, Chicago;
    Conant, NARRATIVE OF REMARKABLE CONVERSIONS, pp. 373ff.
25 DAILY PRESS, Chicago, 27 March 1858; cf. CHRISTIAN TIMES,
    Chicago, 31 March 1858.
26 DAILY PRESS, Chicago, 3 & 20 April 1858.
27 CHRISTIAN TIMES, 19 May 1858.
28 DAILY PRESS, Chicago, 3 & 24 May 1858.
29 R. E. Day, BUSH AGLOW, p. 74.
30 W. R. Moody, THE LIFE OF D. L. MOODY, pp. 55ff.
31 A. T. Andreas, A HISTORY OF CHICAGO, Volume I, pp. 302-336.
32 see THE MENNONITE ENCYCLOPEDIA, pp. 308ff.
33 C. Henry Smith, THE STORY OF THE MENNONITES, passim.
34 S. B. Halliday, THE CHURCH IN AMERICA AND ITS BAPTISMS
    OF FIRE, pp. 526ff.
35 THE EVANGELIST, New York, 24 June 1858.
36 Report, 27 May 1858, THE EVANGELIST, 1 July 1858.
37 THE EVANGELIST, New York, 24 June 1858.
39 Berryessa. (THE EVANGELIST, New York, 6 May 1858)
40 THE EVANGELIST, 10 & 17 June 1858.

Notes on Chapter 5: THE PROBLEM OF THE SOUTH

1   W. M. Gewehr, THE GREAT AWAKENING IN VIRGINIA, pp. 235ff.
2   May & Nicholson, THE NEGROES' CHURCH, pp. 279, 22-27.
3   W. W. Sweet, REVIVALISM IN AMERICA, pp. 157-159.
4   OBERLIN EVANGELIST, 12 May 1858.
5   T. L. Smith, REVIVALISM AND SOCIAL REFORM, p. 153.
6   CHRISTIAN ADVOCATE, New York, cited in T. L. Smith, p. 200.
7   C. G. Finney, MEMOIRS, p. 444.
8   see F. G. Beardsley, A HISTORY OF AMERICAN REVIVALS,
    pp. 227-228.
9   W. A. Candler, GREAT REVIVALS AND THE GREAT REPUBLIC,
    p. 216.   10 SOUTHERN PRESBYTERIAN REVIEW, July 1859.
11 PRESBYTERIAN MAGAZINE, June 1858.

12   Conant, NARRATIVE OF REMARKABLE CONVERSIONS, p. 375.
13   NATIONAL INTELLIGENCER, Washington, 25 March 1858.
14   DAILY COURIER, Louisville, 17 April 1858.
15   W. A. Candler, GREAT REVIVALS AND THE GREAT REPUBLIC, pp. 216-217.
16   see F. G. Beardsley, A HISTORY OF AMERICAN REVIVALS, pp. 240ff.
17   W. W. Sweet, THE STORY OF RELIGION IN AMERICA, pp. 317ff.
18   An Act of Congress required that only regularly ordained ministers in good standing in their denomination be appointed chaplains.
19   see Lemuel Moss, THE ANNALS OF THE UNITED STATES CHRISTIAN COMMISSION.
20   W. R. Moody, THE LIFE OF DWIGHT L. MOODY, pp. 85-86.
21   see W. W. Bennett, THE GREAT REVIVAL IN THE SOUTHERN ARMIES.   22 J. W. Jones, CHRIST IN THE CAMP.
23   W. W. Sweet, THE STORY OF RELIGION IN AMERICA, p. 318.
24   YEARBOOK OF THE AMERICAN CHURCHES, New York, 1933.
25   cf. K. S. Latourette, A HISTORY OF THE EXPANSION OF CHRISTIANITY, Volume IV, pp. 327, 341; & Mays & Nicholson, THE NEGROES' CHURCH.
26   cf. K. S. Latourette, A HISTORY OF THE EXPANSION OF CHRISTIANITY, Volume IV, p. 352; & U.S. Bureau of the Census, Religious Bodies, 1916.
27   see W. E. Burghardt DuBois, editor, THE NEGRO CHURCH, Report of a Social Study, Atlanta University, 1903.
28   MISSIONARY NOTICES of the Wesleyan Methodist Missionary Society, 10 December 1858 & 18 February 1859.
29   J. T. Hamilton, A HISTORY OF THE MORAVIAN CHURCH, p. 457; E. A. Payne, FREEDOM IN JAMAICA, pp. 88ff.
30   see CANADIAN PRESBYTERIAN MISSION TO EAST INDIANS IN TRINIDAD, passim.

Notes on Chapter 6:   APPROVAL—AND DISAPPROVAL

1   CHRISTIAN ADVOCATE, New York, 11 & 25 March 1858.
2   PRESBYTERIAN MAGAZINE, May 1858.
3   T. W. Chambers, THE NOON PRAYER MEETING, p. 36.
4   W. F. P. Noble, A CENTURY OF GOSPEL WORK, p. 422.
5   Conant, NARRATIVE OF REMARKABLE CONVERSIONS, p. 394.
6   ABEND ZEITUNG, quoted in DAILY COMMERCIAL, Cincinnati, 25 March 1858.
7   see McClintock & Strong, BIBLE CYCLOPEDIA, Volume VII, pp. 690-693.
8   DAILY COMMERCIAL, Cincinnati, 12 April 1858.
9   BOSTON COURIER, 5 April 1858.
10   DAILY COMMERCIAL, Cincinnati, 12 April 1858.
11   T. L. Smith, REVIVALISM AND SOCIAL REFORM, pp. 70-71; Conant, NARRATIVE OF REMARKABLE CONVERSIONS, p. 377.
12   CHRISTIAN REGISTER, 3 April 1858.
13   MONTHLY RELIGIOUS MAGAZINE, 1858, pp. 333, 335-336.
14   CHRISTIAN ADVOCATE, New York, 25 March 1858.
15   THE CHURCHMAN, New York, q. in CHRISTIAN ADVOCATE, New York, 11 March 1858.
16   LUTHERAN OBSERVER, 26 March 1858.
17   AMERICAN QUARTERLY CHURCH REVIEW, 1858-59, pp. 352ff: 'Te Religious Awakening.'

18 JOURNAL, XLI ANNUAL CONVENTION OF THE PROTESTANT EPISCOPAL CHURCH IN THE DIOCESE OF OHIO, 1858.

19 C. P. McIlvaine, BISHOP MCILVAINE ON THE REVIVAL OF RELIGION, New York, 1858.

20 JOURNAL, XXI ANNUAL CONVENTION OF THE PROTESTANT EPISCOPAL CHURCH IN THE DIOCESE OF WESTERN NEW YORK, 1858.

21 NATIONAL CYCLOPEDIA OF BIOGRAPHY, I, pp. 187-188 (for biographical notes on Stephen Tyng and his sons).

22 see Philip Schaff, AMERICA: A SKETCH OF THE POLITICAL, SOCIAL AND RELIGIOUS CHARACTER OF THE UNITED STATES, 1855, p. 183.

23 LUTHERAN OBSERVER, 4 January 1856.

24 Report of 12 February 1858, LUTHERAN OBSERVER.

25 LUTHERAN OBSERVER, 12 February 1858.

26 Report of 29 January, 1858, LUTHERAN OBSERVER.

27 LUTHERAN OBSERVER, 5 & 19 February 1858.

28 Report of 26 March, 1858, LUTHERAN OBSERVER.

29 LUTHERAN OBSERVER, 28 May 1858.

30 Reports of 19 & 26 March, 2 & 16 April, & 11 June 1858, following, LUTHERAN OBSERVER.

31 MINUTES OF THE GENERAL ASSEMBLY OF THE PRESBY-TERIAN CHURCH IN THE UNITED STATES OF AMERICA, (Old School) Volume XV, (1858) p. 302.

32 MINUTES Volume XV (1859), pp. 552ff.

33 MINUTES Volume XV (1857), p. 217.

34 MINUTES Volume XV (1858), p. 475.

35 MINUTES Volume XV (1859), p. 747.

36 MINUTES OF THE GENERAL ASSEMBLY OF THE PRESY-TERIAN CHURCH IN THE UNITED STATES OF AMERICA, (New School), Volume XII (1859), pp. 52, 205, 266.

37 CONGREGATIONAL QUARTERLY, New York, January 1859; & January 1860. 38 THE FRIEND, Philadelphia, 29 May 1858.

39 AMERICAN BAPTIST ALMANAC, 1857, p. 47; 1858, p. 48; 1859, p. 48; 1860, p. 48.

40 AMERICAN BAPTIST ALMANAC, 1857, p. 37; 1858, p. 38; 1859, p. 38; 1860, p. 39.

41 Jacob Knapp, AUTOBIOGRAPHY, pp. 164ff.

42 A. B. Earle, BRINGING IN THE SHEAVES, pp. 269ff.

43 CHRISTIAN ADVOCATE, New York, 28 January 1858.

44 CHRISTIAN ADVOCATE, 15 April 1858.

45 W. A. Candler, GREAT REVIVALS AND THE GREAT REPUBLIC, p. 216; cf. CONGREGATIONAL QUARTERLY, April 1859.

46 CONGREGATIONAL QUARTERLY, April & October 185.

47 Old School and New School figures, plus Reformed Church data, CONGREGATIONAL QUARTERLY, Octoer 1859 & January 1860.

48 CONGREGATIONAL QUARTERLY, January 1859.

49 Episcopal totals in CONGREGATIONAL QUARTERLY, April 1859.

50 Also the estimate of L. W. Bacon, THE HISTORY OF AMERICAN CHRISTIANITY, pp. 37-38.

51 MINUTES OF THE GENERAL ASSEMBLY OF THE PRESBY-TERIAN CHURCH IN THE UNITED STATES OF AMERICA, 1863, p. 77; 1864, p. 331; 1865, p. 595; 1866, p. 117; 1867, p. 381; 1868, p. 667. 52 BIBLIOTHECA SACRA, 1859, pp. 279ff.

53 Halliday, THE CHURCH IN AMERICA & ITS BAPTISMS OF FIRE.

54 W. W. Sweet, THE STORY OF RELIGION IN AMERICA, p. 230.

Notes on Chapter 7: THE AWAKENING IN ULSTER

1   MINUTES OF THE GENERAL ASSEMBLY OF THE PRESBY-
    TERIAN CHURCH IN IRELAND, Volume II, p. 678.
2   PROCEEDINGS OF THE GENERAL ASSEMBLY on Revival.
3   G. Müller, AUTOBIOGRAPHY OF GEORGE MULLER, pp. 448ff.
4   D. Adams, THE REVIVAL AT AHOGHILL, p. 7.
5   BALLYMENA OBSERVER, 17 September 1859.
6   J. Weir, THE ULSTER AWAKENING, p. 38.
7   THE REVIVAL, London, 30 July 1859.
8   BELFAST NEWS LETTER, 30 May 1859.
9   W. Gibson, THE YEAR OF GRACE, pp. 66-67.
10 THE REVIVAL, 6 August 1859.
11 J. W. Massie, REVIVALS IN IRELAND, p. 46.
12 BELFAST NEWS LETTER, 23 June 1859.
13 J. Baillie, THE REVIVAL: WHAT I SAW IN IRELAND, p. 45.
14 BELFAST NEWS LETTTER, 30 June 1859.
15 BANNER OF ULSTER, 26 July & 20 August 1859; THE FREE-
    MAN, 10 August 1859.
16 EVANGELICAL CHRISTENDOM, 1859, passim.
17 W. Gibson, THE YEAR OF GRACE, p. 111.
18 W. Arthur, THE REVIVAL IN BALLYMENA AND COLERAINE,
    pp. 12ff.
19 see J. T. Carson, GOD'S RIVER IN SPATE, Chapters IX-X.
    (published just before his election as Moderator in 1959. See also
    A. R. Scott, 'The Ulster Revival of 1859,' the most thorough of all
    studies, a Ph.D. Dissertation, University of Dublin, 1972.
20 W. Gibson, THE YEAR OF GRACE, p. 51.
21 J. Weir, THE ULSTER AWAKENING, p. 73.
22 Quoted in THE REVIVAL, 5 November 1859.
23 W. Gibson, THE YEAR OF GRACE, pp. 55-56.
24 J. Weir, THE ULSTER AWAKENING, p. 130.
25 W. Gibson, THE YEAR OF GRACE, pp. 155ff.
26 THE REVIVAL, 24 September 1859.
27 W. Gibson, THE YEAR OF GRACE, pp. 178ff.
28 W. Reid, AUTHENTIC RECORDS OF REVIVAL, pp. 303ff.
29 THE REVIVAL, 4 February, 21 April & 26 May 1859.
30 J. Edwin Orr, THE SECOND EVANGELICAL AWAKENING IN
    BRITAIN, pp. 56-57.
31 EVANGELICAL CHRISTENDOM, 1859, pp. 363 & 378; & James
    McCosh, THE ULSTER REVIVAL AND ITS PHYSIOLOGICAL
    ACCIDENTS, London, 1859.
32 G. E. Morgan, R. C. MORGAN: HIS LIFE AND TIMES, p. 96;
    cf. THE NONCONFORMIST, 26 March 1860—'an understatement.'
33 EVANGELICAL CHRISTENDOM, 1859, p. 161.
34 cf. THE REVIVAL, 6 August 1859, &   EVANGELICAL CHRIS-
    TENDOM, 1860, pp. 606-607.
35 EVANGELICAL CHRISTENDOM, 1860, pp. 602ff.
36 The official committee of the Irish Churches invited the present
    writer as the speaker in this series commemorating the Revival of
    1859 throughout Ireland, from St. Patrick's Cathedral to Ballymena.

Notes on Chapter 8: THE AWAKENING IN SCOTLAND

1   ACTS OF THE GENERAL ASSEMBLY OF THE CHURCH OF
    SCOTLAND, 26 May 1860.

2 PROCEEDINGS AND DEBATES OF THE GENERAL ASSEMBLY OF THE FREE CHURCH OF SCOTLAND, 1860.
3 UNITED PRESBYTERIAN MAGAZINE, Volume IV, p. 326.
4 W. G. McLoughlin, MODERN REVIVALISM, p. 183.
5 Edinburgh correspondent, NEW YORK OBSERVER, 28 October 1858; cf. THE REVIVAL, 27 August 1859.
6 UNITED PRESBYTERIAN MAGAZINE 1860, Volume IV, p. 333.
7 THE NONCONFORMIST, 16 March, 24 August 1859.
8 NORTH BRITISH DAILY MAIL, 11, 15 & 20 August 1859.
9 SCOTTISH GUARDIAN, 2 August 1859; cf. 23 August 1859.
10 THE REVIVAL, 25 August 1860.
11 Reports of 15 & 22 September 1860, THE REVIVAL.
12 THE REVIVAL, 14 January 1860.
13 G. E. Morgan, R. C. MORGAN, p. 125.
14 cf. A. MacRae, REVIVALS IN THE HIGHLANDS, pp. 154ff, & THE REVIVAL, 8 December 1860.
15 THE REVIVAL, 27 November 1862.
16 THE NONCONFORMIST, 16 March, 24 August 1859, and THE REVIVAL, 30 July, 6 August, 10 September 1859.
17 THE REVIVAL, 3 March 1860.
18 A. McRae, REVIVALS IN THE HIGHLANDS, p. 145.
19 THE REVIVAL, 23 June 1860.
20 UNITED PRESBYTERIAN MAGAZINE, Volume IV, p. 82.
21 THE REVIVAL, 26 November 1859.
22 THE FREEMAN, 28 September 1859.
23 THE REVIVAL, 10 March 1859; THE FREEMAN, 11 January & 21 March 1860.
24 W. Reid, AUTHENTIC RECORDS OF REVIVAL, pp. 321ff.
25 PROCEEDINGS AND DEBATES IN THE GENERAL ASSEMBLY OF THE FREE CHURCH OF SCOTLAND, 1861.
26 THE REVIVAL, 8 December 1864.
27 UNITED PRESBYTERIAN MAGAZINE, Volume IV, p. 371.
28 THE REVIVAL, 19 January 1865.

Notes on Chapter 9: THE AWAKENING IN WALES

1 J. Edwin Orr, THE SECOND EVANGELICAL AWAKENING IN BRITAIN, p. 78. (cf. Eifion Evans, WHEN HE IS COME).
2 J. J. Morgan, THE '59 REVIVAL IN WALES, p. vi.
3 THE REVIVAL, 24 November 1860.
4 J. J. Morgan, THE '59 REVIVAL IN WALES, p. 3.
5 THE REVIVAL, 6 August 1859.
6 Eifion Evans, WHEN HE IS COME, p. 39.
7 J. J. Morgan, THE '59 REVIVAL IN WALES, pp. 3ff.
8 J. J. Morgan, HANES DAFYDD MORGAN YSBYTY A DIWYGIAD.
9 J. J. Morgan, THE '59 REVIVAL IN WALES, pp. 9, 17ff.
10 THE NONCONFORMIST, 21 September 1859.
11 J. Edwin Orr, THE SECOND EVANGELICAL AWAKENING IN BRITAIN, pp. 81-91.   12 THE REVIVAL, 25 February 1860.
13 J. J. Morgan, THE '59 REVIVAL IN WALES, pp. 106-107.
14 THE REVIVAL, 18 May, 22 June 1861.
15 F. Booth-Tucker, THE LIFE OF CATHERINE BOOTH, p. 262.
16 THE REVIVAL, 14 May 1863.
17 THE NONCONFORMIST, 17 December 1859.
18 THE REVIVAL, 19 January 1865.
19 J. J. Morgan, THE '59 REVIVAL IN WALES, p. vi.

20 THE REVIVAL, 24 November 1860.
21 cf. THE NONCONFORMIST, 15 November 1865; THE REVIVAL, 24 November 1860.
22 cf. THE NONCONFORMIST, 30 November 1859; THE FREEMAN, 26 October 1859; & THE REVIVAL, 24 November 1860.
23 Thomas Rees, A HISTORY OF NONCONFORMITY IN WALES.
24 J. J. Morgan, THE '59 REVIVAL IN WALES, p. vi.
25 J. J. Morgan, THE '59 REVIVAL IN WALES, p. vii.
26 Thomas Phillips, THE WELSH REVIVAL, pp. 117-118.
27 Eifion Evans, WHEN HE IS COME, pp. 89-90.

Notes on Chapter 10: AWAKENING IN NORTHERN ENGLAND

1 THE REVIVAL, 17 September, 1 October 1859.
2 THE TIMES, London, 21 September 1859.
3 THE RECORD, 21 September 1859.
4 THE REVIVAL, 1, 22 October 1859.
5 Report of 12 November 1859, THE REVIVAL.
6 THE WATCHMAN, 4 January 1860.
7 THE REVIVAL, 28 July 1864, 21 December 1865.
8 Report of 17 September 1859, THE REVIVAL.
9 WESLEYAN TIMES, 11 May 1863.
10 THE WATCHMAN, 23 May 1860.
11 THE REVIVAL, 26 March 1863.
12 R. Sandall, A HISTORY OF THE SALVATION ARMY, Vol. I, p. 8.
13 F. Booth-Tucker, LIFE OF CATHERINE BOOTH, p. 216.
14 R. Sandall, A HISTORY OF THE SALVATION ARMY, Volume I, pp. 9-11.
15 THE WATCHMAN, 22, 29 February 1860.
16 J. Edwin Orr, THE SECOND EVANGELICAL AWAKENING IN BRITAIN, p. 157.
17 C. G. Finney, MEMOIRS, pp. 458ff.
18 THE NONCONFORMIST, 14 September 1859; cf. J. Edwin Orr, THE SECOND EVANGELICAL AWAKENING IN BRITAIN.
19 C. G. Finney, MEMOIRS, pp. 468-469.
20 THE REVIVAL, 7 and 14 July 1860.
21 H. Pickering, CHIEF MEN AMONG THE BRETHREN, pp. 167ff.
22 J. C. Pollock, MOODY, p. 74.
23 THE RECORD, 28 November 1859 and 10 February 1860.
24 THE REVIVAL, 12 and 26 March 1863.
25 Reports of 8 October 1863; 8 September 1864, THE REVIVAL.
26 cf. Timothy L. Smith, CALLED UNTO HOLINESS, p. 23 (10,000 conversions in 1863); and THE REVIVAL, 5 March 1863.
27 THE REVIVAL, 30 July 1863.
28 F. Booth-Tucker, THE LIFE OF CATHERINE BOOTH, p. 271.
29 THE REVIVAL, 5 November 1863.
30 R. Sandall, A HISTORY OF THE SALVATION ARMY, Vol. I, p. 208.

Notes on Chapter 11: AWAKENING IN SOUTHERN ENGLAND

1 THE REVIVAL, 28 April 1860.
2 Eugene Stock, MY RECOLLECTIONS, pp. 82-83.
3 THE FREEMAN, 25 January 1860.
4 THE REVIVAL, 3 December 1859.
5 E. Hodder, THE LIFE AND WORK OF THE SEVENTH EARL OF SHAFTESBURY, Volume III, p. 100ff.

6   THE REVIVAL, 7 January 1860.
7   E. Hodder, THE LIFE AND WORK OF THE SEVENTH EARL OF SHAFTESBURY, Volume III, p. 3.
8   THE FREEMAN, 4 January 1860.
9   THE REVIVAL, 27 July 1861.
10 J. Edwin Orr, THE SECOND EVANGELICAL AWAKENING IN BRITAIN, p. 99.   11 THE REVIVAL, 2 February 1861.
12 Baptist Noel, of noble birth, resigned his Anglican incumbency to become a Baptist minister, but retained Anglican goodwill.
13 J. Edwin Orr, THE SECOND EVANGELICAL AWAKENING IN BRITAIN, p. 100.
14 THE NONCONFORMIST, 15 November 1865.
15 H. C. G. Moule, MEMORIALS OF A VICARAGE, pp. 48ff.
16 THE REVIVAL, 21 April 1861.
17 J. Edwin Orr, THE SECOND EVANGELICAL AWAKENING IN BRITAIN, pp. 113-116; cf. H. Begbie, THE LIFE OF WILLIAM BOOTH, passim.
18 R. Sandall, A HISTORY OF THE SALVATION ARMY, Vol. I, p. 16.
19 WESLEYAN TIMES, 25 May 1863.
20 THE REVIVAL, 2 and 23 March, 4 and 11 May 1861.
21 C. E. Wood, MEMOIR AND LETTERS OF CANON HAY AITKEN, pp. 76ff; cf. A. C. Downer, A CENTURY OF EVANGELICAL RELIGION IN OXFORD, p. 58.
22 J. B. Lancelot, FRANCIS JAMES CHAVASSE, p. 26.
23 THE REVIVAL, 3 March 1863.

Notes on Chapter 12: APPRECIATION—AND DEPRECIATION

1   NORTHERN WHIG, 31 August 1859 & BELFAST NEWS LETTER, 1 September 1859.
2   THE TIMES, London, 7 March 1860.
3   See issues of 7, 16, 20, 21, 23, 27 September 1859, and 1, 4, 7, 13, 26 October, etc.
4   G. M. Trevelyan, BRITISH HISTORY IN THE NINETEENTH CENTURY, p. 331.
5   Charles Dickens, ALL THE YEAR ROUND, 5 November 1859.
6   Benjamin Scott, THE REVIVAL IN ULSTER: ITS MORAL AND SOCIAL RESULTS, p. 57.
7   W. Gibson, THE YEAR OF GRACE, p. 253; cf. B. Scott, p. 82.
8   THE REVIVAL, 7 April 1860.
9   BRITISH STANDARD, quoted in THE REVIVAL, 21 April 1861.
10 THOM'S DIRECTORY OF IRELAND, Statistics of Ireland; see Criminal Convictions.
11 BELFAST NEWS LETTER, 13 July 1859.
12 W. Gibson, THE YEAR OF GRACE, p. 252.
13 cf. NORTHERN WHIG, 26 May, 12 July, 29 July 1859; and Prof. William Gibson, THE YEAR OF GRACE, p. 254.
14 THOM'S DIRECTORY OF IRELAND, Inspector of Asylums report in the Statistics of Ireland.
15 J. Baillie, THE REVIVAL, p. 63.
16 Benjamin Scott, THE REVIVAL IN ULSTER, p. 42.
17 W. Weir, THE ULSTER AWAKENING, pp. 190, 196.
18 Registrar-General, ILLEGITIMATE BIRTHS IN SCOTLAND.
19 Professor James McCosh, THE ULSTER REVIVAL AND ITS PHYSIOLOGICAL ACCIDENTS. (see J. Edwin Orr, THE SECOND EVANGELICAL AWAKENING IN BRITAIN, pp. 182-183)

20 EVANGELICAL CHRISTENDOM, 1859, p. 363.
21 W. Weir, THE ULSTER AWAKENING, pp. 176ff.
22 A. J. Appasamy, WRITE THE VISION, p. 64.
23 J. Edwin Orr, THE SECOND EVANGELICAL AWAKENING IN BRITAIN, pp. 184-186.
24 A. Ewing, ALEXANDER EWING, Bishop of Argyll, p. 294.
25 THE RECORD, 12 August 1859.
26 J. Edwin Orr, THE SECOND EVANGELICAL AWAKENING IN BRITAIN, p. 187.   27 THE FREEMAN, 11 January 1860ff.
28 G. R. Balleine, HISTORY OF THE EVANGELICAL PARTY IN THE CHURCH OF ENGLAND, pp. 240ff.
29 Eugene Stock, MY RECOLLECTIONS, pp. 82-83.
30 L. E. Binns, THE EVANGELICAL MOVEMENT IN THE CHURCH OF ENGLAND, p. 79.
31 THE FREEMAN, 25 April 1860.
32 Appendix B, in J. Edwin Orr, THE SECOND EVANGELICAL AWAKENING IN BRITAIN, p. 270-271.
33 CONGREGATIONAL YEAR BOOK, 1859, p.33.
34 Appendix C, in J. Edwin Orr, THE SECOND EVANGELICAL AWAKENING IN BRITAIN, p. 272.
35 Appendix D, in J. Edwin Orr, THE SECOND EVANGELICAL AWAKENING IN BRITAIN, pp. 273-275; also pp. 193-198.
36 Appendix E, in J. Edwin Orr, THE SECOND EVANGELICAL AWAKENING IN BRITAIN, pp. 276-277; also pp. 198-201.
37 J. Edwin Orr, THE SECOND EVANGELICAL AWAKENING IN BRITAIN, pp. 201-203.
38 R. M. Jones, THE LATER PERIODS OF QUAKERISM, pp. 951ff.
39 J. Edwin Orr, THE SECOND EVANGELICAL AWAKENING IN BRITAIN, pp. 203-204.
40 J. W. Massie, REVIVALS IN IRELAND, Part II, p. 91.
41 J. Edwin Orr, THE SECOND EVANGELICAL AWAKENING IN BRITAIN, pp. 204-207.

Notes on Chapter 13: MID-CENTURY IN EUROPE

1 M. W. Montgomery, A WIND FROM THE HOLY SPIRIT IN SWEDEN AND NORWAY, p. 58.
2 K. A. Olsson, BY ONE SPIRIT, p. 105.
3 E. Molland, CHURCH LIFE IN NORWAY, passim.
4 SCHAFF-HERZOG ENCYCLOPEDIA, on 'Revivals.'
5 J. O. Andersen, THE CHURCH IN DENMARK, pp. 60ff.
6 H. Koch, GRUNDTVIG (translated by Llewellyn Jones).
7 H. C. Vedder, A SHORT HISTORY OF THE BAPTISTS, p. 395.
8 P. Scharpff, GESCHICHTE DER EVANGELISATION, pp. 249ff.
9 P. Scharpff, GESCHICHTE DER EVANGELISATION, pp. 249ff.
10 EVANGELICAL CHRISTENDOM, 1861, p. 174; 1862, pp. 197ff.
11 G. M. Thomssen, SAMUEL HEBICH OF INDIA, pp. 301ff.
12 J. H. Lohrenz, THE MENNONITE BRETHREN CHURCH, p. 27ff.
13 H. C. Vedder, A SHORT HISTORY OF THE BAPTISTS, p. 406.
14 R. S. Latimer, LIBERTY OF CONSCIENCE UNDER THREE TSARS, pp. 71-76.
15 R. S. Latimer, DR. BAEDEKER AND HIS APOSTOLIC WORK IN RUSSIA, passim.
16 P. Milukow, SKIZZEN RUSSISCHER KULTURGESCHICHTE, p. 185.
17 see THE MENNONITE ENCYCLOPEDIA, pp. 308ff.
18 C. Henry Smith, THE STORY OF THE MENNONITES, passim.

Notes on Chapter 14: REVIVALS IN THE SOUTH SEAS

1 MINUTES OF THE METHODIST CONFERENCE, 1852-54, p. 75, pp. 243, 444.
2 WESLEYAN MAGAZINE, 1852, p. 818; 1853, pp. 582-583, 770.
3 MINUTES OF THE METHODIST CONFERENCE, 1852-54; cf. MINUTES OF THE FIRST CONFERENCE OF THE AUSTRALIAN WESLEYAN METHODIST CHURCH, 1854, pp. 57ff.
4 WESLEYAN MAGAZINE, 1857, p. 1134.
5 Letter of the Rev. James Bickford, 15 July 1857, in above issue.
6 Letter of the Rev. Isaac Harding, 15 February 1858, in WESLEYAN MAGAZINE, 1858, p. 468.
7 cf. CHRISTIAN PLEADER, Sydney, 14 May 1959, & WESLEYAN CHRONICLE, 1858, pp. 243, 284 and 207 (1st September 1859).
8 CHRISTIAN PLEADER, Sydney, 1859, pp. 138, 170, 178, 258-259; 1860, pp. 6-7, 195, 198, 245.
9 CHRISTIAN PLEADER, Sydney, 10 September 1859, p. 180.
10 Reports of 15 & 22 October 1859, pp. 220 & 226; cf. 18 February, 1860, CHRISTIAN PLEADER.
11 WESLEYAN CHRONICLE, Melbourne, 1 June 1859.
12 CHRISTIAN PLEADER, Sydney, 21 January 1860.
13 THE REVIVAL, London, 24 December, & CHRISTIAN PLEADER, 12 November 1859.
14 CHRISTIAN PLEADER, Sydney, 28 January, 4, 11 and 18 August, 10 November 1860.
15 AUSTRALIAN EVANGELIST, Melbourne, 22 August 1860, 18 July 1861, and CHRISTIAN PLEADER, 1861, p. 7.
16 WESLEYAN CHRONICLE, August 1860, pp. 188, 213, etc; and AUSTRALIAN EVANGELIST, 22 August and 1 September 1860.
17 WESLEYAN CHRONICLE, September 1860, p. 213; AUSTRALIAN EVANGELIST, 22 August 1860.
18 THE REVIVAL, 28 January 1860.
19 WESLEYAN MAGAZINE, 1860, p. 847.
20 THE SPECTATOR, Melbourne, 1900-1901, 'HISTORY OF THE BENDIGO CIRCUIT,' issues 13-24.
21 'HISTORY OF THE BENDIGO CIRCUIT,' part II, p. 1 and part IV, pp. 12-13. 22 WESLEYAN CHRONICLE, 22 May 1859, p. 157.
23 WESLEYAN CHRONICLE, October 1860, p. 234; AUSTRALIAN EVANGELIST, 22 August 1860.
24 WESLEYAN CHRONICLE, February & March 1860, pp. 47 and 69.
25 WESLEYAN CHRONICLE, July, p. 155; September 1859, p. 207.
26 E. I. Watkin, A JUBILEE HISTORY OF WESLEY CHURCH, in Melbourne, 1858-1908, pp. 11ff.
27 AUSTRALIAN EVANGELIST, 18 July, 19 August 1861.
28 CHRISTIAN ADVOCATE, August 1860; WESLEYAN CHRONICLE, August 1860, p. 205; and September 1860, p. 215.
29 WESLEYAN CHRONICLE, December 1860, p. 269.
30 cf. MINUTES OF THE CONFERENCES OF THE AUSTRALASIAN METHODIST CHURCH, 1863 & 1864; and THE SPECTATOR, Melbourne, 1900-1901, 'HISTORY OF THE HOBART CIRCUIT,' issues 13-24.
31 K. S. Latourette, A HISTORY OF THE EXPANSION OF CHRISTIANITY, Volume IV, p. 191.
32 see W. Taylor, SEVEN YEARS AS A STREET PREACHER IN CALIFORNIA, passim; also THE STORY OF MY LIFE, 1895, pp. 73-75, 218-228.

33 WESLEYAN CHRONICLE, 1 July 1858; 1 July 1864.
34 THE SPECTATOR, 1900-1901, issues 13-24, 'HISTORY OF THE HOBART CIRCUIT' & 'HISTORY OF THE LAUNCESTON CIRCUIT.'
35 E. I. Watkin, A JUBILEE HISTORY OF WESLEY CHURCH, in Melbourne, 1858-1908, p. 12.
36 cf. MINUTES OF THE METHODIST CONFERENCES, London, 1852-1854, and MINUTES OF THE CONFERENCE OF THE AUSTRALASIAN METHODIST CHURCH, 1854-1867.
37 see Circuit Histories, THE SPECTATOR, Melbourne, 1900-01, issues 13-24.
38 WESLEYAN METHODIST MAGAZINE, 1860, p. 568; 1861, p. 815; 1862, p. 818; 1863, p. 813; cf. REPORTS OF THE WESLEYAN METHODIST MISSIONARY SOCIETY, 1860-1863.
39 CHURCH MISSIONARY GLEANER, 1861, pp. 128-129.
40 YEAR BOOKS, Australasian Methodist Church.
41 MINUTES OF THE HAWAIIAN EVANGELISTIC ASSOCIATION, 1858-1862; cf. THE MESSENGER, London.
42 S. B. Halliday, THE CHURCH IN AMERICA AND ITS BAPTISMS OF FIRE, p. 533; AMERICAN BOARD OF COMMISSIONERS FOR FOREIGN MISSIONS, 1862, pp. 136, 163.
43 J. Rauws, THE NETHERLANDS INDIES, pp. 53-54; CHRISTIAN OBSERVER, Philadelphia.
44 BAPTIST MISSIONARY MAGAZINE, 1902, p. 687.

Notes on Chapter 15: REVIVAL IN SOUTHERN AFRICA

1 REPORT OF THE AMERICAN BOARD, Boston, 1859, p. 45.
2 WESLEYAN METHODIST MAGAZINE, London, January 1960.
3 Archives, METHODIST CHURCH OF SOUTH AFRICA, in Cory Library, Rhodes University; MS lists of 'Awakened,' 29 June 1859, in Bechuana District.
4 REPORT OF THE AMERICAN BOARD, 1861, p. 30.
5 REPORTS of 1862, p. 62; 1863, p. 48; 1867, pp. 53ff; 1868, pp. 9ff.
6 MINUTES OF METHODIST DISTRICT MEETINGS, 1854-58, in Albany and Kaffraria, Cory Library, Indexed References.
7 see DE KERKBODE, Cape Town, 1859-60. (Dutch)
8 DE KERKBODE, 1860, pp. 47, 92-94, 141-144.
9 J. du Plessis, THE LIFE OF ANDREW MURRAY OF SOUTH AFRICA, passim.
10 Jan Christiaan de Vries, cousin of Field Marshal Jan C. Smuts.
11 J. du Plessis, THE LIFE OF ANDREW MURRAY, pp. 194ff.
12 Ds. J. C. de Vries, cited in J. du Plessis above.
13 GODSDIENSVERSLAG (State of Religion Report), Andrew Murray, Worcester, 1860; Archives, Dutch Reformed Church, Cape Town.
14 J. du Plessis, THE LIFE OF ANDREW MURRAY, pp. 194ff.
15 GODSDIENSVERSLAG, Andrew Murray, Worcester, 1861.
16 ARCHIVES, Dutch Reformed Church, Cape Town.
17 DE KERKBODE, Cape Town, Indexed References.
18 Prof. N. Hofmeyr, ADDRESS, 20 October 1860.
19 GODSDIENSVERSLAG, G. W. A. van der Lingen, Paarl, 1860-1861, Archives, Dutch Reformed Church, Cape Town.
20 W. Taylor, THE STORY OF MY LIFE, passim.
21 see W. Taylor, CHRISTIAN ADVENTURES IN SOUTH AFRICA, pp. 38ff, 62ff & 41ff.
22 WESLEYAN METHODIST MAGAZINE, 1 June 1866.
23 see W. Taylor, CHRISTIAN ADVENTURES, pp. 120ff.

24 WESLEYAN METHODIST MISSIONARY REPORTS, 1866–68; cf. Report of William Impey and Letter of William Sargent, in the WESLEYAN METHODIST MAGAZINE, October & November 1866, pp. 928 and 1036.
25 W. Taylor, CHRISTIAN ADVENTURES IN SOUTH AFRICA, pp. 120; cf. MINUTES, QUARTERLY MEETING, FORT BEAUFORT, on 9 November 1866, in Archives, Cory Library; & WESLEYAN METHODIST MISSIONARY REPORTS, 1866–68.
26 SERMON of the Rev. H. H. Dugmore, 15 July 1866.
27 REPORT, Kamastone Circuit, 1866, in Archives, Cory Library.
28 Basil F. Holt, 'BLAZING FIREBRAND,' Article.
29 REPORT, Clarkesbury Circuit, 1866, in Archives, Cory Library.
30 REPORTS, Butterworth Circuit, 1866, Osborn Circuit, 1866.
31 W. Taylor, CHRISTIAN ADVENTURES IN SOUTH AFRICA, p. 316.
32 WESLEYAN METHODIST MAGAZINE, November 1867, pp. 1038ff.
33 MINUTES OF THE METHODIST CONFERENCES, London, 1865–1869, pp. 318; 550; 121; 355 and 584.

Notes on Chapter 16: THE IMPACT ON INDIA

1 Marshall Broomhall, HUDSON TAYLOR, p. 103.
2 E. Stock, HISTORY OF THE CHURCH MISSIONARY SOCIETY, Volume II, p. 34.
3 MISSIONARY HERALD, Boston, 1867, p. 73.
4 Reports in MISSIONARY HERALD, 1867, pp. 43, 79, 145.
5 see AMERICAN BOARD OF COMMISSIONERS FOR FOREIGN MISSIONS, 1861, pp. 54ff; 1862, p. 90.
6 D. A. Stoddard, NARRATIVE OF THE LATE REVIVAL AMONG THE NESTORIANS, Boston, 1847; cf. AMERICAN BOARD OF COMMISSIONERS FOR FOREIGN MISSIONS, 1859, pp. 80ff.
7 S. C. Neill, A HISTORY OF CHRISTIAN MISSIONS, p. 279.
8 C. H. Swavely, THE LUTHERAN ENTERPRISE IN SOUTH INDIA, p. 55.   9 THE REVIVAL, London, 3 December 1859.
10 E. B. Bromley, THEY WERE MEN SENT FROM GOD, p. 163.
11 G. Smith, THE LIFE OF ALEXANDER DUFF, p. 302.
12 THE REVIVAL, 31 December 1859.
13 OVERLAND ATHENAEUM, Madras, 16 September 1859.
14 R. E. Speer, GEORGE BOWEN OF BOMBAY, pp. 232–233.
15 THE REVIVAL, 22 September 1860.
16 see G. H. Lang, THE HISTORY AND DIARIES OF AN INDIAN CHRISTIAN, pp. 9 and 29.
17 THE HISTORY AND DIARIES OF AN INDIAN CHRISTIAN, p. 141.
18 E. Stock, A HISTORY OF THE CHURCH MISSIONARY SOCIETY, Volume II, p. 289.
19 cf. INDIAN WATCHMAN, October 1860; CHURCH MISSIONARY INTELLIGENCER, August 1860; CHURCH MISSIONARY RECORD, August 1860.
20 W. S. Hunt, THE ANGLICAN CHURCH IN TRAVANCORE AND COCHIN, Volume II, p. 154.
21 cf. MISSIONARY RECORD, Madras, December 1873; Report of MISSIONARY CONFERENCE ON SOUTH INDIA, p. 164; Hunt, THE ANGLICAN CHURCH IN TRAVANCORE & COCHIN, p. 115, pp. 154–156.
22 E. Stock, A HISTORY OF THE CHURCH MISSIONARY SOCIETY, Volume III, pp. 179ff.
23 W. S. Hunt, THE ANGLICAN CHURCH IN TRAVANCORE, p. 157.

24 E. Stock, A HISTORY OF THE CHURCH MISSIONARY SOCIETY, Volume III, pp. 179ff.
25 W. S. Hunt, THE ANGLICAN CHURCH IN TRAVANCORE, p. 158.
26 MISSIONARY CONFERENCE ON SOUTH INDIA, p. 167.
27 W. S. Hunt, THE ANGLICAN CHURCH IN TRAVANCORE, p. 160.
28 A. W. Carmichael, WALKER OF TINNEVELLY, p. 231.
29 W. S. Hunt, THE ANGLICAN CHURCH IN TRAVANCORE, p. 152.
30 E. B. Bromley, THEY WERE MEN SENT FROM GOD, pp. 163ff.
31 E. R. Clough, SOCIAL CHRISTIANITY IN THE ORIENT, p. 92; E. B. Bromley, pp. 161-162.
32 E. R. Clough, SOCIAL CHRISTIANITY IN THE ORIENT, p. 98.
33 The Ludhiana-proposed, Evangelical Alliance-sponsored 'Week of Prayer,' see E. R. Clough, p. 137.
34 E. R. Clough, SOCIAL CHRISTIANITY IN THE ORIENT, p. 275.
35 cf. S. C. Neill, A HISTORY OF CHRISTIAN MISSIONS, pp. 364-365; and E. R. Clough, p. 136.
36 J. W. Pickett, CHRISTIAN MASS MOVEMENTS IN INDIA, p. 5.
37 J. N. Hollister, CENTENARY OF THE METHODIST CHURCH IN SOUTHERN ASIA, pp. 45ff.
38 C. H. Swavely, THE LUTHERAN ENTERPRISE IN SOUTH INDIA, pp. 19-20.   39 C. H. Swavely, pp. 55ff.
40 J. N. Hollister, CENTENARY OF THE METHODIST CHURCH IN SOUTHERN ASIA, p. xxv.
41 see J. M. Thoburn, MY MISSIONARY APPRENTICESHIP.
42 J. M. Thoburn, ISABELLA THOBURN, pp. 99ff.
43 W. Taylor, FOUR YEARS' CAMPAIGN IN INDIA, pp. 303-313.
44 E. G. K. Hewat, CHRIST AND WESTERN INDIA, p. 231.
45 J. N. Hollister, CENTENARY OF THE METHODIST CHURCH IN SOUTHERN ASIA, p. 115.
46 W. Taylor, FOUR YEARS' CAMPAIGN IN INDIA, p. 355; cf. J. N. Hollister, p. 120.
47 J. N. Hollister, p. 123.
48 see R. E. Speer, GEORGE BOWEN OF BOMBAY, pp. 260ff, & J. M. Thoburn, ISABELLA THOBURN, p. 106.

Notes on Chapter 17: EMPOWERED PREACHERS

1 F. G. Beardsley, A HISTORY OF AMERICAN REVIVALS, p. 231.
2 M. B. Cheney, LIFE AND LETTERS OF HORACE BUSHNELL, pp. 412-413.
3 T. L. Cuyler, STIRRING THE EAGLE'S NEST, p. 301.
4 see Lyman Abbott, HENRY WARD BEECHER, Boston, 1904.
5 NEW YORK TIMES, 20 March 1858.
6 C. G. Finney, MEMOIRS, passim.
7 C. G. Finney, LECTURES ON REVIVALS OF RELIGION.
8 W. F. P. Noble, A CENTURY OF GOSPEL WORK, p. 522.
9 cf. Notes by R. Jeffry in Jacob Knapp, THE AUTOBIOGRAPHY OF ELDER JACOB KNAPP, pp. xv, xix-xxvi.
10 Jacob Knapp, AUTOBIOGRAPHY, pp. 175ff.
11 C. L. Thompson, TIMES OF REFRESHING, p. 171.
12 A. B. Earle, BRINGING IN THE SHEAVES, passim.
13 C. K. Whipple, in THE RADICAL, 1865-66, pp. 429-38.
14 A. B. Earle, BRINGING IN THE SHEAVES, pp. 269ff.
15 cf. J. Caughey, METHODISM IN EARNEST, Richmond, 1852; & SHOWERS OF BLESSING, New York, 1859; and G. E. Morgan, R. C. MORGAN, pp. 119, 128.

16 R. Wheatley, THE LIFE AND LETTERS OF MRS. PHOEBE PALMER, 1876; G. Hughes, THE BELOVED PHYSICIAN, Walter C. Palmer, 1884.
17 P. C. Headley, E. PAYSON HAMMOND: THE REAPER AND THE HARVEST, London 1909; cf. THE CHRISTIAN, 11 February 1909.
18 P. C. Headley, THE HARVEST WORK OF THE HOLY SPIRIT.
19 THE CHRISTIAN, 11 February 1909.
20 PRESBYTERIAN MAGAZINE, q. in THE REVIVAL, 29 December 1864.   21 THE CHRISTIAN, 30 June 1910.
22 C. E. Wood, MEMOIR AND LETTERS OF CANON HAY AITKEN, London, 1928; cf. THE CHRISTIAN, 3 June 1909.
23 see J. B. Lancelot, FRANCIS JAMES CHAVASSE, London, 1929; J. B. Harford and F. C. MacDonald, HANDLEY C. G. MOULE, London, 1922.
24 cf. MINUTES OF THE METHODIST CONFERENCE, London, 1903, pp. 28ff; and DICTIONARY OF NATIONAL BIOGRAPHY, supplement 1901-1911, Volume I, p. 320.
25 see G. F. Barbour, THE LIFE OF ALEXANDER WHYTE, 1923; A. Gammie, PREACHERS I HAVE HEARD, London, 1946.
26 THE CHRISTIAN, 10 June 1894.
27 W. Y. Fullerton, THE LIFE OF F. B. MEYER, London, 1929.

Notes on Chapter 18: CHRISTIAN ACTION

1 W. A. Candler, GREAT REVIVALS AND THE GREAT REPUBLIC, pp. 215-216; cf. also L. W. Bacon, HISTORY OF AMERICAN CHRISTIANITY, pp. 37-38.
2 See Appendices, J. Edwin Orr, THE SECOND EVANGELICAL AWAKENING IN BRITAIN, pp. 269ff.
3 THE FREEMAN, 4, 11 January 1860; and THE REVIVAL, 7 April 1860.
4 W. G. McLoughlin, MODERN REVIVALISM, p. 183.
5 cf. CONGREGATIONAL QUARTERLY, April 1859; October 1859; January 1860, for American statistics; Appendix B, J. Edwin Orr, THE SECOND EVANGELICAL AWAKENING IN BRITAIN, for British figures.
6 The Congregationalists in the United States increased by 60,407 (one third) in the decade 1855-65, of which 21,582 were added in the single year 1858. In the United Kingdom, 90,000 were gained in the 1859 Revival period.
7 Methodist gains were equally divided between the United States and and Great Britain.
8 In the United States, approximately 100,000 converts were won by the Presbyterian and Reformed Churches.
9 W. A. Candler, GREAT REVIVALS AND THE GREAT REPUBLIC, pp. 222-223.
10 F. G. Beardsley, A HISTORY OF AMERICAN REVIVALS, p. 230.
11 Conant, NARRATIVE OF REMARKABLE CONVERSIONS, pp. 401ff
12 F. G. Beardsley, A HISTORY OF AMERICAN REVIVALS, p. 237.
13 BAPTIST MISSIONARY MAGAZINE, October 1858.
14 W. Canton, HISTORY OF THE BRITISH AND FOREIGN BIBLE SOCIETY, Volume III, pp. 74-75.
15 In the same volume, cf. pp. 33ff, & p. 16.
16 G. E. Morgan, R. C. MORGAN, p. 159.
17 G. R. Balleine, HISTORY OF THE EVANGELICAL PARTY, p. 245.
18 MINUTES OF THE METHODIST CONFERENCE, 1903, pp. 128ff

19 R. Sandall, HISTORY OF THE SALVATION ARMY, Volume I, Chapter I-IV, passim.
20 THE REVIVAL, 6 August 1859.
21 J. E. Hodder-Williams, THE LIFE OF SIR GEORGE WILLIAMS, pp. 187, 203.
22 see E. W. Rice, THE SUNDAY SCHOOL MOVEMENT.
23 cf. THE REVIVAL, 27 August 1859; & Appendix D, J. Edwin Orr, THE SECOND EVANGELICAL AWAKENING IN BRITAIN.

Notes on Chapter 19: THE MISSIONARY EXTENSION

1 E. Stock, HISTORY OF THE CHURCH MISSIONARY SOCIETY, Volume II, pp. 32ff.
2 CONFERENCE ON MISSIONS, held at Liverpool, 1860, passim.
3 W. R. Hogg, ECUMENICAL FOUNDATIONS, pp. 37-47.
4 K. S. Latourette, A HISTORY OF CHRISTIAN MISSIONS IN CHINA, pp. 357ff.   5 W. E. Soothill, TIMOTHY RICHARD OF CHINA.
6 J. Edwin Orr, THE SECOND EVANGELICAL AWAKENING IN BRITAIN, pp. 226-229.
7 Mrs. Howard Taylor, daughter-in-law and biographer of J. Hudson Taylor, on her death bed shared unpublished information with the writer; cf. H. & G. Taylor, HUDSON TAYLOR IN EARLY YEARS; HUDSON TAYLOR AND THE CHINA INLAND MISSION, etc; and Marshall Broomhall, HUDSON TAYLOR; see also THE REVIVAL, 2 December 1860, 2 November 1861, 3 August, 14 & 28 September 1865, and 31 May 1866.
8 see Griffith John, A VOICE FROM CHINA, pp. 187ff; R. Lovett, JAMES GILMOUR OF MONGOLIA, passim; Blodgett & Baldwin, SKETCHES OF THE MISSIONS OF THE AMERICAN BOARD IN CHINA, pp. 43ff; L. S. Ashmore, THE SOUTH CHINA MISSION OF THE AMERICAN BAPTIST FOREIGN MISSION; McGillivray, A CENTURY OF PROTESTANT MISSIONS IN CHINA, pp. 32ff, 297, 322, 384ff, 429ff; W. Campbell, SKETCHES FROM FORMOSA
9 K. S. Latourette, A HISTORY OF THE EXPANSION OF CHRISTIANITY, Volume VI, p. 336.
10 National Bible Society of Scotland, ANNUAL REPORT, 1865.
11 J. D. Davis, THE LIFE OF REV. JOSEPH HARDY NEESIMA.
12 American Baptist Missionary Union, ANNUAL REPORT, 1873.
13 see C. Hamlin, MY LIFE AND TIMES; Anonymous, A CENTURY OF MISSION WORK IN IRAN, 1834-1934; R. Sinker, MEMORIAL OF THE HON. ION KEITH-FALCONER OF ARABIA.
14 J. Rauws, THE NETHERLANDS INDIES, pp. 53-54.
15 J. Warneck, LUDWIG I. NOMMENSEN, EIN LEBENSBILD.
16 J. Edwin Orr, THE SECOND EVANGELICAL AWAKENING IN BRITAIN, p. 67; Lovett, JAMES CHALMERS, AUTOBIOGRAPHY AND LETTERS, passim.
17 J. Flierl, CHRIST IN NEW GUINEA; Brown, AUTOBIOGRAPHY OF GEORGE BROWN; J. Rauws, NETHERLANDS INDIES, p. 116.
18 see AMERICAN BOARD OF COMMISSIONERS FOR FOREIGN MISSIONS, 1862, pp. 136, 163; cf. S. B. Halliday, THE CHURCH IN AMERICA AND ITS BAPTISMS OF FIRE, p. 533.
19 Freeman & Jones, A NARRATIVE OF THE PERSECUTIONS OF CHRISTIANS IN MADAGASCAR, London, 1840.
20 W. Ellis, THE MARTYR CHURCH OF MADAGASCAR, pp. 373ff.
21 E. Stock, HISTORY OF THE CHURCH MISSIONARY SOCIETY, Volume II, pp. 473ff.

22 A. Burgess, ZANAHARY IN SOUTH MADAGASCAR, p. 132.
23 C. F. Pascoe, TWO HUNDRED YEARS OF THE S. P. G., p. 306.
24 P. B. Hinchliff, JOHN WILLIAMS COLENSO.
25 W. P. Livingstone, CHRISTINA FORSYTHE OF FINGOLAND; &
    J. Wells, THE LIFE OF JAMES STEWART.
26 W. C. Holden, THE STORY OF KAMA AND HIS TRIBE, pp. 24ff.
27 J. Whiteside, A HISTORY OF THE WESLEYAN METHODIST
    CHURCH IN SOUTH AFRICA.
28 see L. A. Hewson, AN INTRODUCTION TO SOUTH AFRICAN
    METHODISTS, p. 74.
29 G. & N. Pamla, AMABALANA NGO BOMI BUKA, (notes from the
    Xhosa by Dr. Basil F. Holt); cf. MINUTES OF THE METHODIST
    CONFERENCE, Cape Town, 1913.
30 cf. E. W. Smith, THE MABILLES OF BASUTOLAND.
31 C. W. Mackintosh, COILLARD OF THE ZAMBESI.
32 J. Wells, THE LIFE OF JAMES STEWART.
33 E. Baker, THE LIFE AND EXPLORATIONS OF F. S. ARNOT.
34 D. Crawford, THINKING BLACK: CENTRAL AFRICA.
35 J. W. Springer, THE HEART OF CENTRAL AFRICA, pp. 19ff.
36 G. Hawker, THE LIFE OF GEORGE GRENFELL.
37 Mrs. H. G. Guinness, THE NEW WORLD OF CENTRAL AFRICA,
    p. 175.
38 BAPTIST MISSIONARY MAGAZINE, 1887; cf. J. du Plessis, THE
    EVANGELIZATION OF PAGAN AFRICA, pp. 211-212.
39 BAPTIST MISSIONARY MAGAZINE, 1887, p. 70.
40 J. du Plessis, THE EVANGELIZATION OF PAGAN AFRICA,
    pp. 211ff.
41 cf. J. H. Speke, WHAT LED TO THE DISCOVERY OF THE
    SOURCE OF THE NILE, p. 366; DAILY TELEGRAPH, London,
    15 November 1875.
42 E. Stock, HISTORY OF THE CHURCH MISSIONARY SOCIETY,
    Volume III, pp. 98-102, 410-412, 441-448.
43 W. P. Livingstone, MARY SLESSOR OF CALABAR.
44 J. Page, THE BLACK BISHOP, SAMUEL ADJAI CROWTHER.
45 Rutherfurd & Glenny, THE GOSPEL IN NORTH AFRICA, pp. 135ff
46 G. E. Beskow, DEN SVENSKA MISSIONEN I OST-AFRIKA.
47 F. C. Macdonald, BISHOP STIRLING OF THE FALKLANDS,
    pp. 68-70.
48 E. F. Every, 25 YEARS IN SOUTH AMERICA, pp. 81ff.
49 Braga & Grubb, THE REPUBLIC OF BRAZIL, pp. 50ff, pp. 59ff
50 Browning, Ritchie & Grubb, THE WEST COAST REPUBLICS OF
    SOUTH AMERICA, pp. 27ff; 79ff.
51 W. Taylor, THE STORY OF MY LIFE, p. 680.
52 Braga & Grubb, THE REPUBLIC OF BRAZIL, pp. 54ff, 61ff, 63ff.
53 Melinda Rankin, TWENTY YEARS AMONG THE MEXICANS,
    pp. 88ff, 120ff.

Notes on Chapter 20: THE HOLINESS MOVEMENT

1 W. E. Boardman, THE HIGHER CHRISTIAN LIFE, Boston, 1858;
   London, 1860; see M.M. Boardman, THE LIFE AND LABOURS
   OF THE REV. W. E. BOARDMAN, New York, 1887.
2 W. B. Sloan, THESE SIXTY YEARS, p. 10.
3 J. C. Pollock, THE KESWICK STORY, pp. 30ff.
4 W. B. Sloan, THESE SIXTY YEARS, p. 19.
5 J. Harford Battersby, MEMOIR OF T. D. HARFORD-BATTERSBY.

6   W. B. Sloan, THESE SIXTY YEARS, indexed references.
7   T. L. Smith, REVIVALISM AND SOCIAL REFORM, p. 27.
8   see J. C. Pollock, THE KESWICK STORY, passim.
9   T. L. Smith, REVIVALISM AND SOCIAL REFORM, pp. 114ff;
    cf. R. Wheatley, LIFE & LETTERS OF MRS. PHŒBE PALMER,
    & G. Hughes, THE BELOVED PHYSICIAN: WALTER C. PALMER.
10 W. Taylor, THE STORY OF MY LIFE, pp. 219-228.
11 see A. B. Earle, BRINGING IN THE SHEAVES.
12 T. L. Smith, REVIVALISM AND SOCIAL REFORM, p. 139.
13 P. Scharpff, GESCHICHE DER EVANGELISATION, pp. 220ff.

Notes on Chapter 21;   THE EVANGELISTIC EXTENSION

1   W. R. Moody, THE LIFE OF DWIGHT L. MOODY: the standard
    text; and a recent biography, J. F. Findlay, DWIGHT L. MOODY.
2   J. C. Pollock, MOODY : A BIOGRAPHICAL PORTRAIT, pp. 14ff
3   Moody wrote home to describe his involvement in the 1858 Revival
    in Chicago. The only satisfactory explanation of the date of Moody's
    letter is that he wrote it in the New Year of 1858; cf. Moody, p. 47.
4   W. R. Moody, THE LIFE OF DWIGHT L. MOODY, pp. 55ff.
5   F. G. Beardsley, A HISTORY OF AMERICAN REVIVALS, p. 237.
6   W. R. Moody, THE LIFE OF DWIGHT L. MOODY, pp. 131ff.
7   J. McPherson, HENRY MOORHOUSE, pp. 48 and 66.
8   W. R. Moody, THE LIFE OF DWIGHT L. MOODY, p. 149.
9   see THE CHRISTIAN, 3 June 1909, on HENRY VARLEY; cf.
    W. R. Moody, p. 134ff.
10 R. Braithwaite, THE REV. WILLIAM PENNEFATHER.
11 W. R. Moody, THE LIFE OF DWIGHT L. MOODY, pp. 152ff.
12 cf. EDINBURGH COURANT, December 1873; THE CHRISTIAN,
    January and February 1874.
13 W. R. Moody, THE LIFE OF DWIGHT L. MOODY, pp. 197ff.
14 see DUBLIN EVENING NEWS, November 1874.
15 Moody, THE LIFE OF DWIGHT L. MOODY, pp. 215ff, 223ff.
16 F. Engels, SOCIALISM, UTOPIAN AND SCIENTIFIC, introduction.
17 see NEW YORK TIMES, 4 February 1876.
18 W. R. Moody, THE LIFE OF DWIGHT L. MOODY, pp. 291ff.
19 J. C. Pollock, MOODY: A BIOGRAPHICAL PORTRAIT, pp. 241ff.
20 see THE CHRISTIAN, 6 July 1882.
21 W. R. Moody, THE LIFE OF DWIGHT L. MOODY, pp. 297ff.
22 MISSIONARY REVIEW OF THE WORLD, May 1895.
23 W. R. Moody, THE LIFE OF DWIGHT L. MOODY, pp. 409ff.
24 see KANSAS CITY STAR, 11-18 November 1899.
25 W. W. Sweet, REVIVALISM IN AMERICA, p. 169.
26 G. Loud, EVANGELIZED AMERICA, pp. 290ff.
27 S. D. Clark, CHURCH AND SECT IN CANADA, p. 401.
28 see W. Holcolmb, SAM JONES, passim.
29 Luther A. Weigle, B. Fay Mills, DICTIONARY OF AMERICAN
    BIOGRAPHY.
30 J. C. Ramsay, JOHN WILBUR CHAPMAN, p. 74 (cf. FAMILY
    CALL, 23 November 1896); and H. Murray, SIXTY YEARS AN
    EVANGELIST: GIPSY SMITH.
31 DE KERKBODE, Cape Town, 1874-75, indexed; see J. du Plessis,
    THE LIFE OF ANDREW MURRAY, p. 322 and passim.
32 E. Weeks, W. SPENCER WALTON.
33 E. Amdahl, in INTERNATIONAL REVIEW OF MISSIONS, Volume
    XXIX, pp. 358ff.

34 G. M. Stephenson, THE RELIGIOUS ASPECTS OF SWEDISH IM-
    MIGRATION, pp. 103ff.
35 M. W. Montgomery, A WIND FROM THE HOLY SPIRIT IN
    SWEDEN AND NORWAY, p. 58.
36 G. M. Stephenson, p. 109.
37 M. Gidland, KYRKA OCH VACKELSE, 1849-1880, pp. 344ff.
38 G. M. Stephenson, THE RELIGIOUS ASPECTS OF SWEDISH IM-
    MIGRATION, pp. 278ff.
39 O. Grauer, FREDRIK FRANSON, pp. 21ff.
40 P. Scharpff, GESCHICHTE DER EVANGELISATION, pp. 249ff.
41 F. Siegmund-Schultze, EVANGELISCHE KIRCHE IN POLEN.
42 K. S. Latourette, THE NINETEENTH CENTURY IN EUROPE,
    Volume II, pp. 198ff.
43 Revesz, Kovats & Ravasz, HUNGARIAN PROTESTANTISM; cf.
    M. Bucsay, GESCHICHTE DES PROTESTANTISMUS IN UNGARN,
    p. 185.
44 see R. S. Latimer, LIBERTY OF CONSCIENCE UNDER THREE
    TSARS, pp. 71-76.
45 R. S. Latimer, DR. BAEDEKER AND HIS APOSTOLIC WORK
    IN RUSSIA, passim.
46 cf. W. C. Emhart, RELIGION IN THE SOVIET UNION, p. 284;
    R. P. Casey, RELIGION IN RUSSIA, pp. 42ff.

Notes on Chapter 22: VOLUNTEERS FOR SERVICE

1 C. P. Shedd, TWO CENTURIES OF STUDENT CHRISTIAN MOVE-
   MENTS, pp. 110-111.
2 J. C. Pollock, A CAMBRIDGE MOVEMENT, pp. 41ff.
3 THE CHRISTIAN, 19 February 1885.
4 G. A. Smith, THE LIFE OF HENRY DRUMMOND.
5 N. P. Grubb, C. T. STUDD: CRICKETER AND PIONEER.
6 J. C. Pollock, A CAMBRIDGE MOVEMENT, p. 57.
7 W. R. Moody, THE LIFE OF DWIGHT L. MOODY, pp. 350ff.
8 J. C. Pollock, A CAMBRIDGE MOVEMENT, pp. 59-60.
9 J. C. Pollock, MOODY: A BIOGRAPHICAL PORTRAIT, pp. 228ff
10 J. C. Pollock, A CAMBRIDGE MOVEMENT, p. 58.
11 CAMBRIDGE REVIEW, Issues of November 1882.
12 W. R. Moody, THE LIFE OF DWIGHT L. MOODY, pp. 350-357.
13 J. C. Pollock, A CAMBRIDGE MOVEMENT, p. 70.
14 THE CHRISTIAN, 23 November 1882.
15 Wilfred Grenfell, A LABRADOR DOCTOR (Autobiography)
16 J. C. Pollock, A CAMBRIDGE MOVEMENT, passim.
17 COLLEGE BULLETIN, New York, March 1885.
18 P. Thompson, D. E. HOSTE: A PRINCE WITH GOD; Marshall
   Broomhall, W. W. CASSELS: FIRST BISHOP IN WEST CHINA.
19 Luther D. Wishard, 'The Student Era in Christian History,' p. 138.
20 Basil Matthews, JOHN R. MOTT, WORLD CITIZEN.
21 COLLEGE BULLETIN, New York, April 1880.
22 Luther D. Wishard, 'The Student Era in Christian History,' p. 129.
23 C. P. Shedd, TWO CENTURIES OF STUDENT CHRISTIAN MOVE-
   MENTS, pp. 248ff.
24 see REPORT OF THE FIRST INTERNATIONAL CONVENTION
   OF THE STUDENT VOLUNTEER MOVEMENT, pp. 161-163.
25 C. P. Shedd, STUDENT CHRISTIAN MOVEMENTS, pp. 259-262.
26 cf. SPRINGFIELD REPUBLICAN, 2 August 1886; & John R. Mott,
   HISTORY OF THE STUDENT VOLUNTEER MOVEMENT, p. 12.

27 cf. C. P. Shedd, STUDENT CHRISTIAN MOVEMENTS, p. 267; THE INTERCOLLEGIAN, May 1887; & W. R. Moody, THE LIFE OF DWIGHT L. MOODY, p. 358.
28 cf. C. P. Shedd, STUDENT CHRISTIAN MOVEMENTS, p. 275; J. H. Oldham, STUDENT CHRISTIAN MOVEMENT OF GREAT BRITAIN AND IRELAND, p. 13; G. A. Smith, THE LIFE OF HENRY DRUMMOND, pp. 370ff.
29 C. K. Ober, LUTHER D. WISHARD, pp. 122ff.
30 L. D. Wishard, 'The Students' Era in Christian History,' pp. 178ff.
31 THE INTERCOLLEGIAN, December 1889; SPRINGFIELD UNION, 7 July 1892; J. H. Oldham, STUDENT CHRISTIAN MOVEMENT OF GREAT BRITAIN AND IRELAND, pp. 14-15.
32 G. A. Smith, THE LIFE OF HENRY DRUMMOND, pp. 386ff.
33 Basil Matthews, JOHN R. MOTT, WORLD CITIZEN, pp. 112ff.
34 J. H. Oldham, STUDENT CHRISTIAN MOVEMENT OF GREAT BRITAIN AND IRELAND, pp. 21ff.
35 C. P. Shedd, STUDENT CHRISTIAN MOVEMENTS, Chapter XXII.
36 K. S. Latourette, A HISTORY OF THE EXPANSION OF CHRISTIANITY, Volume IV, pp. 97-98.
37 J. C. Pollock, MOODY: A BIOGRAPHICAL PORTRAIT, pp. 261ff.
38 see G. T. B. Davis, TORREY AND ALEXANDER.
39 A. E. Thompson, THE LIFE OF A. B. SIMPSON, pp. 26ff.
40 The Gospel Tabernacle has remained the Mother Church of the denomination, which still excels in missionary enterprise.
41 A. E. Thompson, THE LIFE OF A. B. SIMPSON, pp. 128ff.
42 S. B. Halliday, THE CHURCH IN AMERICA AND ITS BAPTISMS OF FIRE, pp. 347ff.

Notes on Chapter 23: MISSIONARY REINFORCEMENT

1 Student Volunteer Movement, STUDENTS AND THE WORLDWIDE EXPANSION OF CHRISTIANITY, p. 195.
2 R. H. Glover, PROGRESS OF WORLD WIDE MISSIONS, p. 109.
3 D. McConaghy, PIONEERING WITH CHRIST, pp. 26ff.
4 F. A. Mackenzie, BOOTH-TUCKER: SADHU AND SAINT.
5 THE CHRISTIAN ENDEAVOUR MANUAL, Agra, 1909.
6 H. & G. Taylor, HUDSON TAYLOR AND THE CHINA INLAND MISSION, passim.
7 Marshall Broomhall, W. W. CASSELS, FIRST BISHOP IN WEST CHINA; cf. J. C. Pollock, MOODY, pp. 252ff.
8 CHINA'S MILLIONS, 1906.
9 R. B. Ekvall, AFTER FIFTY YEARS (Christian and Missionary Alliance story).
10 K. S. Latourette, A HISTORY OF THE EXPANSION OF CHRISTIANITY, Volume VI, pp. 341-342.
11 RECORDS OF THE GENERAL CONFERENCE OF THE PROTESTANT MISSIONARIES OF CHINA, 1890.
12 C. W. Iglehart, A CENTURY OF PROTESTANT CHRISTIANITY IN JAPAN, pp. 42 and 72.
13 Otis Cary, A HISTORY OF CHRISTIANITY IN JAPAN, p. 167.
14 C. W. Iglehart, A CENTURY OF PROTESTANT CHRISTIANITY IN JAPAN, pp. 73.
15 Otis Cary, Chapter IV; so also Iglehart, Chapter III.
16 K. S. Latourette, A HISTORY OF THE EXPANSION OF CHRISTIANITY, Volume VI, pp. 392ff.
17 C. W. Iglehart, A CENTURY OF PROTESTANT CHRISTIANITY IN JAPAN, p. 75.

18 Otis Cary, A HISTORY OF CHRISTIANITY IN JAPAN, p. 216.
19 K. S. Latourette, A HISTORY OF THE EXPANSION OF CHRIS-TIANITY, Volume VI, p. 420.
20 cf. A. Vanderbosch, THE DUTCH EAST INDIES, pp. 48ff; and J. Rauws, THE NETHERLANDS INDIES, pp. 56ff.
21 J. B. Rogers, FORTY YEARS IN THE PHILIPPINES, p. 2; & F. Laubach, THE PEOPLE OF THE PHILIPPINES, pp. 137ff.
22 J. Sibree, THE MADAGASCAR MISSION, pp. 77ff.
23 A. Burgess, ZANAHARY IN SOUTH MADAGASCAR, pp. 130ff.
24 S. B. Halliday, THE CHURCH IN AMERICA AND ITS BAPTISMS OF FIRE, p. 529.
25 J. L. Barton, DAYBREAK IN TURKEY, pp. 174-175.
26 E. R. Pitman, MISSIONARY HEROINES IN MANY LANDS.
27 E. Stock, HISTORY OF THE CHURCH MISSIONARY SOCIETY, Volume III, p. 515.
28 see J. C. Wilson, AN APOSTLE TO ISLAM: A BIOGRAPHY OF SAMUEL M. ZWEMER, passim.
29 cf. A. Watson, THE AMERICAN MISSION IN EGYPT; W. J. W. Roome, "BLESSED BE EGYPT"
30 C. R. Watson, SORROW AND HOPE OF THE EGYPTIAN SUDAN.
31 see Rutherfurd & Glenny, THE GOSPEL IN NORTH AFRICA, pp. 165-166.
32 J. H. Hunter, A FLAME OF FIRE: THE LIFE AND WORK OF ROWLAND V. BINGHAM.
33 R. L. McKeown, TWENTY-FIVE YEARS IN QUA IBOE, pp. 52ff.
34 E. Stock, HISTORY OF THE CHURCH MISSIONARY SOCIETY, Volume III, pp. 441-448 cf. A. W. Tucker, EIGHTEEN YEARS IN UGANDA AND EAST AFRICA.
35 C. F. Harford-Battersby, PILKINGTON OF UGANDA, Chapter XII.
36 N. C. Sargant, THE DISPERSION OF THE TAMIL CHURCH, pp. 74ff. cf. Y. Samuel, DAVID—AMBASSADOR FROM INDIA. A cloud shadowed Tamil David's later minstry; like his namesake, he repented and renewed his commitment to evangelism.
37 PROCEEDINGS OF THE CHURCH MISSIONARY SOCIETY, 1894, p. 59; cf. Statistics of the Uganda Mission, 1892 and 1907.
38 Prof. J. du Plessis has supplied (without sources) somewhat larger figures, not subtracting C. M. S. gains in other parts of East Africa.
39 PROCEEDINGS OF THE CHURCH MISSIONARY SOCIETY, 1893, p. 41; 1894, p. 9.
40 W. S. Churchill, MY AFRICAN JOURNEY, London, 1908.
41 SCRIBNER'S MAGAZINE, New York, August 1910.
42 J. Richter, GESCHICHTE DER EVANGELISCHEN MISSION IN AFRICA, p. 485.
43 J. du Plessis, THE EVANGELIZATION OF PAGAN AFRICA, pp. 329-330.
44 Mrs. A. Macaw, CONGO: THE FIRST ALLIANCE MISSION FIELD.
45 J. E. Lundahl, NILS WESTLIND. (Swedish biography).
46 cf. A. J. Brown, ONE HUNDRED YEARS, p. 217; P. Steiner, KAMERUN ALS KOLONIE UND MISSIONFELD.
47 G. & N. Pamla, AMABALANA NGO BOMI BUKA, (Notes from the Xhosa by the South African scholar, Dr. Basil F. Holt)
48 see E. Weeks, W. SPENCER WALTON, passim.
49 A. E. Thompson, THE LIFE OF A. B. SIMPSON, p. 228.
50 K. G. Grubb, RELIGION IN CENTRAL AMERICA.
51 H. B. Grose, ADVANCE IN THE ANTILLES, pp. 104, 208.
52 J. T. Hamilton, HISTORY OF THE MORAVIAN CHURCH, p. 530.

Notes on Chapter 24: THE SOCIAL INFLUENCE, I

1   G. Seldes, THE STAMMERING CENTURY, New York, 1928, p. 141.
2   cf. L. A. Weigle, AMERICAN IDEALISM, p. 188, & J. W. Jones, CHRIST IN THE CAMP, passim.
3   see T. L. Smith, REVIVALISM AND SOCIAL REFORM, Chapters XII & XIII.
4   G. M. Trevelyan, ENGLISH SOCIAL HISTORY, pp. 492ff.
5   THE CHRISTIAN, 3 June 1909.
6   W. Canton, HISTORY OF THE BRITISH AND FOREIGN BIBLE SOCIETY, Volume III, pp. 1-2.
7   J. W. Bready, LORD SHAFTESBURY AND SOCIAL-INDUSTRIAL PROGRESS, pp. 313, 318ff, 326, 333.
8   cf. K. S. Latourette, THE NINETEENTH CENTURY IN EUROPE, Volume II, p. 376; & J. W. Bready, LORD SHAFTESBURY, p. 402.
9   see THE REVIVAL, 27 August 1859.
10 K. S. Latourette, THE NINETEENTH CENTURY IN EUROPE, Volume II, pp. 355ff.
11 J. W. Bready, DR. BARNARDO: PHYSICIAN, PIONEER, AND PROPHET, p. 50.
12 see THE CHRISTIAN, 22 April 1886, on Quarrier's Homes; & G. E. Morgan, R. C. MORGAN, pp. 144, 156, on Fegan's Homes.
13 Young and Ashton, BRITISH SOCIAL WORK, p. 41.
14 ENCYCLOPEDIA BRITANNICA, 1970, 'Probation.'
15 Young and Ashton, BRITISH SOCIAL WORK, pp. 159, 165, 174.
16 J. Butler, REMINISCENCES OF A GREAT CRUSADE, passim.
17 cf. J. Baillie, THE REVIVAL, p. 63; & W. Weir, THE ULSTER AWAKENING, pp. 151, 190, 196.
18 G. E. Morgan, R. C. MORGAN, p. 145; cf. THE REVIVAL, 1860 onwards, with many reports upon 'The Midnight Movement.'
19 Young and Ashton, BRITISH SOCIAL WORK, pp. 205ff.
20 see J. Butler, REMINISCENCES OF A GREAT CRUSADE; cf. G. E. Morgan, R. C. MORGAN, pp. 298ff; & Millicent Fawcett, JOSEPHINE BUTLER, passim.
21 Young and Ashton, BRITISH SOCIAL WORK, pp. 209ff, 221.
22 Charles Dickens, ALL THE YEAR ROUND, 1859, pp. 32-53.
23 cf. Registrar-General's QUARTERLY RETURNS OF BIRTHS, DEATHS AND MARRIAGES, 1858-65; and MONTHLY RETURNS.
24 C. P. Shedd, A HISTORY OF THE WORLD'S ALLIANCE OF YOUNG MEN'S CHRISTIAN ASSOCIATIONS, pp. 82ff.
25 M. T. Boardman, UNDER THE RED CROSS FLAG, p. 32.
26 see M. Gumpert, DUNANT: THE STORY OF THE RED CROSS.
27 B. & S. Epstein, HENRI DUNANT, p. 22.
28 T. L. Smith, REVIVALISM AND SOCIAL REFORM, p. 148.
29 A. F. C. Bourdillon, VOLUNTARY SOCIAL SERVICES, p. 45.
30 J. Spargo, KARL MARX: HIS LIFE AND WORK.
31 F. Engels, SOCIALISM, UTOPIAN & SCIENTIFIC: Introduction.

Notes on Chapter 25: THE SOCIAL INFLUENCE, II.

1   J. Whiteside, A HISTORY OF THE WESLEYAN METHODIST CHURCH IN SOUTH AFRICA.
2   J. S. Dennis, CHRISTIAN MISSSIONS AND SOCIAL PROGRESS, Volume II, p. 69.
3   ZAMBESI INDUSTRIAL MISSION MONTHLY, November 1903.
4   J. S. Dennis, Volume II, p. 69.

5   M. A. Sherring, THE INDIAN CHURCH, p. 218.
6   J. Richter, A HISTORY OF MISSIONS IN INDIA, pp. 347ff.
7   W. C. Barclay, HISTORY OF METHODIST MISSIONS, pp. 507ff.
8   cf. C. Reynolds, PUNJAB PIONEER, Life of Dr. Edith Brown;
    W. Wanless, AN AMERICAN DOCTOR AT WORK IN INDIA; &
    M. P. Jeffrey, DR. IDA : INDIA, passim.
9   Christian Medical Association, TALES FROM THE INNS OF
    HEALING, p. 144.
10 see J. Jackson, LEPERS—A HISTORY OF THE MISSION TO
    LEPERS IN INDIA AND THE EAST.
11 S. Higginbotham, THE GOSPEL AND THE PLOW; G. R. Hess,
    SAM HIGGINBOTHAM OF ALLAHABAD.
12 see A. D. Lindsay, CHRISTIAN HIGHER EDUCATION IN INDIA,
    p. 298.
13 Nurullah & Naik, HISTORY OF EDUCATION IN INDIA, pp. 881ff.
14 cf. K. S. Latourette, A HISTORY OF CHRISTIAN MISSIONS IN
    CHINA, pp. 441-451.
15 cf. J. J. Morgan, THE '59 REVIVAL IN WALES, pp. 85-86; &
    E. W. Price Evans, TIMOTHY RICHARD, p. 10.
16 C. H. Peake, NATIONALISM AND EDUCATION IN MODERN
    CHINA, pp. 43-44.
17 T. Richard, FORTY-FIVE YEARS IN CHINA, p. 297.
18 see Beach & St. John, WORLD STATISTICS OF CHRISTIAN
    MISSIONS, p. 78.
19 WORLD STATISTICS OF CHRISTIAN MISSIONS.
20 cf. H. G. Underwood, THE CALL OF KOREA, pp. 112ff; THE
    CHRISTIAN MOVEMENT IN THE JAPANESE EMPIRE (Annual),
    1915, pp. 476-477, 491; REPORT OF THE BOARD OF MISSIONS,
    METHODIST EPISCOPAL CHURCH, SOUTH, 1908.
21 see W. E. Griffis, HEPBURN OF JAPAN.
22 W. E. Griffis, A MAKER OF THE NEW ORIENT—SAMUEL
    ROBBINS BROWN.
23 W. E. Griffis, VERBECK OF JAPAN.
24 J. D. Davis, A SKETCH OF THE LIFE OF REV. JOSEPH
    HARDY NEESIMA.
25 A. S. Hardy, THE LIFE AND LETTERS OF JOSEPH HARDY
    NEESIMA.
26 Otis Cary, HISTORY OF CHRISTIANITY IN JAPAN, Volume II,
    pp. 165ff, 209.
27 F. de Azevedo, BRAZILIAN CULTURE, p. 419.
28 Braga & Grubb, THE REPUBLIC OF BRAZIL, pp. 33, 61, 76.
29 W. R. Wheeler, MODERN MISSIONS IN CHILE AND BRAZIL,
    Chapter IX.
30 q. in W. E. Browning, THE RIVER PLATE REPUBLICS, p. 72.
31 Martinez & Lewandowski, THE ARGENTINE IN THE TWENTIETH
    CENTURY, p. 120.
32 W. E. Browning, THE RIVER PLATE REPUBLICS, pp. 67-68;
    see J. G. Guerra, SARMIENTO, SU VIDA Y SUS OBRAS.
33 A. H. Luiggi, SIXTY-FIVE VALIANTS, pp. 17, 35ff.
34 J. B. Zubiaur, SINOPSIS DE LA EDUCACION EN LA REPUBLICA
    ARGENTINA, pp. 31-44.
35 Browning, Ritchie & Grubb, THE WEST COAST REPUBLICS OF
    SOUTH AMERICA, pp. 29ff.
36 see Melinda Rankin, TWENTY YEARS AMONG THE MEXICANS,
    pp. 88ff; cf. Camargo & Grubb, RELIGION IN THE REPUBLIC
    OF MEXICO, p. 44.

BIBLIOGRAPHY

ACTS of the General Assembly of the Church of Scotland, 1860.
AMERICAN BAPTIST ALMANAC, Philadelphia, 1857, 1858, 1859, 1860.
AMERICAN BOARD OF COMMISSIONERS FOR FOREIGN MISSIONS, Boston, 1859-62.
AMERICAN QUARTERLY CHURCH REVIEW, New Haven, 1859.
ANNUAL REPORT, American Baptist Missionary Union, Boston, 1873.
ANNUAL REPORT, American Missionary Association, Boston, 1865.
ANNUAL REPORT, National Bible Society of Scotland, Glasgow, 1865.
AUSTRALIAN EVANGELIST, Melbourne, 1860-1861.
BALLYMENA OBSERVER, Ballymena, Ireland, 1859.
BANNER OF ULSTER, Belfast, 1859.
BAPTIST MISSIONARY MAGAZINE, 1858, 1887 & 1902.
BELFAST NEWSLETTER, 1859.
BIBLIOTHECA SACRA, Andover, 1859.
BOSTON COURIER, 1858.
BRITISH STANDARD, London, 1861.
CHINA'S MILLIONS, London, 1885, 1906.
CHRISTIAN ADVOCATE AND JOURNAL, New York, 1857-58.
CHRISTIAN ENDEAVOUR MANUAL, Agra, 1909.
CHRISTIAN MOVEMENT IN THE JAPANESE EMPIRE, Tokyo, 1915.
CHRISTIAN OBSERVER, Philadelphia, 1858-59.
CHRISTIAN PLEADER, Sydney, 1859.
CHRISTIAN REGISTER, Boston, 1858.
CHRISTIAN TIMES, Chicago, 1858, 1859, 1860.
CHURCH MISSIONARY GLEANER, London, 1861.
CHURCH MISSIONARY INTELLIGENCER, London, 1860.
CHURCH MISSIONARY RECORD, Madras, 1860.
THE CHURCHMAN, New York, 1858.
CONGREGATIONAL QUARTERLY, New York, 1859-1860.
DAILY COMMERCIAL, Cincinnati, 1858.
DAILY COURIER, Louisville, 1858.
DAILY PRESS, Chicago, 1858.
DAILY TRANSCRIPT, Boston, 1858.
DAILY TRIBUNE, New York, 1858.
DE KERKBODE, Cape Town, 1859-60; 1874-75.
ENCYCLOPEDIA BRITANNICA, Chicago, 1960.
EVANGELICAL CHRISTENDOM, London, 1858-1860 (Quarterly).
EVANGELICAL REPOSITORY, New York, 1858.
THE EXAMINER, New York, 1858.
THE FREEMAN, London, 1859-60.
THE FRIEND, Philadelphia, 1858.
GODSDIENSVERSLAG (State of Religion Report), Andrew Murray of Worcester, Archives of the Dutch Reformed Church, Cape Town.
THE INDEPENDENT, New York, 1858.
INDIAN WATCHMAN, Madras, 1860.
JOURNAL of the XLI Annual Convention of the Protestant Episcopal Church in the Diocese of Ohio, 1858.
JOURNAL of the Annual Convention of the Diocese of New York, 1858.
KANSAS CITY STAR, 1899.
LUTHERAN OBSERVER, Ohio, 1858-59.
MINUTES of the Conferences of the Australasian Methodist Church, 1863-1864.

MINUTES of the First Conference, Australian Wesleyan Methodist
Church, 1854.
MINUTES of the General Assembly of the Presbyterian Church in
Ireland, 1859.
MINUTES of the General Assembly of the Presbyterian Church of
the United States of America, Volume XV, 1857-1859.
MINUTES of the Hawaiian Evangelistic Association, Honolulu, 1858-62.
MINUTES of the Methodist Conference, Cape Town, 1913.
MINUTES of the Methodist District Meetings, in the Archives, Cory
Library, in Rhodes University, Grahamstown.
MINUTES of the Wesleyan Methodist Conferences, London, 1852-54.
MISSIONARY NOTICES of the Wesleyan Methodist Missionary Society,
London, 1858-1859.
MISSIONARY RECORD, Madras, 1873.
MISSIONARY RECORD, Presbyterian Church of Nova Scotia, 1858.
MISSIONARY REVIEW OF THE WORLD, London & New York, 1895.
MONTHLY RELIGIOUS MAGAZINE, Boston, 1858.
NATIONAL INTELLIGENCER, Washington, 1858.
NEW YORK HERALD, 1858.
NEW YORK OBSERVER, 1858.
NEW YORK TIMES, 1858 & 1876.
THE NONCONFORMIST, London, 1860.
NORTH BRITISH DAILY MAIL, Glasgow, 1859.
NORTHERN WHIG, Belfast, 1859.
OBERLIN EVANGELIST, Oberlin, Ohio, 1858.
OVERLAND ATHENAEUM, Madras, 1859.
PRESBYTERIAN MAGAZINE, Philadelphia, 1858.
PROCEEDINGS AND DEBATES of the General Assembly of the Free
Church of Scotland, 1860.
PROCEEDINGS of the Church Missionary Society, London, 1894.
PROCEEDINGS of the General Assembly of the Presbyterian Church
in Ireland, Belfast, 1859, on 'Revival.'
THE RECORD, London, 1859.
RECORDS OF THE GENERAL CONFERENCE OF THE PROTESTANT
MISSIONARIES OF CHINA, Shanghai, 1890.
REPORT of the American Board, Boston, 1859.
REPORT of the Missionary Conference on South India, Madras, 1879.
REPORT, Board of Missions, Methodist Episcopal Church South, 1908.
REPORTS, Wesleyan Methodist Missionary Society, London, 1860-63.
THE REVIVAL, London, 1859 & 1860ff.
SCRIBNER'S MAGAZINE, New York, 1910.
SCOTTISH GUARDIAN, Edinburgh, 1859.
SOUTHERN PRESBYTERIAN REVIEW, Columbia, 1859.
THE SPECTATOR, Melbourne, 1900-1901.
THE TIMES, London, 1859, 1860.
UNITED PRESBYTERIAN MAGAZINE, Edinburgh, 1860.
THE WATCHMAN, Boston, 1857-58.
WESLEYAN CHRONICLE, Melbourne, 1858.
WESLEYAN METHODIST MAGAZINE, London, 1852, 1857, 1863.
WESLEYAN METHODIST MISSIONARY REPORTS, London, 1866-68.
WESLEYAN TIMES, London, 1863.
WESTERN CHRISTIAN ADVOCATE, Cincinnati, 1858.
WORLD STATISTICS OF CHRISTIAN MISSIONS, edited by Beach
and St. John, New York, 1916.
YEARBOOK OF THE AMERICAN CHURCHES, New York, 1933.
ZAMBESI INDUSTRIAL MISSION MONTHLY, London, 1903.

Abbott, Lyman, HENRY WARD BEECHER, Boston, 1904.

Adams, D., THE REVIVAL AT AHOGHILL, Belfast, 1859.

Andersen, J. O., A HISTORY OF THE CHURCH IN DENMARK, Copenhagen, 1930.

A CENTURY OF MISSION WORK IN IRAN, 1834—, Beirut, 1934.

Appasamy, A. J., WRITE THE VISION, London, 1964.

Arthur, W., THE REVIVAL IN BALLYMENA AND COLERAINE, London, 1859.

Ashmore, L. S., THE SOUTH CHINA MISSION OF THE AMERICAN BAPTIST FOREIGN MISSION, Shanghai, 1920.

Bacon, L. W., THE HISTORY OF AMERICAN CHRISTIANITY, New York, 1897.

Baillie, J., THE REVIVAL: or What I Saw in Ireland; London, 1860.

Baker, E., THE LIFE AND EXPLORATIONS OF F. S. ARNOT, London, 1921.

Balleine, G. R., A HISTORY OF THE EVANGELICAL PARTY IN THE CHURCH OF ENGLAND, London, 1908.

Barbour, G. F., THE LIFE OF ALEXANDER WHYTE, London, 1923.

Barclay, W., HISTORY OF METHODIST MISSIONS, New York, 1949.

Barton, J. L., DAYBREAK IN TURKEY, Boston, 1908.

Beardsley, F. G., A HISTORY OF AMERICAN REVIVALS, New York, 1912.

Begbie, Harold, THE LIFE OF WILLIAM BOOTH, London, 1926.

Bennett, W. W., THE GREAT REVIVAL IN THE SOUTHERN ARMIES, Philadelphia, 1877.

Beach & St John, WORLD STATISTICS OF CHRISTIAN MISSIONS, New York, 1916.

Beskow, G. E., SVENSKA MISSIONEN I OST AFRIKA, Stockholm, 1884.

Blodgett and Baldwin, SKETCHES OF THE MISSIONS OF THE AMERICAN BOARD IN CHINA, Boston, 1896.

Boardman, M. M., THE LIFE AND LABOURS OF THE REV. W. E. BOARDMAN, New York, 1887.

Boardman, M. T., UNDER THE RED CROSS FLAG, Philadelphia, 1915.

Boardman, W. E., THE HIGHER CHRISTIAN LIFE, Boston, 1858.

Booth-Tucker, F., THE LIFE OF CATHERINE BOOTH, London, 1924.

Bourdillon, A. F. C., VOLUNTARY SOCIAL SERVICES, London, 1945.

Braga & Grubb, THE REPUBLIC OF BRAZIL, London, 1932.

Braithwaite, R., THE REV. WILLIAM PENNEFATHER: LIFE AND LETTERS, London, 1878.

Bready, J. W., LORD SHAFTESBURY AND SOCIAL-INDUSTRIAL PROGRESS, London, 1926.

Bromley, E. B., THEY WERE MEN SENT FROM GOD, Bangalore, 1937.

Broomhall, Marshall, HUDSON TAYLOR: THE MAN WHO BELIEVED GOD, London, 1929.

Broomhall, M., W. W. CASSELS, Bishop in West China; London, 1926.

Brown, A. J., ONE HUNDRED YEARS: History of the Foreign Mission Work of the Presbyterian Church in the U.S.A.; New York, 1937.

Brown, George, AN AUTOBIOGRAPHY, London, 1908.

Browning, W. E., THE RIVER PLATE REPUBLICS, London, 1928.

Browning, Ritchie & Grubb, WEST COAST REPUBLICS OF SOUTH AMERICA, London, 1930.

Bucsay, M., GESCHICHTE DES PROTESTANTISMUS IN UNGARN, Stuttgart, 1959.

Burgess, A. ZANAHARY IN SOUTH MADAGASCAR, Minneapolis, 1932.

Butler, J., PERSONAL REMINISCENCES OF A GREAT CRUSADE, London, 1913.
Camargo & Grubb, RELIGION IN THE REPUBLIC OF MEXICO, London, 1935.
Campbell, W., SKETCHES FROM FORMOSA, London, 1915.
Candler, W.A., GREAT REVIVALS AND THE GREAT REPUBLIC, Nashville, 1904.
Canton, W., HISTORY OF THE BRITISH AND FOREIGN BIBLE SOCIETY, London, 1904-1910 (Four Volumes).
Cary, Otis, A HISTORY OF CHRISTIANITY IN JAPAN, New York, 1909 (Two Volumes).
Carson, J. T., GOD'S RIVER IN SPATE, Belfast, 1958.
Casey, R. P., RELIGION IN RUSSIA, New York, 1946.
Caughey, J., METHODISM IN EARNEST, Richmond, 1852.
Caughey, J., SHOWERS OF BLESSING, New York, 1876.
Christian Medical Assn., TALES FROM THE INNS OF HEALING, Nagpur, 1942.
Chambers, T. W., THE NOON PRAYER MEETING, New York, 1858.
Cheney, M. B., LIFE AND LETTERS OF HORACE BUSHNELL, New York, 1880.
Churchill, W. S., MY AFRICAN JOURNEY, London, 1908.
Clark, S. D., CHURCH AND SECT IN CANADA, Toronto, 1948.
Clough, Emma R., SOCIAL CHRISTIANITY IN THE ORIENT, New York, 1914.
Conant, W.C., NARRATIVE OF REMARKABLE CONVERSIONS, New York, 1858.
CONFERENCE ON MISSIONS HELD AT LIVERPOOL, London, 1860.
Crawford, Dan, THINKING BLACK, London, 1912.
Cuyler, T. L., STIRRING THE EAGLE'S NEST, New York, 1892.
Daniels, J., THE LIFE OF WOODROW WILSON, New York, 1924.
Davis, J. D., A SKETCH OF THE LIFE OF Rev. JOSEPH HARDY NEESIMA, Chicago, 1894.
Davis, G. T. B., TORREY AND ALEXANDER, New York, 1905.
Day, R. E., BUSH AGLOW, Philadelphia, 1936.
De Azevedo, F., BRAZILIAN CULTURE, New York, 1950.
Dennis, J. S., CHRISTIAN MISSIONS AND SOCIAL PROGRESS, New York, 1897-1906.
Dickens, Charles, ALL THE YEAR ROUND, London, 1859.
DICTIONARY OF NATIONAL BIOGRAPHY, London, 1901-1911.
Downer, A.C. CENTURY OF EVANGELICAL RELIGION IN OXFORD, London, 1938.
Du Plessis, J., THE EVANGELIZATION OF PAGAN AFRICA, Cape Town, 1930.
Du Plessis, J., LIFE OF ANDREW MURRAY OF SOUTH AFRICA, London, 1919.
Earle, A. B., BRINGING IN THE SHEAVES, Boston, 1868.
Ekvall, R. B., AFTER FIFTY YEARS (C. & M.A.), Harrisburg, 1939.
Ellis, W., THE MARTYR CHURCH IN MADAGASCAR, London, 1870.
Emhart, W.C., RELIGION IN THE SOVIET UNION, New York, 1961.
Engels, F., SOCIALISM, UTOPIAN AND SCIENTIFIC, New York, 1935.
Epstein, B. & S., HENRI DUNANT, New York, 1963.
Evans, Eifion, WHEN HE IS COME, (Welsh Revival '59), London, 1959.
Every, E. F., 25 YEARS IN SOUTH AMERICA, London, 1929.
Ewing, A., MEMOIR OF ALEXANDER EWING, London, 1879.
Faulkner, H. U., AMERICAN ECONOMIC HISTORY, New York, 1938.
Fawcett, Millicent, JOSEPHINE BUTLER, London, 1927.

Findlay, J. F., DWIGHT L. MOODY, Chicago, 1969.
Finney, C. G., LECTURES ON REVIVALS OF RELIGION, New York, 1833, London, 1928.
Finney, C. G., MEMOIRS OF CHARLES G. FINNEY, New York, 1876.
Flierl, J., CHRIST IN NEW GUINEA, Tanunda, South Australia, 1932.
Fullerton, W. Y., THE LIFE OF F. B. MEYER, London, 1929.
Gammie, A., PREACHERS I HAVE HEARD, London, 1946.
Gewehr, W. M., THE GREAT AWAKENING IN VIRGINIA, Durham, North Carolina, 1930.
Gibson, W., THE YEAR OF GRACE, Edinburgh, 1860 (1909).
Gidland, M., KYRKA OCH VACKELSE, 1849-1880, Uppsala, 1955.
Glover, R. H., THE PROGRESS OF WORLD WIDE MISSIONS, New York, 1925.
Grauer, O. C., FREDRIK FRANSON, Chicago, 1940.
Griffis, W. E., A MAKER OF THE NEW ORIENT: SAMUEL ROBBINS BROWN, Chicago, 1902.
Griffis, W. E., HEPBURN OF JAPAN, Philadelphia, 1913.
Griffis, W. E., VERBECK OF JAPAN, New York, 1900.
Grose, H. B., ADVANCE IN THE ANTILLES, New York, 1910.
Grubb, K. G., RELIGION IN CENTRAL AMERICA, London, 1937.
Guinness, Mrs. H. G., THE NEW WORLD OF CENTRAL AFRICA, London, 1890.
Gumpert, M., DUNANT: THE STORY OF THE RED CROSS, New York, 1938.
Halliday, S. B., THE CHURCH IN AMERICA AND ITS BAPTISMS OF FIRE, New York, 1896.
Hamilton, J. T., HISTORY OF THE MORAVIAN CHURCH, Bethlehem, Pennsylvania, 1900.
Hamlin, C., MY LIFE AND TIMES, Boston, 1892.
Hardy, A. S., LIFE AND LETTERS OF JOSEPH HARDY NEESIMA, Boston, 1892.
Harford & Macdonald, HANDLEY C. G. MOULE, London, 1922.
Harford-Battersby, J., MEMOIR OF T. D. HARFORD-BATTERSBY, London, 1890.
Harford-Battersby, C. F., PILKINGTON OF UGANDA, London, 1898.
Hawker, G., GEORGE GRENFELL, London, 1909.
Headley, P. C., E. PAYSON HAMMOND, London, 1885.
Hewat, E. G. K., CHRIST AND WESTERN INDIA, Bombay, 1950.
Hewson, L. A., INTRODUCTION TO SOUTH AFRICAN METHODISTS, Cape Town, 1950.
Higginbotham, S., THE GOSPEL AND THE PLOW, New York, 1921.
Hinchliff, P. B., JOHN WILLIAM COLENSO, London, 1964.
Hodder, E., THE LIFE AND WORK OF THE SEVENTH EARL OF SHAFTESBURY, London, 1887.
Hodder-Williams, J. E., THE LIFE OF SIR GEORGE WILLIAMS, London, 1906.
Hogg, W. R., ECUMENICAL FOUNDATIONS, New York, 1952.
Holcomb, W., LIFE AND SAYINGS OF SAM JONES, Atlanta, 1906.
Holden, W., THE STORY OF KAMA AND HIS TRIBE, London, undated.
Hollister, J. N., CENTENARY OF THE METHODIST CHURCH IN SOUTHERN ASIA, Lucknow, 1956.
Hughes, G., THE BELOVED PHYSICIAN: WALTER C. PALMER, New York, 1884.
Humphrey, H., REVIVAL SKETCHES AND MANUAL, New York, 1859.
Hunt, W. S., THE ANGLICAN CHURCH IN TRAVANCORE AND COCHIN, Kottayam, 1933.

Hunter, J. H., A FLAME OF FIRE: THE LIFE AND WORK OF ROWLAND V. BINGHAM, Toronto, 1961.
Iglehart, C. W., A CENTURY OF PROTESTANT CHRISTIANITY IN JAPAN, Tokyo, 1959.
Jackson, J., A HISTORY OF THE MISSION TO LEPERS IN INDIA, London, 1910.
Jeffrey, M. P., DR. IDA: INDIA, New York, 1938.
John, Griffith, A VOICE FROM CHINA, London, 1907.
Jones, J. W., CHRIST IN THE CAMP, Richmond, 1887.
Jones, Rufus M., LATER PERIODS OF QUAKERISM, London, 1921.
Knapp, Jacob, THE AUTOBIOGRAPHY OF ELDER JACOB KNAPP, New York, 1868.
Koch, Hal, GRUNDTVIG (translated by Llewellyn Jones), Antioch, Ohio, 1952.
Lancelot, J. B., FRANCIS JAMES CHAVASSE, London, 1929.
Lang, G. H., HISTORY AND DIARIES OF AN INDIAN CHRISTIAN, London, 1939.
Latimer, R. S., DR. BAEDEKER AND HIS APOSTOLIC WORK IN RUSSIA, London, 1907.
Latimer, R. S., UNDER THREE TSARS: LIBERTY OF CONSCIENCE IN RUSSIA, 1856-1909, London, 1909.
Latourette, K. S., A HISTORY OF CHRISTIAN MISSIONS IN CHINA, London, 1929.
Latourette, K. S., HISTORY OF THE EXPANSION OF CHRISTIANITY, Volumes IV, V & VI, New York and London, 1938-1945.
Latourette, K. S., THE NINETEENTH CENTURY IN EUROPE, New York, 1959.
Laubach, F., THE PEOPLE OF THE PHILIPPINES, New York, 1925.
Lindsay, A. D., editor, CHRISTIAN HIGHER EDUCATION IN INDIA, Oxford, 1931.
Livingstone, W. P., CHRISTINA FORSYTHE OF FINGOLAND, London, 1919.
Livingstone, W. P., MARY SLESSOR OF CALABAR, London, 1916.
Loud, Grover C., EVANGELIZED AMERICA, New York, 1928.
Lovett, R., JAMES CHALMERS: AUTOBIOGRAPHY AND LETTERS, London, 1902.
Lovett, R., JAMES GILMOUR OF MONGOLIA, London, 1935.
Luiggi, A. H., SIXTY-FIVE VALIANTS, Gainesville, 1965.
Lundahl, J. E., NILS WESTLIND, Stockholm, 1915.
McClintock & Strong, BIBLE CYCLOPEDIA, Volume III, New York, 1874.
McConaghy, D., PIONEERING WITH CHRIST, New York, 1941.
McCosh, James, THE ULSTER REVIVAL AND ITS PHYSIOLOGICAL ACCIDENTS, London, 1859.
McGillivray, D., A CENTURY OF PROTESTANT MISSIONS IN CHINA, 1807-1907, Shanghai, 1907.
McIlvaine, Charles P., BISHOP McILVAINE ON THE REVIVAL OF RELIGION, Philadelphia, 1859.
McKeown, R. L., TWENTY-FIVE YEARS IN QUA IBOE, London, 1912.
McLoughlin, W. G., MODERN REVIVALISM, New York, 1959.
Macdonald, F.C., BISHOP STIRLING OF THE FALKLANDS, London, 1929.
Mackenzie, F. A., BOOTH-TUCKER: SADHU AND SAINT, London, 1930.
MacPherson, J., HARRY MOORHOUSE: THE ENGLISH EVANGELIST, London, 1920.
MacRae, A., REVIVALS IN THE HIGHLANDS, Stirling, 1906.
Macaw, Mrs. A., CONGO: FIRST ALLIANCE FIELD, Harrisburg.

Massie, J. W., REVIVALS IN IRELAND, London, 1860.
Matthews, B., JOHN R. MOTT: WORLD CITIZEN, New York, 1934.
Mays & Nicholson, THE NEGROES' CHURCH, New York, 1933.
Molland, Einar, CHURCH LIFE IN NORWAY, Minneapolis, 1957.
Montgomery, M. W., A WIND FROM THE HOLY SPIRIT IN SWEDEN AND NORWAY, New York, 1884.
Moody, W. R., THE LIFE OF DWIGHT L. MOODY, New York, 1900.
Morgan, G. E., R. C. MORGAN, HIS LIFE AND TIMES, London, 1909.
Morgan, J.J., HANES DAFYDD MORGAN YSBYTTY A DIWGIAD '59, Mold, 1906.
Morgan, J.J., THE '59 REVIVAL IN WALES, Mold, 1909.
Moss, Lemuel, THE ANNALS OF THE UNITED STATES CHRISTIAN COMMISSION, Philadelphia, 1868.
Müller, George, THE AUTOBIOGRAPHY OF GEORGE MULLER, (edited by A. T. Pierson), London, 1905.
Murray, Harold, SIXTY YEARS AN EVANGELIST: GIPSY SMITH, London, 1937.
Neill, S. C., A HISTORY OF CHRISTIAN MISSIONS, London, 1964.
Newcomb, H., THE HARVEST AND THE REAPERS, Boston, 1858.
Nichol, F. D., THE MIDNIGHT CRY, Washington, 1944.
Noble, W. F. P., A CENTURY OF GOSPEL WORK, Philadelphia, 1876.
Nurullah & Naik, A HISTORY OF EDUCATION IN INDIA, (First Edition), Bombay, 1951.
Olsson, K. A., BY ONE SPIRIT, Mission Covenant, Chicago, 1962.
Orr, J. Edwin, THE SECOND EVANGELICAL AWAKENING IN BRITAIN, London, 1949.
Page, J., THE BLACK BISHOP: SAMUEL ADJAI CROWTHER, New York, undated.
Pamla, G. & N., AMABALANA NGO BOMI BUKA: CHARLES PAMLA, Palmerton, South Africa, 1934.
Pascoe, C. F., TWO HUNDRED YEARS OF THE S. P. G., London, 1901.
Peake, C. H., NATIONALISM AND EDUCATION IN MODERN CHINA, London, 1932.
Pickering, H., CHIEF MEN AMONG THE BRETHREN, London, 1931.
Pickett, J. W., CHRISTIAN MASS MOVEMENTS IN INDIA, New York, 1933.
Pitman, E. R., MISSIONARY HEROINES IN MANY LANDS, London.
Pollock, J. C., MOODY: A BIOGRAPHICAL PORTRAIT, London, 1963.
Prime, S. I., THE POWER OF PRAYER, New York, 1858.
Ramsay, J. C., JOHN WILBUR CHAPMAN, New York, 1962.
Rankin, M., TWENTY YEARS AMONG THE MEXICANS, Cincinnati, 1875.
Rauws, J. et al, THE NETHERLANDS INDIES, London, 1935.
Rees, Thomas, A HISTORY OF PROTESTANT NONCONFORMITY IN WALES, London, 1860.
Reid, W., AUTHENTIC RECORDS OF REVIVAL, London, 1860.
Revesz, Kovats & Ravasz, HUNGARIAN PROTESTANTISM, Cleveland, 1927.
Reynolds, Charles, PUNJAB PIONEER, the Life of Dr. Edith Brown; New York, 1969.
Rice, E. W., THE SUNDAY SCHOOL MOVEMENT, Philadelphia, 1917.
Richard, Timothy, FORTY-FIVE YEARS IN CHINA: Reminiscences; New York, 1916.
Richter, J. GESCHICHTE DER EVANGELISCHEN MISSION IN AFRIKA, Gütersloh, 1922.
Richter, J., INDISCHE MISSIONSGESCHICHTE, Gütersloh, 1924.

Rodgers, J. B., FORTY YEARS IN THE PHILIPPINES, New York, 1940.

Roome, W. J. W., "BLESSED BE EGYPT!" London, 1898.

Rudolph, F., THE AMERICAN COLLEGE AND UNIVERSITY, Boston.

Rudolph, F., MARK HOPKINS AND THE LOG, Boston, 1956.

Rutherford & Glenny, THE GOSPEL IN NORTH AFRICA, London, 1900.

Samuel, Y., DAVID—AN AMBASSADOR FROM INDIA, Madras, (u.d.)

Sandall, R., THE HISTORY OF THE SALVATION ARMY, Volume I, London, 1947.

Sargant, N. C., DISPERSION OF THE TAMIL CHURCH, Madras, 1940.

Schaff, Philip, AMERICA: THE POLITICAL, SOCIAL & RELIGIOUS CHARACTER OF THE UNITED STATES, New York, 1855.

Schaff-Hertzog, THE NEW SCHAFF-HERTZOG ENCYCLOPEDIA OF RELIGIOUS KNOWLEDGE, London, 1908ff, Grand Rapids, 1949ff.

Scharpff, P., GESCHICHTE DER EVANGELISATION, Giessen, 1964.

Scott, Benjamin, THE REVIVAL IN ULSTER: MORAL AND SOCIAL RESULTS, London, 1859.

Seldes, Gilbert, THE STAMMERING CENTURY, New York, 1928.

Shaw, J., TWELVE YEARS IN AMERICA, London, 1867.

Shedd, C. P., TWO CENTURIES OF STUDENT CHRISTIAN MOVEMENTS, New York, 1934.

Shedd, C. P., HISTORY OF THE WORLD'S ALLIANCE OF YOUNG MEN'S CHRISTIAN ASSOCIATIONS, London, 1955.

Sherring, M. A., THE INDIAN CHURCH DURING THE GREAT REBELLION, London, 1859.

Sibree, James, THE MADAGASCAR MISSION, London, 1907.

Siegmund-Schultze, F., EVANGELISCHE KIRCHE IN POLEN, Leipzig, 1938.

Sinker, R., MEMORIALS OF THE HON. ION KEITH-FALCONER, Cambridge, 1888.

Sloan, W. B., THESE SIXTY YEARS: THE KESWICK CONVENTION, London, 1935.

Smith, C. H., THE STORY OF THE MENNONITES, Newton, 1950.

Smith, E. W., THE MABILLES OF BASUTOLAND, London, 1939.

Smith, G., THE LIFE OF ALEXANDER DUFF, London, 1899.

Smith, G. A., THE LIFE OF HENRY DRUMMOND, New York, 1898.

Smith, M. H., MARVELS OF PRAYER, New York, 1858.

Smith, T. L., CALLED UNTO HOLINESS, Kansas City, 1962.

Smith, T. L., REVIVALISM AND SOCIAL REFORM, New York, 1957.

Spargo, J., KARL MARX: HIS LIFE AND WORK, New York, 1910.

Speer, R. E., GEORGE BOWEN OF BOMBAY, New York, 1938.

Speke, J. H., WHAT LED TO THE DISCOVERY OF THE SOURCE OF THE NILE, London, 1864.

Springer, J. M., THE HEART OF CENTRAL AFRICA, Cincinnati, 1909.

Steiner, P., KAMERUN ALS KOLONIE & MISSIONFELD, Basel, 1909.

Stephenson, G. M., THE RELIGIOUS ASPECTS OF SWEDISH IMMIGRATION, Minneapolis, 1932.

Stock, Eugene, HISTORY OF THE CHURCH MISSIONARY SOCIETY, London, 1899ff.

Stock, Eugene, MY RECOLLECTIONS, London, 1909.

Stoddard, D. A., THE LATE REVIVAL AMONG THE NESTORIANS, Boston, 1847.

Student Volunteer Movement, STUDENTS AND THE WORLDWIDE EXPANSION OF CHRISTIANITY, Kansas City, 1914.

Swavely, C.H., THE LUTHERAN ENTERPRISE IN SOUTH INDIA, Madras, 1952.

Sweet, W. W., THE STORY OF RELIGION IN AMERICA, New York, 1931.

Sweet, W. W., REVIVALISM IN AMERICA, New York, 1945.

Taylor, H. & G., HUDSON TAYLOR IN EARLY YEARS, New York, 1945.

Taylor, William, CHRISTIAN ADVENTURES IN SOUTH AFRICA, London, 1867.

Taylor, William, FOUR YEARS' CAMPAIGN IN INDIA, London, 1876.

Taylor, William, SEVEN YEARS' STREET PREACHING IN SAN FRANCISCO, New York, 1857.

Taylor, William, THE STORY OF MY LIFE, London, 1897.

Thoburn, J. M., MY MISSIONARY APPRENTICESHIP, New York, 1884.

Thoburn, J. M., ISABELLA THOBURN, New York, 1903.

Thompson, A. E., THE LIFE OF A. B. SIMPSON, New York, 1920.

Thompson, C. L., TIMES OF REFRESHING, Chicago, 1877.

Trevelyan, G. M., ENGLISH SOCIAL HISTORY, London, 1944.

Trevelyan, G. M., BRITISH HISTORY IN THE NINETEENTH CENTURY, London, 1922.

Tucker, A. W., EIGHTEEN YEARS IN UGANDA AND EAST AFRICA, London, Two Volumes, London, 1908.

Underwood, Horace, THE CALL OF KOREA, Chicago, 1908.

Vanderbosch, A., THE DUTCH EAST INDIES, Grand Rapids, 1933.

Vedder, H. C., SHORT HISTORY OF THE BAPTISTS, Philadelphia, 1907.

Wanless, W., AN AMERICAN DOCTOR AT WORK IN INDIA, New York, 1932.

Warneck, J., LUDWIG I. NOMMENSEN, Lebensbild, Barmen, 1928.

Washington, Booker T., UP FROM SLAVERY, New York, 1901.

Watkin, E.J., JUBILEE HISTORY, WESLEY CHURCH, MELBOURNE, 1858-1908, Melbourne, 1908.

Watson, Andrew, THE AMERICAN MISSION IN EGYPT, 1854-1896, Pittsburgh, 1904.

Watson, C. R., THE SORROW AND HOPE OF THE EGYPTIAN SUDAN, Philadelphia, 1913.

Weeks, E., W. SPENCER WALTON, London, 1907.

Weigle, L. A., AMERICAN IDEALISM, New Haven, 1928.

Wells, J., THE LIFE OF JAMES STEWART, London, 1909.

Wheatley, R., THE LIFE AND LETTERS OF Mrs. PHŒBE PALMER, New York, 1876.

Wheeler, W. R., MODERN MISSIONS IN CHILE AND BRAZIL, Philadelphia, 1926.

Whiteside, J., HISTORY OF THE WESLEYAN METHODIST CHURCH IN SOUTH AFRICA, London, 1926.

Wilder, R. P., THE GREAT COMMISSION AND THE MISSIONARY RESPONSE, London, 1936.

Wilson, J. C., AN APOSTLE TO ISLAM: SAMUEL M. ZWEMER, Grand Rapids, 1932.

Wood, C. E., MEMOIR AND LETTERS OF CANON HAY AITKEN, London, 1928.

Young and Ashton, BRITISH SOCIAL WORK IN THE NINETEENTH CENTURY, London, 1936.

Zubiaur, J. B., SINOPSIS DE LA EDUCACION EN LA REPUBLICA ARGENTINA, Buenos Aires, 1901.

INDEX